Beyond Harm

Toward Justice, Healing and Peace

Derek R. Brookes

RELATIONAL APPROACHES

First published in 2019 by Relational Approaches

www.relationalapproaches.com

A catalogue record for this book is available from the National Library of Australia. http://catalogue.nla.gov.au

Cover art and design by Lynelle Brookes

ISBN 978-0-6485601-0-4 (pbk)
ISBN 978-0-6485601-1-1 (ebk)

With Lynelle

Preface

Many of us are looking for an alternative way of responding to the harms we have all experienced in life. We want an approach that will focus more on 'making things right', rather than merely causing even more suffering. We want to do what we can to repair the harm that was done, rather than remain 'stuck' in brokenness and hurt. We can't change what happened, but we so much want to move beyond it.

This is not a new idea, of course. The search for this kind of alternative has ancient roots. In recent years, it has come to be embodied in a (still evolving) range of processes that fall under the umbrella of 'restorative justice'. But how does this distinctive kind of 'justice' work? What does it mean for harm to be 'repaired'? How do these processes enable people to change how they think and feel about what happened? What sort of 'healing' is possible? What are the risks and limitations? Why would anyone want to take part in this kind of facilitated process? Why not simply 'go it alone'? And how were these processes designed? Why are they organised and structured as they are? Can they be improved? How can participants be assured that they are receiving the best possible service from a facilitator?

For largely practical reasons, these (and many other) important questions very often fall outside the usual 'introduction to restorative justice' that participants receive. The problem is that, as a result, people may not gain the maximum benefit possible from taking part; or they go into it without really understanding what they are doing or why they are feeling as they do. They may also have unrealistic expectations about what can be achieved; or they may feel pressured into doing or saying things that they are not yet comfortable with, and for good reason. They may never have experienced this kind of approach before, and so they may not realise when things are not working as well as they could be, or that there are a number of different ways in which they could reach the same goals.

Again, for similar reasons, the training that restorative justice facilitators undergo is often heavily weighted toward equipping them with practical skills and procedural knowledge. Comparatively little time is given to the theoretical foundations of restorative justice. The problem with this practice-based focus is that it can limit a facilitator's capacity to be creative, flexible and sensitive to context. Provided with little more than a set of pre-scripted procedures, they will be less able to adapt to the variation they will face when dealing with real people in real situations.[1] In other words, facilitators do not only need a 'road map from A to B', they also need to know the general 'lay of the land'. If the given 'road map' does not quite fit the needs of the participants, facilitators will then be able to suggest alternative routes to the same restorative destination.

Beyond Harm was written primarily to meet the 'real-world' need that both participants and facilitators may have for a deeper understanding of restorative justice.[2] I hope that it may also be of some use to readers who are, for whatever reason, interested in exploring what lies at the heart of restorative justice, and how it has the potential to help us move beyond the harms we have experienced and toward the kind of justice that can bring healing and a sense of peace.[3]

CONTENTS

PART 1.

Moral Repair

1. Introduction

1.1 A MORAL DILEMMA

Moral questions are usually thought to be about actions that have not yet taken place. When someone says that they are facing 'a moral dilemma', we usually take them to mean that they are considering several possible actions they could take at some point in the future. For instance, they might be wondering whether to go out to a restaurant or make a donation to help prevent the spread of malaria. So they ask themselves this kind of question:

'What is the right thing to do?'

But what happens when the action is in the past? Suppose we have hurt someone, or we have been wronged in some way. Would it not make sense to ask this sort of question:

'What is the right thing to do *now*?'[1]

It might be thought that there is no 'moral dilemma' here, since there is only one choice available: the only thing we can do after a wrongdoing is face up to the fact that 'what's done is done'. It's too late *now* for anyone to do the 'right thing'. The 'right thing' would have been for the wrong never to have been committed in the first place. But the past cannot be changed. The wrong cannot be undone. So the only way of dealing with it is to leave it well alone, and get on with our lives.

But there is a well-known problem with this response: it doesn't take into account the way in which the past can continue to affect us in the present—especially when it comes to wrongdoing. For many of us, we cannot just 'move on' and forget what has happened. It has left an indelible stain on our lives. It still hurts. The guilt over what we have done persists. It haunts our dreams. It taints our moments of happiness. The aching loss rises up in waves, day after day. But these feelings of rage, or guilt, or grief are not 'dead and buried' in an unchangeable past. They are fully alive in the present. What this means is that something can be done about them. We can change how we feel *now* about what happened. We may not be able to undo the wrong that was done. But we can do something to address the harm that it *continues* to do in our lives.

So what are our options here? If the wrongdoing is a crime or a breach of some rule (in a school, workplace or prison, for instance), then there are institutional responses that can take place. For instance, they can establish the truth about who was responsible; and they can hold them to account in an authoritative, public manner. These are often important things that need to be done, and they can contribute in powerful ways to our healing. But they also tend to be very formal, involuntary, legalistic processes, usually led by third-parties or officials, rather than those directly involved. As a consequence, institutional processes can feel distant or abstract—far removed from the feelings and wishes of the individual people who were responsible for or affected by the wrongdoing. For that reason, they can be frustrating, demeaning, incomprehensible and can even cause additional harm. [2]

In other words, institutional processes may be important, and even necessary. But in terms of repairing the personal harm that people may continue to experience after a wrongdoing, they are rarely sufficient. What remains is the kind of 'repair work' that can only be carried out by those directly involved. For example: if we have *caused harm*, then we need to be honest and fully own up to what we have done. We need to apologise to those we have wronged and do what we can to make amends. If we have *been harmed*, then we may feel that it is important to find a way to make sure that our 'voice' is heard and validated. We may want to ensure that the truth comes out and that responsibility is placed where it is due. We may need to have a say in what would count as reparation or amends for what was taken from us or destroyed. We might even, at some point, feel that we want to meet with the one who has wronged us, to tell them how their actions have affected us. If what we hear is remorse and a real desire to do whatever they can to make amends, then there might come a time when we feel we can offer them forgiveness.

We might think that, in an ideal world, this kind of 'repair work' would be the right thing for everyone to do. But moral dilemmas often arise for us simply because our world is far from ideal. This is especially the case when it comes to how each of us respond to wrongdoing. No one has lived our lives.

They have not walked in our shoes. They have not suffered as we have. So no one is entitled to judge us if we feel unable to take this path at this moment in our lives. And there should be no illusions that this kind of repair work is 'the easy way out' or a 'soft option'. It is one of the most challenging things that anyone can do. So people need to explore the alternatives, weigh up the risks and acknowledge their fears. There can be very good reasons for someone to decide that this option is not for them—at least not right now, not in their current situation.

Yet there will be some who come to the view that being directly involved in repairing the harm done by a wrongdoing is something that they not only can do, but also need to do. They might, for instance, believe that it reflects who they want to be and the kind of world in which they want to live. They may also come to see that it is an essential part of their journey toward healing and peace. And so, despite all the demands and the risks, they feel it is the right thing for them to do.

1.2 WHY USE RESTORATIVE JUSTICE?

In the following pages, I will be suggesting that the primary role of restorative justice is *to enable and support those who want to repair the harm caused by a wrongdoing* (which I will now call 'moral repair'). But before doing so, it will be important to address an immediate problem for this view. The social practices involved in moral repair appear to be instinctive, a part of our natural make-up.[3] Presumably then, we should all be experts. Moral repair should be as commonplace and straightforward as speaking our native language or laughing at a joke. Yet if this were so, why would we need anyone to help us? Would that not be like offering training wheels to a professional cyclist? There might be grounds for offering some help to children. Perhaps like the language instinct, a child's natural disposition to engage in moral repair needs to be socially activated. But when an adult fails to offer a genuine apology for their wrongdoing, would that not be due to their own choice rather than a lack of 'know-how'? So why do we need restorative justice?

As mentioned above, there are undoubtedly numerous cases in which people know what moral repair involves, but feel that, due to their circumstances, they are simply not in a position to take this path. And yet it is also likely that many people very much want moral repair, but genuinely don't know how to go about it. Most of us have an intuitive sense of how to repair minor harms. We quickly offer an apology after carelessly bumping into a stranger on the train. This kind of repair-work is typically accepted without much thought or resistance. But which of us is a 'natural expert' on repairing the harm caused by the murder of a loved one, or the death of a parent due to medical negligence, or the historical genocide of indigenous people, or the betrayal of a marriage partner, or years of child abuse, or the loss of a limb caused by an unsafe workplace, or the stress and humiliation of bullying at work, or the brain injury of a child caused by a drunk driver? How many of us have a clear sense of what could bring about moral repair in such cases?

Worse still, we might have serious doubts about whether the usual processes of moral repair even apply. For instance, suppose your child has been killed by a drunken driver. How could being offered an apology make any (or enough) difference? What would you need from the individual who has wounded you and your loved ones in such an unspeakable way? What would you want them to do? How could you possibly forgive, when your rage and fight for justice are the very things that keep you going? Or again, suppose you were the drunk driver: the one responsible for bringing about such immense hurt. How could you ever come close to 'repairing' what you have done? How could you hope to make amends for a wrong that has affected so many, and in ways that are too horrifying to imagine? Even if you think that you ought to do *something* to communicate how profoundly remorseful you are, how can you be sure that you will not just make things worse?

Despite these obstacles, we might still feel that the work of moral repair could be what is missing. Nothing else seems to have brought us the peace or the kind of healing that we crave. Yet we scarcely know where to start. Nor can we simply brush aside our reservations and fears. So if we are to have any chance of moving forward, we will almost certainly need some guidance and support, as well as a 'tried and tested' process that we can work through.

There is a second kind of problem that arises for the view that moral repair doesn't (or shouldn't) need any assistance. Take the so-called 'minor' types of crimes. In such cases, the work of moral repair might feel less inconceivable, but there are a host of practical obstacles to overcome. Suppose a teenager is caught and charged with breaking into your house and stealing your precious valuables. How would you go about contacting them? The police are unlikely to hand out their phone number or address. Confronting them on the street outside the courthouse is probably not going to turn out well—at least if moral repair is what you have in mind. Even if you somehow managed to arrange a private meeting with the teenager, how could you be sure they were motivated to work toward the goal of moral repair? Maybe they just want to persuade you to drop the charges. Their plan might be to manipulate you into thinking that *they* are the real victim. Or again, suppose you are the teenager in this case. How could you be sure that what you said in any such meeting would be 'heard' as a genuine effort to make things right? Would you not worry that the home-owners might have already made up their minds about what they think of you? Would they believe anything you say? Maybe they just want to find some legal ammunition they can use against you? All in all, what are the chances that this kind of 'do-it-yourself' meeting would be safe, let alone effective?

These are precisely the kind of obstacles to moral repair that have inspired the development of what is now called 'restorative justice'. In other words, restorative justice is a practical solution to the hurdles of 'know-how' and 'no-way' that can so easily prevent us from finding some measure of moral repair after a wrongdoing.

1.3 A QUALIFICATION

There is a qualification that needs to be made here. To say that restorative justice is a 'solution' is not to claim that it can *guarantee* a successful outcome. It is true that, under certain conditions, most people will behave and respond in fairly predictable ways. If that were not the case, using a structured process like restorative justice would make no difference. However, it would be a mistake to assume that we can simply 'trust the process', as if moral repair is akin to 'painting-by-numbers'. Following a 'how-to-paint' manual to the letter will not, on its own, produce a work of art. In the same way, even if a facilitator has a solid theoretical understanding of restorative justice, or strictly follows a best practice guide, it does not follow that the damaged moral relations they are working with will always be fully repaired. Human beings are far too messy and complex for that.

In other words, using a restorative justice process is not an 'all-or-nothing' affair. Even with the best designed and facilitated process, a wide spectrum of outcomes is possible—ranging from 'passable' to 'astonishing'. No one can guarantee, let alone predict, where people will end up. This can be, in part, due to circumstantial issues, such as timing or the availability of key people. But what matters above all are the moral resources and character that each person brings to the process. The quality of restorative justice depends crucially upon whether everyone, including the facilitators, come together with 'the right heart'. They need to bring hope, honesty, compassion, humility and 'good faith'. And no amount of theory, good process design or facilitation skills can produce 'the right heart' in this sense. For this reason, a 'passable' state of moral repair may, in some cases, be the best outcome available, given the unique mix of circumstances and individuals involved.

In short, understanding how moral repair works and using a carefully designed process *will* make a difference to the quality of restorative justice. (There are too many examples in which people have been obstructed and frustrated by a poorly designed or facilitated process.) But it does not follow that 'knowing-why' and 'knowing-how' are, in and of themselves, sufficient.

2. Moral Harm

2.1 WHAT IS MORAL HARM?

The work of moral repair is not about healing physical wounds; nor is it about recovering material or financial losses, although these matters can enter into the process. Rather its primary focus is (what I will call) the 'moral harm'[1] that has been caused. This kind of harm is frequently overlooked or dismissed. That is partly because moral wounds are invisible to the naked eye. A moral injury can be excruciatingly painful, but it does not literally bleed. It is not equivalent to a flooded home, a crushed limb or the death of a loved one. All of these can take place without anyone having been wronged. They could have occurred due to a genuine accident or an unforeseen natural disaster. Yet if moral harm is added to a physical or material loss, the suffering can be magnified beyond telling.[2] So what is this mysterious, intangible thing called 'moral harm'? Why does it hurt so much?

2.2 UNDERLYING MESSAGES

One of the keys to unlocking the nature of moral harm is the concept of 'underlying messages'.[3] It is easy to assume that *what we communicate* is a simple matter of *what we say*. For example, we might, at first glance, assume that when someone says to us: 'I'd love to meet you for lunch on Friday,' then that is what they mean, no more and no less. But this is too simplistic. When someone agrees to meet us for lunch they might also be saying: 'I enjoy your company'. In other words, when we do or say something, there are messages that lie beneath the surface. This is true even when we fail to act or speak. If someone does not take up our invitation to lunch they might be saying: 'I don't want that kind of relationship with you'.

Underlying messages are also conveyed by *how* we say or do something. We can say the same words sarcastically or respectfully—and, in doing so, communicate very different messages.

What is said or done   *How* it is said or done

Underlying Messages

what we think of ourselves

what we think of the other person

how we would like them to respond

what we think our relationship is with them

what we think our social status is relative to theirs

what we would like our relationship with them to be

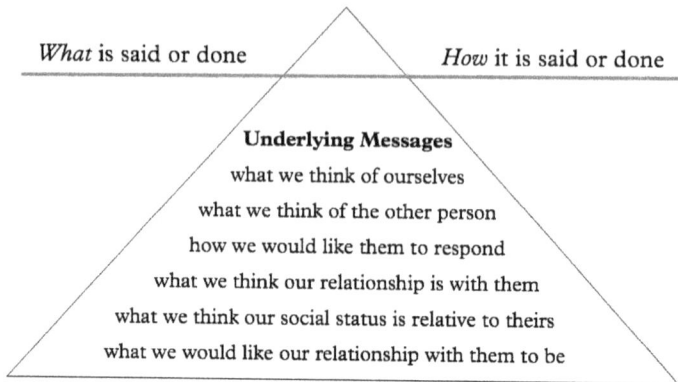

If we voiced our underlying messages out loud they would, in many cases, be socially inept, awkward, presumptuous or even highly offensive and hurtful (e.g. 'Remember: you work for me', 'I find you quite attractive', 'Don't think you can push me around', 'I don't feel safe with you', 'I want you to like me', 'I'm your boss, not your friend'). So, to minimise the chances of conflict or embarrassment, we hide them under the surface of our actions and words.[4]

The fact that underlying messages are concealed in this way does not necessarily mean we want them to go unnoticed. Normally, we want the person on the receiving end to interpret our actions and words as we intended. But in many instances, the evidence we offer them will be far too ambiguous or sketchy. Sometimes we do this so that they will find it hard to accuse us of being deliberately offensive. But we often do or say things that are thoughtless, in the sense that we convey messages we don't mean. In certain situations, a blank look, a terse email, not responding to a greeting, or a touch on the shoulder might be entirely harmless. But it's not hard to imagine other contexts in which they would convey a hurtful or offensive message—whether intended or not.

When our actions or words have been misunderstood, we can try to remedy the situation by making the underlying message more explicit.[5] So we use phrases like the following:

- 'Sorry, I didn't mean to suggest that_____.'

- 'When I said _____, I meant_____.'

- 'I only smiled at what you said because _____.'

One might argue that it is possible to communicate messages of disrespect directly or explicitly, without needing to use hidden or underlying messages. There are certainly expressions that seem to be patently clear and unambiguous (e.g. 'you are nothing to me'). But even such overtly disrespectful messages still need to be interpreted. After all, they could mean very different things depending on what is also being communicated by the speaker's tone of voice, their body language, and so on.[6] But these additional non-verbal communications are exactly what we have been calling 'underlying messages'. In other words, *every* communication comes with an underlying message that tells us how to interpret what is being said or done—especially in terms of how the other person sees us and what kind of relationship they want to have with us. Whether we like it or not, we cannot communicate without also sending an underlying message.[7]

So what, then, is the connection between underlying messages and moral harm? We have seen that underlying messages are usually about *what we think of others*. Our underlying messages provide others with evidence about how we see them. They are like a mirror in which other people can see themselves through our eyes.[8] To harm someone else *morally* is to communicate that we think they are of less value or worth than ourselves, or even of no value at all. So we have wronged someone when we send the message that we see them as little more than an object. Rather than being our equal, we regard them as nothing more than a means to our ends. We see them as being useful for our own purposes, regardless of what they want or how they might feel.[9] So the connection between underlying messages and moral harm could scarcely be stronger: they are the chief mechanism by which this kind of injury is inflicted.

2.3 SELF-CONSCIOUS EMOTIONS

It would be a mistake, however, to think that underlying messages of disrespect are doing all the work. We care about these messages not simply because we think they are untrue or unfair, but because of how they make us *feel*. To explain, underlying messages typically trigger an emotional response. Like ordinary mirrors, we tend not to react to an image of ourselves in a cold, matter-of-fact way. When we see our reflections, we respond emotionally. What we feel will depend on whether we like what we see in the reflection. If an underlying message suggests that we are seen as attractive, highly skilled, intelligent, morally virtuous or high up on the social ladder, then we will feel a sense of pride or satisfaction in ourselves. If it suggests that we are seen as flawed, defective, bad, incompetent, ugly, stupid, repulsive or inferior, then we will feel terrible about ourselves or ashamed.[10] For example, suppose I pass on some ugly gossip about you to Jane. She smiles knowingly as I talk, and I see myself in Jane's eyes as someone who is self-confident and discerning. I feel good about myself, even a sense of pride. But suppose you then find out what I said to Jane and you confront me. I see the hurt and anger in your eyes. I grasp immediately what kind of person you must think I am. I see a malicious coward in the mirror you are holding up to me, and I feel terribly ashamed of myself.

The family of emotions that are typically elicited by underlying messages are called 'self-conscious emotions'. There are two features that distinguish these emotions: first, they are, as the name suggests, *what we feel about ourselves*; second, they arise *when we become aware of how we are seen in the eyes of others*.[11] We can classify the self-conscious emotions under two headings. Under the term *shame* are included all those emotions in which we feel bad about ourselves. Under the term *pride* are all those emotions in which we feel good about ourselves.

We can also distinguish self-conscious emotions from each other by how it is that they arise. For example, *embarrassment* is a kind of shame that arises when we realise (or imagine) that other people have seen us breaching a social convention or etiquette—such as sneezing without covering one's mouth.[12] *Guilt* involves feeling bad about ourselves when we find out (or imagine) that others know we have done something morally wrong.[13] We feel *humiliation* when it seems to us that we have been insulted, disrespected, patronised, belittled, rejected or abandoned.[14] Pride can include feelings of *self-esteem* that arise when we feel (or imagine) that another person is treating us with respect or recognises our accomplishments. *Arrogance* or *vanity* also involve feeling good about ourselves. But they arise when we believe that others are right to treat us with excessive admiration or deference.

Self-Conscious Emotions

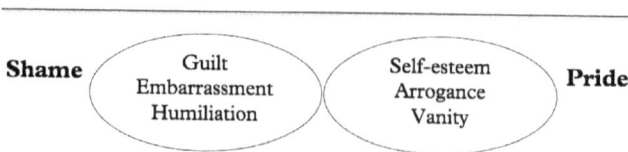

Shame   (Guilt / Embarrassment / Humiliation)   (Self-esteem / Arrogance / Vanity)   **Pride**

Of the two primary self-conscious emotions, shame seems more likely than pride to relate to moral harm. But what is this connection? Why should we think that dealing with an emotion like shame might be relevant to repairing a moral harm? Should we not put our efforts into more objective concerns, like investigating a person's culpability, demanding reparation, or imposing punishment? To address this kind of question, we need to explore the role of shame in more depth.

2.4 SHAME

Shame signals a threat

Shame is one of the most painful emotions we can experience. But it is not a useless accessory, an accident of nature that we could well live without. The capacity to feel shame has a purpose. The pain it causes us serves an important function. Shame is very like fear in this respect. The primary role of fear is to signal a threat to our *physical self* (our sense of what our bodies look and feel like, how we want to be situated within our physical environment, etc.). Shame also signals a kind of threat. Each shame-inducing message is in some way a threat to our *social self* (who we think we are, how we want others to think of us and our connection to them).

Our survival and well-being depends not only upon achieving the *physical goals* of safety and nourishment, but also the *social goals* of connection ('getting along') and advancement ('getting ahead').[15] What counts as a failure to 'get along' or 'get ahead' will depend almost entirely upon our surrounding culture or social context. For example, 200 years ago, no one would have felt guilty for driving a car over the speed limit. Hence, the kind of things that cause us to feel shame will, for the most part, be learnt or acquired from our social context, and so will differ across cultures or social groups. What is universal, however, is the fact that all (properly functioning) human beings experience shame when faced with a threat to their social self. This can be readily explained by the benefits of meeting the two social goals of 'getting along' and 'getting ahead'.[16]

The role of shame can also be explained by looking at how it reveals to us the way that things *ought* to be with respect to our social self. It may be helpful to use an analogy with our physical self. We are generally aware of our body and the state in which it happens to be. We are also aware of what it feels like to be in a normal or healthy physical state. We have some grasp of how our body *ought* to work, of what it feels like when our body is functioning as it should. Pain alerts us to the fact that, in this respect, things are not how they *should* be. In other words, pain tells us that our physical self is under threat. Shame performs a similar function to pain, except that it affects our social self. We are, in general, aware of what we think about ourselves, other people and our connections with them. We are also conscious of who we *ought* to be, how others *should* treat us and what a *right* relationship with them would be like. For instance, we know that we are in a right relationship with another person when we are both experiencing (and communicating to each other) feelings of gratitude, respect, appreciation, and trust. Shame alerts us to the fact that something has gone wrong: it tells us that our social self is, in some way, under threat.[17] As the words 'ought', 'right' and 'should' suggest, there will be some cases in which this threat has a moral quality. Indeed, the emotion of shame is the primary means by which we come to believe, even if mistakenly, that we have been wronged or that we have committed a wrong.[18]

Shame reveals what we value

We know that pain usually signifies a genuine physical problem. If we are uncertain, we can confirm the matter by going to the doctor. But on what grounds can we claim that our shame signifies that there is a genuine moral problem? How can we know for sure that our shame is telling us that we *ought not* to have done something, or that we *ought not* to have been treated in a certain way? Who would we consult to check that our emotions are tracking moral reality?

This is a complex philosophical question, and it is not easy to provide an answer—or at least not one that would be universally convincing. But we can say this much: the 'in-built' role of shame only makes sense if we assume that this emotion is capable of alerting us to the fact that we have committed or experienced a wrong. For instance, most of us can readily sense when we are treated with disrespect, derision or contempt. Even if there are cultural differences about *which* words or actions communicate disrespect, this kind of treatment is universally held to be profoundly threatening. But what is the source of disrespect? What is it that triggers this feeling that we have not been treated as we ought to have been? There appear to be two situations that cause this feeling. In both cases, someone has disregarded or refused to acknowledge something that we consider to be of value or worth. To understand this in more depth, we need to distinguish between two kinds of value: acquired and inherent.[19]

1. Acquired value: We generally feel that others should give us due respect for our accomplishments, our talent or expertise, our property, intelligence, attractiveness, power, social status, virtues, and so on. There are scales, rankings or hierarchies that are used to measure where we stand on such matters, relative to other people. Many of us claim that we don't pay much attention to these scales or rankings. We know how short-lived, random and superficial they often are. So we feel that it's best not to put too much weight on how others 'position' us. Yet our emotions give us away. When someone tramples on our hard-won achievements, or mocks our chosen profession, it feels as if we've been robbed of something we have earned: a due measure of respect for what we have made of ourselves. It is rightfully ours, and so we experience its absence as a kind of injustice.[20] Alternatively, someone may look down on us or treat us unfairly simply because we are 'beneath' them on some particular scale or hierarchy. Either way, we can feel demeaned, humiliated or insulted as a consequence. This emotional response suggests that how others perceive or respond to our status, position or achievements matters to us. Shame provides us with a kind of social litmus test.[21] It can alert us to the fact that we are not being valued or respected as we feel we ought to be; and so we can feel 'wronged' as a consequence.[22]

2. Inherent value: There is another, very different kind of respect that can cause us to feel shame when it is withheld. This is the respect we feel we are owed *regardless* of our achievements, possessions, moral virtues or social status. We recognise just how important this type of respect is to us when we discover that certain people look down on us, discriminate against us or treat us as inferior *simply because of qualities that we can do nothing about*—such as our gender, ethnicity, age, disability, sexuality, and so on. It follows that the object of this second type of respect—what it is directed towards—must be something of value that is *intrinsic* to every human being. The only candidate here would appear to be *our humanity itself*. It is in virtue of being members of the human species that we have equal and inherent worth. This kind of value is our birthright. No one is exempt. It cannot be bestowed upon us by another human being or an institution. It is not something we can earn. It cannot be taken away or diminished. It cannot be increased or improved. No one has more of this kind of value than anyone else.[23]

It might be questioned whether this egalitarian view of human worth can be justified. But there would be severe repercussions if we rejected it. This view underpins universally held principles of fairness and reciprocity. It is the foundation for the claim that we all share basic human rights.[24] It explains why we feel that things are not as they *ought* to be when other people treat us like an object, an inferior being, or a mere means to their ends. These feelings only make sense if we assume that every human being has intrinsic and equal worth or value. And this assumption can be a matter of life or death. Those who are considered less than fully human are far more likely to be subjected to the horrors of genocide, social exclusion, murder, slavery, sexual abuse, racism, and so on.[25] That is why being the target of this kind of disrespect feels life threatening in a way that is not dissimilar to suffering physical violence.[26] It is the feeling of shame—or, more exactly, humiliation—that alerts us to the fact that our intrinsic human worth has been violated, and that we have therefore been seriously wronged.

We may have no universally accepted answer to the question of where our intrinsic worth comes from or how it might be rationally justified.[27] But human beings seem to come with an in-built psychological mechanism that would not make sense without this assumption. That mechanism is the experience of shame.[28]

How others see or treat our acquired value can inflict moral harm

It might be thought that we can only experience moral harm when our *inherent* value is directly threatened or undermined, as in the wrongs of racism, sexism, murder, slavery and the like. But why then do we feel 'wronged' when someone fails to acknowledge or respect our achievements, our property, or our status in a particular job or institution? Why do we react with anger and resentment when someone 'looks down on us' *merely* because they happen to be 'above' us in rank or status? We *say* that we believe all humans are of equal inherent worth. But do we in fact think that our worth or value depends entirely on our position in some scale or hierarchy? Or are we egalitarians only when it comes to certain areas of our lives (which we can't do anything about—such as race, gender or sexuality), but non-egalitarians when it comes to every other aspect of our lives (where we have at least some control)?[29]

This *could* be how we think about human worth. But not necessarily. There is another explanation for why we feel 'wronged'. It may not be that we think our worth is determined by our acquired value. Instead, it might be that someone is (mis)using our relative position on some particular scale or hierarchy as *evidence* that we have less worth as a human being, or even no worth at all. In other words, the value we have (or have not) acquired in life is exploited as a *reason* for challenging or threatening our inherent worth. To do so is, of course, completely unjustified. Indeed, this kind of threat is the very definition of 'moral harm'. But we need more detail.

There is nothing wrong with scales or rankings *per se*: they can have genuine utility. For instance, educational and employment rankings can make sure that people are matched to positions that best suit their particular talents, interests and skill-sets. (No one asks for a hospital orderly to perform open heart surgery on the grounds of 'equal opportunity'). Again, a bit of competition can motivate us to reach beyond our perceived limitations. But scales and rankings can also be horribly mis-used if we see our position as evidence of our relative value or worth as a human being. There are two ways of doing this: First, we can appeal to our higher position on a particular scale as evidence for our 'superiority' over those who are below us on that scale. ("People on income support are low-life scroungers.") Second, if we are lower than someone on one particular scale, we can still claim 'superiority' over them simply by (a) rejecting wholesale the value of *that* scale or ranking, whilst (b) appealing to the evidence of our higher position on a *different* scale or ranking. ("You may have loads of money, but who cares? You're ugly and you have no friends.")

And this is not simply about how we *see* others. This way of thinking can have a terribly harmful impact on the lives of others. One reason why we find scales and hierarchies so problematic is not simply that those at the 'top' so often *see* themselves as 'superior', although that is objectionable enough. It is that they tend to *treat* those 'below' them as having less worth, or even no worth at all. This can happen in several ways: First, those at the 'top' can treat those 'below' them as little more than tools for them to use and dispose of as they wish. In other words, the people 'beneath' them on this particular scale are not treated as ends in themselves, as persons with equal inherent worth. Instead, they are treated merely as a *means* of achieving the ends of those 'above' them. And that is the very definition of what it is to cause someone moral harm. Second, those at the 'top' of a scale can use their position to claim far more than they deserve, in comparison with those 'below' them. In other words, simply because of their 'higher' position in the hierarchy, they claim advantages for themselves that are objectively unfair. For instance, they give themselves wages that are far above anything that could be warranted by their actual contribution. Or they use their position to hire their friends or lackeys, rather than people who are most qualified for the job. Or they think that their 'higher' position gives them the right to humiliate, embarrass, demean and bully those 'beneath' them. In each case, the people who engage in these behaviours are acting as if those who are 'lower' than them on a particular scale are *thereby* 'inferior', and so do not need to be shown the kind of respect that would be owed to someone of equal worth.

In short, moral harm can come to our door in a variety of ways. But it is *always* due to the fact that our equal and inherent worth has been threatened or challenged in some way. This can happen directly, through acts such as racism, violence or sexism; or it can happen more indirectly, when our relative position on some scale or hierarchy is (mis)used as evidence that we are of lesser worth than others. Either way, it is shame that alerts us to the fact that, in these situations, we are being wronged.

Shame explains why we care

We now have a partial answer to the question: 'What is moral harm and why does it hurt so much?' When someone wrongs us, they are sending us a particular kind of underlying message. They are saying that they see us as somehow inferior or even worthless. But we do not merely register this negative message about ourselves intellectually. It also *hurts*. We feel the impact of wrongdoing primarily because its underlying message causes us to experience the intense pain of shame. It is this emotional response that explains why we care so much about moral injuries—often far more than any physical, financial or material losses. [30]

Likewise, if we have caused harm, we feel the weight of guilt primarily because of what our actions say about us. On the one hand, we care deeply about people honouring and respecting *our own* worth or value (whether acquired or intrinsic). Yet we have violated or withheld our recognition of the worth or value of *another* person. But then it follows that, in doing so, we have failed to treat them as we would want them to treat us. More accurately, we have not treated them as we feel we ought to be treated ourselves. We have not only been utterly selfish: we have wronged them. There may be some who can register this fact about themselves in a detached, purely intellectual way. But most of us will know we have wronged someone because we begin to suffer the anguish of a guilty conscience. Once again, we care about the fact that we have done something wrong primarily because the underlying message of wrongdoing—what it says about the kind of person we are—causes us to experience shame.

So what can we do about moral harm? How should we respond? Is it possible to heal from these invisible wounds? What would it take to repair a moral injury? To answer these questions, there is yet more that we need to learn about shame. In particular, we need to explore the various automatic and habitual ways in which we react to shame. We will discover that the journey to moral repair cannot get off the ground without some of these shame-reactions. But it can also be obstructed, delayed and undermined by a range of other shame-reactions.

3. The Shame Experience

3.1 THE PROCESS OF SHAME

Like other emotions, shame only occurs as part of a sequence of events. This sequence starts with an initial *trigger*—like an insult—that elicits the feeling of *shame*. As with any painful feeling, shame often produces immediate and involuntary *bodily responses*, such as blushing. It can also spark *memories* of similar shame experiences, even from childhood. Finally, there will be emotional and behavioural *reactions* to the feeling of shame, such as anger or returning the insult with an offensive remark of your own. The whole shame experience can thus be set out as follows:

Phase 1. *Shame Triggers*
Someone says or does something and we hear an underlying message of rejection, disrespect, contempt, or censure.

Phase 2. *Shame*
The emotion of shame arises within us.

Phase 3. *Bodily Responses*
Our eyes lower, shoulders droop, we blush or wince.

Phase 4. *Shame Memories*
We recall similar shame-experiences, thereby increasing the duration and intensity of our current feelings of shame.

Phase 5. *Shame-reactions*
We undergo emotional and behavioural responses to shame, such as denial, avoidance, self-harm, anger, or retaliation.

Several points should be emphasised about this process. First, once the shame trigger has been heard, the remaining responses will arise almost immediately. The time it takes to move from a trigger to a shame-reaction will typically be measured in microseconds. This means that we will scarcely notice these five phases as distinct or successive. Second, each phase is automatic and involuntary: none of them are within our control.[1] Nevertheless, as we shall see, we can have some control over how we *respond* to our shame-reactions, but only if we become conscious of them. It is precisely this capacity that allows us to engage in the work of moral repair. But we first need to understand a little more about the phases that lead up to and follow the emotion of shame.

Shame Triggers

As we have seen, shame is triggered by underlying messages that communicate how we think others see us.[2] When we feel that we have been treated with contempt, disrespected, insulted or humiliated, the emotion of shame will be triggered within us, whether we like it or not. The kinds of underlying messages that trigger shame can be classified as follows:

- *Performance*: 'You are stupid, weak, incompetent'.
- *Dependence*: 'You can't make it on your own'.
- *Competition*: 'You are a loser.' 'I will always beat you.'
- *Morality*: 'You are nothing but a monster.' 'You are evil.'
- *Attractiveness*: 'You are ugly, deformed, disgusting'.
- *Sexuality*: 'There is something wrong with you sexually'.
- *Privacy*: 'I know what you are like.' 'I saw you doing X.'
- *Closeness*: 'You are unlovable.' 'I don't like your company.'
- *Recognition*: 'You are nothing to me.'

Bodily Responses

Like most emotions, shame will produce an immediate and involuntary bodily response.[3] Some of these responses can resemble how we react when we are physically assaulted. For example, people often respond to insults by saying: 'It felt like he punched me in the stomach'. Other common reactions include facial and postural changes, such as wincing, blushing, shoulders drooping, lowered eyes, and so on.[4]

Shame Memories

Shame can automatically and involuntarily release memories of similar experiences from the past, usually those that were caused by the same kind of trigger.[5] For instance, a manager who seems impossible to please may trigger memories of how we were treated by our parents.[6] One unfortunate side effect is that our experience of shame can be far more intense than the present situation warrants. To an observer, our reactions appear all out of proportion. This is because we are reacting not only to how someone is treating us in the present, but also to how someone from the past treated us—usually someone we were too afraid to stand up to at the time.[7] The following list includes the kinds of shame memories that many people carry with them from their early childhood:

- I never felt like my father really approved of me.

- I was made to feel stupid and inferior by my older siblings.

- I was always 'wrong' and my parents were always 'right'.

- Whenever I got into a fight with my parents, they always brought up everything bad I'd ever done.

- I kept trying to please my parents, but nothing seemed to work.

Shame-Reactions

We all experience a range of emotional and behavioural reactions to shame. It is likely that some reactions are, to a large degree, a result of our genetic inheritance. But most are probably a result of learning the repertoire of shame-reactions displayed by our family members and others within our social context. Eventually, we settle into our own unique catalogue of shame-reactions, fine-tuned and spring-loaded by years of repetition.

We can broadly categorise our reactions to shame as falling into either a 'Fight' or 'Flight' response. Adapting Donald Nathanson's 'shame compass', we can then locate two main types of shame-reactions within each category. The types of shame-reactions that Nathanson calls 'Avoidance' and 'Withdrawal' naturally fall into the 'flight' category; whilst the types called 'Attack Other' and 'Attack Self' can be seen as 'fight' reactions.[8] Under each of these four reactions-types, there is a wide range of emotional and behavioural responses—as illustrated in the diagram below.

Avoidance	Attack other
deny, minimise, justify, distract, display, compete	resentment, anger, revenge, punish, humiliate, abuse

Flight ⟸ **Shame** ⟹ Fight

Withdrawal	Attack Self
hiding, fear of intimacy, isolation, dissociation	self-blame, remorse, self-ridicule, self-harming, suicide

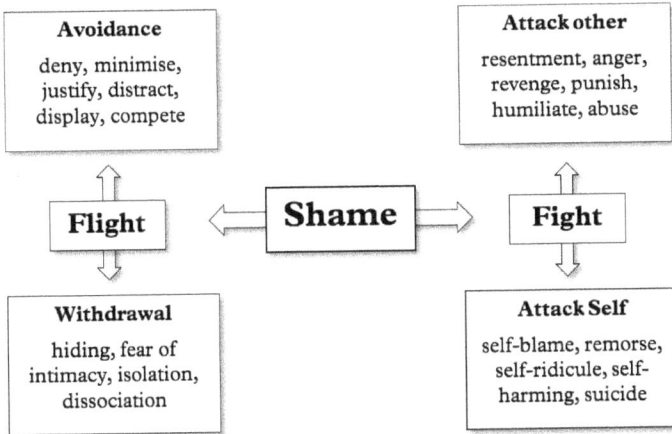

3.2 THE PURPOSE OF SHAME-REACTIONS

The fact that both shame and our reactions to it are automatic or involuntary is not necessarily something we should lament. Our ancient ancestors would not have lasted very long if, when faced with a hungry predator, they first had to think about whether or not they were in danger, and then ponder the question of whether or not they should run. They would have survived only because they immediately and involuntarily experienced fear, and their automatic response was to run as fast as they could. A similar explanation can be given for the way in which the emotion of shame and our reactions to it arise.

Nevertheless, there are two areas over which we do have control. First, for any particular instance of shame, we can choose how we *respond* to the shame-reactions that arise. We can ignore them and let them continue to control us. Or we can do the hard work of digging beneath the surface, uncovering the cause, and then doing what we can to release our shame. Second, moral repair can have a long-term positive impact on our well-being. If we continue to choose the path of moral repair in our lives, then, over time, that is likely to *transform* how we react to shame in the future.

The activity of *responding* to our shame-reactions is most relevant to the work of moral repair, and so this will be the focus of this book. The practice of *transforming* our shame-reactions is related more to the long-term impact of moral repair, and so is still worth considering in this context. So I will briefly explore this second area in the following section.

4. Responding to Shame-Reactions

4.1 TRANSFORMING OUR SHAME-REACTIONS

Why would we want to change the way we react to our feelings of shame? The main reason is this: in certain contexts, these reactions can be terribly destructive, both to ourselves and those around us. If we can modify these patterns, this will bring about an increase in our well-being, and we will experience healthier and more resilient relationships. There are three things that we can do to transform our shame-reactions: we can *increase our awareness* of the shame we are feeling; we can do things that will *enhance our self-esteem*; and we can *heal our emotional wounds*.

Increasing awareness of our shame

To become more aware of our shame, we need to spend time reflecting not only on particular incidents, but also on patterns that seem to be recurring. For example, we can ask ourselves questions like the following:

- What kind of messages are most likely to *trigger* shame within me?
- What are the shame *memories* that make me over-react?
- What are my most common *reactions* to shame?

The more we learn about ourselves, the more likely it is that we will be able to anticipate and even plan for particular incidents. For example, suppose that, looking over my history, I discover that one family member always seems to 'press my buttons'. I begin to realise why that is: they consistently treat me in a condescending manner. Then I start to observe how it is that I react when this person speaks to me: I sense my shoulders hunching, blood rushing to my face, and my eyes looking down. I notice that, almost immediately afterwards, I feel small, vulnerable or childlike. At other times, I find that I am filled with a burning rage, fantasising about how I could bring this person down a peg or two.

With this self-awareness at hand, it will be easier for me to manage how I react the next time around. Now I can plan ahead. I can anticipate my automatic reactions. This will ensure that when they happen, they are less likely to be overwhelming. I may even think about how I could 'contain' or manage my reactions, so they are not so overt or dominating. For example, I might think about how I would like to respond to this person. I can ask myself what sort of reaction would be respectful and dignified, and what might prevent the situation from happening again. Perhaps I could be more assertive and confront this person about their patronising manner. Planning what I want to say, and even rehearsing the words in my mind are good ways of ensuring that my usual automatic reactions are 'contained' or managed.

The point is that, as with other ingrained patterns of behaviour or habits, practise makes perfect. If we are consistent in applying this kind of shame management in our dealings with others, then over time this will modify our shame-reactions. It will change the ways in which we automatically respond to our feelings of shame.

Enhancing our self-esteem

Another way of changing the way we react to shame is to enhance or deepen our self-esteem. Violent rage is more likely to arise in someone who is insecure or lacking in self-confidence. This shame reaction is more severe than is strictly necessary because it is not only a response to the present situation, but also to background feelings of inferiority. Again, someone who already feels bad about themselves is likely to be more susceptible to verbal abuse, betrayal, rejection, demeaning looks and other shame triggers.

In either case, improving self-esteem will make it easier for them to 'bounce back' from experiences of shame. This kind of resiliency is best instilled in childhood. But it is still possible for adults to develop a more secure positive self-regard. This will have a significant impact on the intensity and duration of their shame-reactions.

Healing our emotional wounds.

Finally, it is possible to release the shame that we carry with us from past experiences, whether from childhood or more recent events. This process, as we will see, involves uncovering our shame and then finding ways to convince ourselves that the messages that triggered this shame are false. For example, we may come to the realisation that, contrary to what we were told, we are not inferior, and we did not deserve to be neglected or exploited. In severe cases, the process of releasing our shame may need the assistance of a professional therapist. But as we will see, it is also possible for us to do so on our own. This kind of healing will make it less likely that shame memories invade our present experience with such intensity, if at all.

4.2 RELEASING OUR SHAME

It was suggested above that we can choose how we respond to our shame-reactions. We can either let these automatic behaviours and emotions control us; or we can do the hard work of re-tracing what has happened, uncovering what triggered this reaction, and then taking steps to release our shame. This is the kind of choice that will be our focus from now on.

First, we need to understand how it is possible for us to release our shame. Then we need to look at what it is about the nature of shame that makes shame release so difficult. Second, we will examine the way in which shame-reactions arise in response to the inherent difficulty of releasing our shame. Rather than overcome the problem, shame-reactions are designed to avoid it altogether. We react as we do precisely so that we do not have to do the painful work of shame release. Finally, we will look at what we need to do to get around the roadblock put up by our shame-reactions; and then how we can work through the process of releasing our shame. Once we have understood this process, we will have grasped the essence of moral repair—and so, of restorative justice.

The role of shame-beliefs

It is easy to imagine that emotions are nothing more than a *feeling*: that is, a complex set of bodily sensations or physiological responses. But emotions, as we have seen, are loaded with meaning. The emotion of shame is not 'mute': it tells us something about how we see the world around us. The reason for this is that emotions have cognitive content. They are not only composed of feelings, but also *beliefs*.

We can often tell emotions apart by the way they feel. Fear feels very different from embarrassment. But we can only identify what emotions *mean* because they include a belief, appraisal or evaluation about the world.[1] For example, fear consists of the belief that we are in danger. Without this belief, we would not realise that we are feeling *fear*, rather than, say, an emotion like embarrassment. Likewise, any instance of shame will include both feelings and a belief about ourselves. We can call these 'shame-feelings' and 'shame-beliefs' respectively. Shame-beliefs are *negative appraisals or evaluations about ourselves that are based upon how we think others see us.* So how does this distinction between shame-beliefs and shame-feelings help us to understand how we can release our shame? The short answer is this: since we cannot feel shame without having a shame-belief, it follows that if we can get rid of the relevant shame-belief, the feeling of shame will dissipate as well. But we need more detail.

First, beliefs do not magically appear out of thin air. They cannot arise within us unless it seems to us that they are supported by evidence. (Try to believe that there is a hippo sitting next to you right now!) This is not to suggest that all our beliefs are well founded or rational. Clearly, we can make mistakes. We can be careless, lazy, or ignorant. What we take to be 'good evidence' may be nothing of the sort.[2] Nevertheless, we cannot believe something to be true unless *it seems to us* to be based upon good evidence. That is the psychological mechanism for generating beliefs.[3]

Second, since beliefs are an essential component of emotions, it follows that if we can change the relevant belief, we can change how we feel.[4] How do we change a belief? We need to discover that the evidence upon which it rests is false or that it is undermined or outweighed by new evidence. For example, the belief that we are in physical danger is an essential component of fear. So if we discover that this belief is false, the fear will dissolve. If we find that the danger is not as serious as we thought, then the intensity of our fear will decrease.

This same process can be applied to shame. Suppose you feel embarrassed about being late for an important meeting. But you then discover that no one has noticed you are late. So your embarrassment subsides. In this case, your embarrassment was made up of a shame-belief (e.g. 'I am incompetent'), which was based on an assumption about how your colleagues would see you. Then you discovered that they did not see you that way at all. Since the evidence no longer supported your shame-belief, it vanished along with your shame-feelings.

The role of shame-feelings

We have seen that getting rid of a shame-belief can release our shame. But what role, if any, does the *feeling* aspect of our shame have to play in shame release? To answer this, we need to look at the basic function of this feeling component of our emotions. Why do our emotions feel the way they do? Why can we not just make do with beliefs?

We are all interested in truth. We try to make sure that most of what we believe corresponds to reality. But we are not mere data processors, designed to clock up true beliefs about the world. We must *engage* with our immediate physical and social environment. Our survival depends on being able to act or react in real-time. In this context, true beliefs are (usually) necessary. But they are not enough to motivate us to take action. For example, we might assume that, in cases of an external danger, what propels us to act is a sound assessment of the risks posed to us by the threat. But we have too many counterexamples. Human beings often know that they are under serious threat (e.g. from smoking or climate change), and yet they fail to take evasive action.

The missing ingredient, it would seem, is the *feeling* of fear. We can believe that we are facing a real and deadly threat. But if the danger is too distant or remote, then our fear is less likely to be activated—or at least not to a level that would motivate us to do something about it. That's because our capacity to experience intense, action-inducing fear generally responds to more immediate or proximate threats. So when it comes to a distant threat, we are likely to do nothing—or too little too late. In other words, our reactions to danger are propelled or energised primarily by the *feeling* aspect of fear, rather than the *belief* or evaluative aspect. The feeling that comes with fear is so uncomfortable and distressing that we will be strongly motivated to do something that will rid ourselves of this feeling as soon as we can.

As we have seen, we can only remove the feeling of fear by changing or eliminating our belief that we are under threat. Fortunately, nature has equipped us with the capacity to bring about this objective. We react immediately and automatically when we experience fear. We either attack the threat (*fight*) or run from it (*flight*). Both strategies, if successful, will have the effect of undermining or defeating the evidence for our belief that we are in danger, in which case our feelings of fear will dissipate. But what propels or motivates us to react in these ways is not the belief, but the desire to reduce the discomfort of our feelings of fear.

Shame-reactions work in the same way. We instinctively react to shame by employing a range of self-protective strategies.[5] For example, suppose we do something that violates a code of conduct that our social group cares about deeply: so much so, that it virtually defines them as a group. To avoid being thrown out, we need to rectify the situation. What we *should* do is acknowledge what we have done, sincerely apologise and make amends ('getting along'). Assuming this 'repair-work' is accepted and we are allowed to remain in the group, we will then need to start the long and arduous process of rebuilding our reputation and status ('getting ahead'). And yet, astonishingly, we do the very opposite. We start out by claiming it never happened. But when confronted with the evidence, we become furious, insisting that we had nothing to do with it. And then we viciously point the finger at someone else. What is going on here? Why would we react in these counter-productive ways? The truth is that we are running from shame, and we don't even realise it. Underneath the hood of our conscious awareness, these 'avoidance' reactions are all being driven by our desperate need to suppress the excruciating pain of feeling shame.[6]

What this means is that *releasing* our shame will be the very last thing we feel like doing. Why is this? On the one hand, one would think that releasing our shame would be exactly what we want. After all, this will rid us of an emotion that is intensely painful. In a contest between shame suppression and shame release, one would think that the latter would always win. In one sense, this is true. Shame release is ultimately the better option. But this does not take into account the fact that the process of releasing our shame requires that we bring this painful emotion into the forefront of our consciousness.

In other words, what makes it so hard to release our shame is not the shame-belief, but the shame-feeling. It is the terrible pain of this emotion that compels us to keep it buried in the dark corners of our conscious awareness. There is hardly anything worse than the feelings of humiliation, guilt, disgrace, inferiority, degradation, and the like. There is nothing more excruciating than having our self-worth, the core of who we are, come under attack. But we have no choice. We must wrench our shame out of the shadowy depths of our subconscious, and place it under the glaring spotlight of our conscious awareness. That is the only way to release this emotion. If our shame remains hidden or obscure, we will not be able to identify the shame-belief that is driving it. Without this awareness, we will not know how to remove the shame-belief in question, and so release the shame.

So how do we become aware of our shame? By feeling it. We must dig this emotion out from wherever we have buried it, and allow ourselves to feel the full force of its raw pain. Since shame release, as we shall see, is central to moral repair, this is precisely why engaging in this kind of work should never be seen as a 'soft option'. It is one of the most demanding, vulnerable, courageous, and agonizing things that anyone can do.[7]

5. Withdrawal

5.1 WITHDRAWAL FROM OTHERS

We have seen how it is possible to release our shame, and also how difficult that process can be. But we have yet to grasp how our shame-reactions can put up another obstacle to shame release. To do this, we need to explore the four main types of shame-reactions ('Withdrawal', 'Avoidance', 'Attack Other', 'Attack Self') and how they each work to suppress or displace our shame. Then we can examine how best to overcome these reactions so as to uncover and release the shame from which they are designed to protect us. We begin with the shame-reaction called 'Withdrawal'.

Being harmed

Suppose I am in the heat of an argument with my manager at work. At some point, he calls me an 'incompetent idiot'. The accusation is loud, aggressive and heard by all my colleagues. Even worse, no one comes to my defence. The silence is deafening. So now I am confronted with what appears to be powerful evidence that not only my manager, but also all my colleagues think I'm an incompetent idiot. Before I know it, my face is turning red, my shoulders start to droop, and I feel like I've just been punched in the stomach. I feel utterly humiliated.

What can I do? How can I escape this terrible situation? Since my manager and colleagues are the source of my shame, one option is simply to withdraw from them: I can leave the room, ask to be transferred, or resign from my job. If successful, this reaction will have the effect of suppressing or decreasing the intensity of my shame. How does this work? If I am no longer *directly and immediately* confronted by evidence that other people see me as an 'incompetent idiot', my shame-belief that people see me this way will weaken accordingly. Out of sight, out of mind. As we have seen, the intensity of a shame-feeling will depend on the strength of the corresponding shame-belief; and that strength is, in turn, linked to how much evidence we think we have for that belief.[1]

It should be said that withdrawing from people who are hurting you is not necessarily a bad thing—especially when you do not (yet) have the strength to stand up to them. Removing yourself may be a matter of self-protection, even survival. It may also give you a safe space in which to recover and tend to your wounds.[2]

Causing harm

Take another scenario: suppose that I have wronged you in some way. The last thing I want to see is the hurt and the anger in your eyes. I certainly don't want to hear about the pain and suffering for which I am responsible. That would be too much to bear. So I do my best to avoid meeting you. I even try not to think about you. If we do happen to meet, I find that I cannot look you in the eyes.[3] I am like a child who has been caught by his mother doing something naughty, and responds by covering his eyes ('if I can't see her, she can't see me'). These are all withdrawal strategies, designed to suppress or reduce the shame that I feel. There may come a time when I am ready to face you. But my immediate self-protecting instinct is to hide.

Again, this behaviour is not necessarily a bad thing. It can have some benefits, even for the person harmed. As we shall see, it is often better that people take some time out to process what they have done or what has happened to them. This self-reflection will make it far more likely that they will be able to respond in a way that is constructive and healing. Notwithstanding the possible benefits, there are deep problems with this strategy. The more we withdraw from others—hiding our true selves, shutting people out of our lives—the more likely it is that we will experience an ever-increasing loss of intimacy, openness and trust in our relationships. In extreme cases, we can find ourselves in complete social isolation, with no close relationships or social attachments.[4]

5.2 WITHDRAWAL FROM OURSELVES

Suppose I have killed another human being while driving over the speed limit. My guilt is all consuming. I cannot forgive myself. Or suppose I am suffering violence and emotional abuse from my spouse. I am humiliated, demeaned and bruised—day after day. The only reason I stay is because I feel worthless, ugly and unlovable, and therefore 'deserving' of the abuse.

These cases involve people who are overwhelmed by the shame of what they have done or of what has happened to them. They see themselves as 'bad', 'worthless' or 'inferior'. Even worse, they can find no way to undermine or challenge the evidence that is causing them to form these negative beliefs about themselves. Suppose they reach a point where they can no longer tolerate this situation. They feel so bad about who they are that they cannot live with themselves. One 'way out' would be to commit suicide. But another possibility is to split into a *good self* and a *bad self*. This allows them to channel any pride they feel into bolstering their good self, whilst quarantining their shame so it can only affect their bad self.[5]

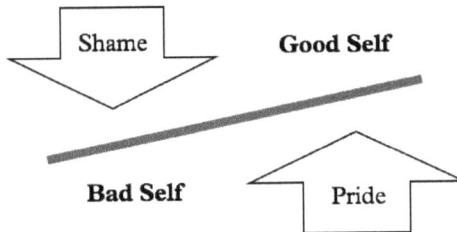

Shame   **Good Self**

Bad Self   Pride

This kind of splitting is something that happens *to* us, rather than being a result of deliberate choice. It is an automatic self-protective mechanism. There are varying degrees to which this 'split' occurs. In cases of severe physical or sexual violence, it can lead to extreme dissociation. People can experience seeing what is happening to them from a position that seems to them to be located outside or above their bodies. But it can also be found in more common experiences, such as when we say:

- 'I can't believe I did that.'
- 'I wasn't myself.'
- 'It was like they were doing it to someone else'.
- 'It felt like it wasn't really happening.'

5.3 REPAIR-WORK FOR THE PERSON HARMED

Withdrawing from myself

Suppose I have been humiliated, treated as if I was a mere 'thing' to be used and then discarded. My immediate reaction is not to deny these negative messages. Instead, I protect myself from the shame that they make me feel. I split into two selves: a 'good self' and a 'bad self'. Then I focus all my energy on trying to see myself as the 'good self', and put out of my mind the possibility that I might be the 'bad self'. In other words, my shame-reaction has been to dissociate or 'withdraw from myself'. But this solution only works some of the time. More often than not, the 'bad self' leaks into my conscious awareness, stirring up feelings of shame that threaten to overwhelm me. I find myself engaging in self-destructive behaviours in a desperate attempt to get rid of my 'bad self'. What can I do? How can I find some peace?

The answer is that I need to face the situation head on. This means accepting the truth about what was done to me. First, I need to get to the point where I can say: 'This happened to me, and not someone else'. I may have instinctively detached myself, seeing the offence as happening to someone else. But this was only a temporary reprieve. It is *my* body, *my* self that has been hurt. That is the reality. I cannot heal until I see what happened to me *through the eyes of the one who was hurt*—that is, my true, whole self—rather than from the safe distance of an observing, dissociated self. I will then be able to feel the shame from which my withdrawal strategy is protecting me.

As painful as this might be, feeling my shame is the only way I can get a clear focus on the negative-beliefs-about-myself that are built into this emotion. I need to expose these beliefs, bringing them into the full light of my conscious awareness. It is only then that I will be able to see these negative beliefs for what they are: utterly and sickeningly false. I am not worthless. No one is. I have as much right as any other human being to be treated with respect and dignity. I am not 'yours', a mere 'thing' that you can use in whatever way you like. I am a human being with infinite value. The way that you treated me was wrong. I do not have to accept the negative underlying messages about me that I unconsciously 'absorbed' when you hurt me. How you see me is *not* the truth about who I am.

Identifying these negative beliefs and then exposing their falsehood will effectively remove them from my mind. But without those beliefs, the shame and humiliation of what you did to me will also disintegrate. And then I will have no need to keep protecting myself. I won't need to keep up the damaging illusion that I have a 'good self' and a 'bad self'.

To sum up, if a person who has been harmed is stuck in the *Flight* shame-reaction of 'Withdrawal' (from themselves), then they will need to shift to the *Fight* reaction of 'Attack Other' by unearthing and rejecting the false underlying messages that they 'absorbed'. This move from 'Flight to 'Fight' will be an essential first step in their journey toward moral repair. There is yet more repair-work that can be done, as we will see. But this, on its own, is a huge achievement and can be immensely healing.

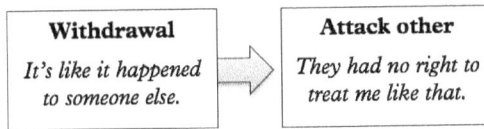

Withdrawal		Attack other
It's like it happened to someone else.	⟹	*They had no right to treat me like that.*

Withdrawing from the person responsible

Suppose that my reaction has not been to withdraw from *myself*. Instead, I have protected myself from the humiliation of what you did to me by withdrawing from *you*. I have done my best to get as far away as possible from you, and any reminders of you or of what happened to me. I resigned from my job, I moved interstate, I stopped seeing friends who knew you, and so on. This reaction worked to some extent: it did reduce the intensity of my humiliation. But the shame of what happened remains lodged in the back of my mind. So whenever I am feeling alone or start to miss my old life, I find my thoughts straying back to the humiliation of what you did to me. And then, stupidly, I lash out and hurt the people I love, which only makes me feel *more* ashamed. So I feel like I am stuck in the past. I am desperate to find a way of moving on. What can I do?[6]

In withdrawing from you (and anything that reminds me of you) I have given you far too much power over my life. But I have only been doing this because I have not yet fully accepted that *how you see me* is false. I have been avoiding you because I don't want to risk the degrading humiliation of seeing myself through your eyes, yet again. You could only have done what you did to me because you saw me as a worthless 'thing' that you could use and throw away. So my greatest fear is that any encounter with you (or reminders of you) will only re-ignite the shame that I want so desperately to 'go away'. In other words, it is not just my own negative-beliefs-about-myself that I need to confront and defeat (and I need to do that as a first step). I also need to stand up to how *you* see me. I need to engage in a more 'outward-directed' process.

To do this, I need to begin by focusing on the *wrongness* of what you did to me. I need to expose the injustice of your actions to the open glare of my conscious awareness. This is not just about making a careful, 'all-things-considered' moral evaluation of what you did (although that is important). This is about *feeling*. It is about giving myself permission to respond emotionally to the fact that what was done to me was undeserved and cruel. I need to feel the full, excruciating pain of being treated as if I had no value. Something will then start to shift inside me. As I come not only to see, but to *feel* the wrongness of what you did to me, I will find myself experiencing an intense anger toward you.

Why is it so important to feel anger? We will look at this emotion in more detail in Chapter 7, but we can mention one of the key roles that it plays here: It is one thing to *believe* that we should be treated as a human being of equal worth and value. But we also need the inner strength, the conviction and the motivation to stand up to someone who challenges our worth. For this, we need the right kind of *emotional* response. If I feel angry at you for the wrong that you did to me, then, if I happen to meet you again, I will be far less likely to see myself through your eyes. But in that case, I don't need to hide from you anymore. You can't touch me. When I am angry at you, then how I see myself—as a person of incalculable worth—is strong enough to resist whatever negative messages you might throw at me.

Of course, very few of us can *stay* angry, nor would we want to. And we might not trust ourselves to respond with the right amount of anger exactly when we need it most—for example, when we happen to meet the person responsible on the street. Moreover, even 'righteous' anger can easily slide into self-destructive malevolence and revenge-fantasies. So there is still some repair-work to be done. But even if I do eventually find a way to 'let go' of my anger (by forgiving you, for instance), feeling this powerful, self-protecting emotion is a crucial part of the journey. [7]

In other words, if I have been harmed and I find that I have been protecting myself with the *Flight* shame-reaction of 'Withdrawal' (from others), then I need to shift to a certain kind of *Fight* reaction: that is, I need to experience the 'Attack Other' response of anger. There is more to be done, but this is an essential step toward the ultimate shame release and healing of moral repair.

Withdrawal	Attack Other	Moral Repair
I don't care. I don't see him anymore.	*You hurt me terribly. I'm so angry at you.*	*I'm no longer angry with you.*

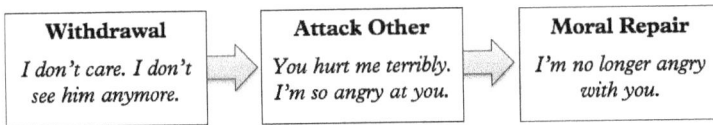

5.4 REPAIR-WORK FOR THE PERSON RESPONSIBLE

Withdrawing from myself

Suppose I have wronged someone, and my way of avoiding shame has been to split into a 'good self' and a 'bad self'. For instance, I might have persuaded myself that the person who did this wasn't the 'real' me: it was completely out of character. I was intoxicated, or beside myself with anger, or not fully aware of what I was doing, or I was provoked, pressured, or tempted by others. Or again, suppose that I have gone so far as to deny, even to myself, that I had anything to do with what happened. When I am accused, I can find no memory of the incident or my part in it. Perhaps I have lied about it so often, over so many years, that I have now come to believe in my own innocence. And yet, there is also something 'dead' inside of me. I know that I am, in some sense, 'shut down' emotionally. Or I may be fearful and anxious at times, but I can't explain why. What can I do? How do I find some peace?

In this sort of case, my self-deceit and disassociation are working to quash the painful feelings of guilt and shame that I would otherwise experience. The only way forward for me is to take the enormously courageous and honourable step of acknowledging, even if only to myself, that *I am the one to blame*. My behaviour may, for whatever reason, have been out of character. But I made a series of choices—such as drinking too much—that made it possible for me to end up hurting someone deeply. Unless I can own up to what I have done, I will not be able to access the feelings of shame that I have suppressed. But it is only by feeling my shame that I will be able to identify and then do something about the negative shame-beliefs that lie behind it. And this, as we have seen, is the only path to shame release and the peace of mind that we crave.

Now if I have been responsible for wrongdoing, 'doing something about my negative shame-beliefs' will be more complicated. Some of those beliefs will be false, but others will be entirely valid. For instance, the shame-belief that would have been responsible for my 'splitting' or dissociation will look something like this: *because I did this wrong, I must be utterly evil and inhuman, a worthless pile of trash.* This is the view that I tried to make sure would only be attributed to my 'bad self', leaving my 'good self' innocent of the charges. But as I begin to feel my shame, and this negative belief comes into focus, I will be able to see, perhaps immediately, that it is completely false. Every human being, no matter what they have done, is of infinite value. I may have committed an evil act, but that does not mean I have lost my humanity. Nothing can remove the equal and inherent worth that is shared by every human being, not even their own actions. Seeing the falsehood of my shame-belief will work to release the feelings of shame that it is supporting; and my self-protective instinct to 'split' or dissociate will then dissolve.

But there is more work to be done here. If I have done something wrong, then there is a sense in which I *should* feel bad about myself. If I have hurt someone, then I *ought* to feel ashamed of myself and what I have done. This is a healthy kind of shame: it alerts me to the fact that my social self is not as it ought to be. I have not treated another person with the respect and dignity that they deserved as a fellow human being. I have fractured my moral relations with them, and I now have an obligation to do whatever I can to repair them. These are the *valid* shame-beliefs that I will start to identify as I open myself up to feeling the shame I have hitherto suppressed. There is more repair-work that I will need to do, but I have at least taken the initial step.

To sum up, when a person responsible for causing harm is stuck in the *Flight* shame-reaction of 'Withdrawal' (from themselves), they need to shift to self-blame, which is an 'Attack Self' type of *Fight* reaction. Again, there is more they will need to do, but this move from 'Flight' to 'Fight' is a vital first step toward moral repair.

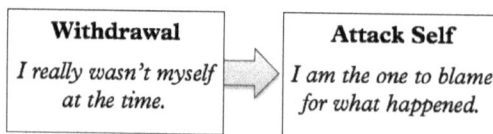

Withdrawal		Attack Self
I really wasn't myself at the time.	⟹	*I am the one to blame for what happened.*

It needs to be mentioned here that the process described above is easier said than done. It is challenging enough to accept that our bad choices led to someone getting seriously hurt. But it is another matter entirely to unpeel the layers of suppression and denial in order to feel the excruciating shame of having done such a thing. It is one of the most demanding things that anyone can do. And there are multiple ways in which our efforts can be blocked or de-railed, especially by the judgments and threats of those around us. To get to a point where we can open up and start to feel the searing pain of our guilt and shame, we must feel safe. No one will strip down naked if they think they will only be met with ridicule or contempt. Piling shame upon shame will only intensify our dissociation and entrench our denials. That is why, as we will see, the concept of a 'safe place' is so central to restorative justice.

Withdrawing from the person harmed

Suppose that I have withdrawn from the person who I have wronged (and anything that reminds me of them). I do whatever I can to make sure I don't meet the person that I hurt. I try not to think about them. I break off a friendship. I find that I want to be alone, more and more. I worry that people will eventually find me out. But I cannot put my finger on why I am doing all these things. How can I recover from this situation?

The first step is to recognise that this kind of reaction is simply a way of protecting myself against the terrible shame of what I have done. What I need to do, then, is stop pretending that it will all go away if no one around me knows what I have done. I may be able to surround myself with people who know nothing about my past, but I can't hide from a guilty conscience. It will follow me wherever I go. So I need to face up to what I have done. I need to admit responsibility for my part in what happened. But this on its own won't deal with the issue of withdrawing from others. I may feel that I have genuinely 'owned' what I have done, and yet still be terrified of meeting the person who I have wronged. Why? Because I don't want to feel the shame of *seeing myself in their eyes*. I know they will see me as a 'monster', 'scum', or 'evil'. In this case, there is only one way forward for me: I need to come out of hiding and face up to this fear.

There are several steps to this process.[8] First, I need to focus on the *wrongness* of what I have done. This means that I will need to take a step back from my own self-interested perspective and make an objective moral assessment of my behaviour. This will involve putting myself in the shoes of the person who I harmed. I need to see what happened *from their perspective*. Even more importantly, I need to *feel* something of the pain and humiliation that they are likely to have felt when I hurt them.

If I can do this, then a shift in me will start to take place. Up to this point, I will have been almost completely wrapped up in my own fears and anxieties about how I am 'seen' by the person harmed. But now I have begun to step out of my own head, and see things from where they are standing. As I start to feel something of their pain and hurt, I will begin to feel the 'outward-directed' emotion of remorse. This is not simply a matter of 'regret', which can be the response of a narcissist who is only disappointed they were caught.[9] Remorse is not compatible with a cold indifference to the human impact of one's actions. Nor can it arise from self-pity or the arrogance of 'impression-management'. On the contrary, to feel this emotion requires *genuine humility and sorrow for having caused unjustifiable harm to another human being.*[10] In other words, remorse is a moral emotion, ignited by the sincere acknowledge-ment of responsibility and fuelled by an empathetic recognition of the hurt and suffering that one has caused to someone else.[11]

Moreover, remorse is precisely the emotion that I need to experience if I am to escape the trap of 'withdrawal' and face the person I have harmed. I might still fear their response. How they see me still *matters*. But the remorse that I feel has overwhelmed those fears. What is driving me now is the need to repair the harm I have caused. Far from wanting to hide from the person I have wronged, I find myself genuinely wanting to meet them and apologise for what I have done, and then do whatever I can to make amends and ease their suffering.[12] There is still much work to be done before I can do this (without causing more harm than good). But experiencing remorse is, as we shall see, an essential step in the right direction. I will now be powerfully motivated to work toward repairing the harm I have caused.

So, to sum up: if I have wronged someone, but find myself trapped in the *Flight* shame-reaction of 'Withdrawal' (from others), then my journey toward healing must involve the kind of 'outward-focused' repair-work that leads to remorse. This can be regarded as a morally appropriate kind of 'Attack Self' reaction. Again, there is more I will need to do, but this is a crucial first step toward moral repair.

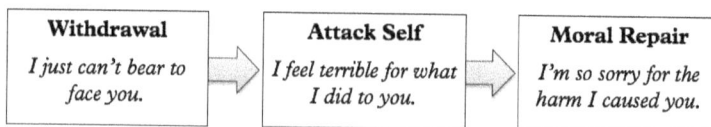

Withdrawal		Attack Self		Moral Repair
I just can't bear to face you.	⟹	*I feel terrible for what I did to you.*	⟹	*I'm so sorry for the harm I caused you.*

6. *Avoidance*

6.1 DISTRACTIONS

One way in which we push our shame into the background of our conscious-ness is to find ways of generating *other* powerful emotions within ourselves—like excitement or pleasure. So we might have a party, go shopping, attend a concert, drive faster than we should, consume drugs or alcohol, and so on.[1] This strategy works because it deflects our attention from the underlying message that is sustaining our shame, which helps us to feel good about our-selves again.

Suppose I feel bruised and humiliated by what someone has said about me. However, I don't want to address this negative message head on, perhaps because I suspect they might be right. What I can do instead is engage in highly emotive activities that will take my mind off this message entirely. The beauty of this strategy is that I don't have to find emotions that counter the shame, in the sense of providing me with positive-beliefs-about-myself. I can leave the risky issue of how I feel about myself to one side. The emotions I am looking for only need one quality: they must be strong enough to take up as much of my attention as possible. This will have the effect of squeezing my feelings of shame out of the picture, reducing their intensity to a point where I scarcely notice they are still there.[2]

Alternatively, I could find ways of countering my shame, but not directly. Rather than defeating the specific underlying message that is driving my shame, I can instead focus all my attention on finding messages that will boost my sense of pride or self-esteem. The effect of doing this will, once again, be to overwhelm or squeeze out my shame. For example, suppose I am feeling shame because I have been caught doing something wrong. I have thereby come to believe that 'I am a bad person'. I could address the evidence that is supporting this belief (i.e. my bad behaviour). But that just seems too hard. And I don't want to face the possibility that my belief might actually be true. So I carefully avoid such evidence, and instead focus all my efforts on trying to find evidence that, on balance, 'I am a good person'—or at least intelligent, important or attractive. So I engage in strategies that will make me look good in the eyes of others. I give a donation to charity, buy a flashy new car, excel in my work, win a contest, lose weight, or wear an attractive outfit to work.[3]

If I am unable to boost my self-esteem by making myself sufficiently wealthy, powerful or attractive, then another option open to me is to identify with those who are. In other words, I can fantasise about what it might be like to live their lives. I can step into their shoes by imagining that I am a lot like them. I can even emulate their behaviour or appearance. If it looks like they feel good about themselves, it follows that I will feel the same—at least to the extent that I am like them.

Again, many of us feel that (what we perceive as) the superior qualities of others can 'rub off' on us, simply due to our association or proximity to them. Witness how people feel a sense of pride when they are noticed by—or are even in the presence of—a member of the Royal family, a movie star, a famous sports person, or some other celebrity.[4] If any of these strategies work, I will have diluted my shame by injecting an extra dose of pride, while at the same time doing what I can to satisfy the dual social imperative to 'get along' and 'get ahead'.

It should be clear that these strategies also work for groups, businesses or corporations. For example, suppose a company has been found guilty of wrongdoing or illegal behaviour—such as fraud, corruption, health and safety breaches, and so on. One option for the company would be to take full responsibility and attempt to repair the harm caused by its actions. But another option would be to divert the public's attention away from the wrongdoing to whatever might make the company look good. Thus, it might engage in an expensive PR exercise—for example, producing commercials that parade the social benefits of the company or making large and highly publicised donations to charity. It might also seek to erase any visible connection it has to the wrongdoing. This might involve placing all the blame on individual employees, sacking or demonising any staff that blow the whistle, refusing to engage with any customers or members of the public who were harmed by the company, and so on.

These strategies are not merely designed to ameliorate the economic loss that can result from bad publicity—although that motivation will invariably play a major role. They also serve a more personal objective. There will be a number of individuals who are closely connected to the company—such as the CEO, upper management, shareholders, employees, and so on. No one wants to be associated with a company that is regarded with contempt or disgust by the public. We all want to feel a sense of pride in the work we do and the institutions with which we are associated.[5] In other words, the emotions of shame and pride are very much operative in corporate decision-making. PR strategies that divert attention from corporate wrongdoing are, to no small degree, motivated by the urge to avoid the painful emotion of shame.

6.2 COGNITIVE DISTORTIONS

Suppose I have harmed someone without any justification. The belief that 'I am a bad person' begins to emerge, along with the early, if faint, feeling of shame. One way of quickly diminishing the intensity of this emotion is to weaken the belief that 'I am a bad person'. I can do this most readily by doing whatever I can to avoid facing up to the evidence upon which it is based. For example, I might deny having done anything wrong. I could also try to minimise, excuse or justify the harm that I have caused. These reactions are known as 'cognitive distortions'.[6]

The use of such distortions is common in more competitive, risk-averse and punitive cultures—where admitting to wrongdoing is regarded, more often than not, as a sign of stupidity or weakness, rather than of integrity, self-respect and moral courage.[7] Cognitive distortions are also most likely to be used where people are fearful of the negative consequences of admitting fault—whether this be a damaged reputation, diminished employment prospects, fractured relationships, someone taking revenge, financial penalties, imprisonment, and so on.

There are several ethical problems with using cognitive distortions. First, I will have harmed someone twice: both in having committed the original offence, and then by having denied, justified or minimised the wrong that I have done to them. Second, this breach with reality could lead to even more offending. What happens when I am faced with a decision about whether or not to perform a similar act? If I decide not to commit this new act on the grounds that it is wrong, then this will expose the fact that I was wrong to have committed the previous act. One way for me to get around this problem is to apply the same cognitive distortions to the new act. Indeed, to be completely safe, I will need to apply these distortions to *any* similar act—whether it is carried out by me or someone else. In other words, I will need to make a permanent adjustment to my moral compass. What I previously took to be wrongful behaviour, I will now regard as morally permissible.[8]

It gets worse. This adjustment will not only entrench my original moral disfigurement. It is likely to erode the boundaries of what I perceive to be ethical behaviour—often in ways that I could not have anticipated. For example, once I accept that, say, back-stabbing a colleague is morally permissible, then I am likely to become far less concerned about harming my colleagues in other, perhaps more serious ways.[9]

Cognitive distortions are also used by *people who have experienced harm.* Suppose I have been a victim of an assault. In the humiliation that I experienced, I have come to believe that 'I am weak and pathetic'. One way that I could suppress this shame is to attack the evidence that is driving it. So I might start to minimise the harm that I experienced. I convince myself that the crime was not as bad as it could have been; or that I am coping much better than other people I know; or that my suffering was actually for the best because it led to a positive outcome.[10]

6.3 REPAIR-WORK

Avoidance strategies can be highly effective ways of alleviating the intensity of shame. But in the end, they all encounter the same problem. They can only work by employing some degree of self-deception, dishonesty, callousness or selective blindness.[11] We have to make ourselves virtually unaware of (or uncaring about) the harm we have caused, or the harm we have suffered.[12] Avoidance is a way of removing the emotion from the forefront of our consciousness. But this means that the shame is never actually released. Instead, it remains in the back of our minds, where it can continue to propel us into activities that are not necessarily ethical or in our best interests.[13]

As with the withdrawal strategy, one of the most effective ways of overcoming avoidance is to engage in the work of moral repair. We have already sketched out the initial stages of this work in the previous Chapter, and we will explore it in far more detail in the Chapters that follow. But it will be useful to reiterate the basic process here, and how it applies to the avoidance strategy.

Repair-work for the person harmed

If I have been harmed, then I first need to feel the shame of what was done to me by the person responsible. This is the only way that I can identify and confront the negative messages that I unconsciously absorbed. It will soon become crystal clear that there was no excuse or justification for what they did to me. Yes, it could have been much worse, but it could also have been much better. If the person responsible had made different choices, it would not have happened at all. I may have learnt some important life lessons, but these positives do not magically turn the wrong into a right.

Even if I have defeated these negative messages, I might still feel a formidable dread or anxiety about meeting the person responsible, and so I continue doing whatever I can to avoid them. To move forward, I need to focus on the *wrongness* of what was done. And I need to give myself permission to feel outrage and resentment toward the person who did this. It is only when I've felt *anger* toward the person who hurt me that I will feel enough self-respect and motivation to continue on my journey toward healing and moral repair.

Thus, if I have been wronged by you, and I am stuck in the *Flight* shame-reaction of 'Avoidance', then I need to shift to two respective 'Attack Other' reactions: first, I need to place responsibility at your feet, where it is due; and then I need to experience anger at you for what you did to me. This move from 'Flight' to 'Fight' will be an essential first step toward moral repair.

Repair-work for the person responsible

If I have wronged someone, I cannot even begin the process of moral repair until I feel the shame that I have been avoiding. Only then will I be able to see the extent to which I have been justifying my actions, finding excuses, or minimising the harm. I can then put aside all of these self-protecting distortions, and 'own' who I am and what I have done.

But that is not enough. I can admit what I have done, but still be intensely fearful of meeting the person who I have hurt. The shame of seeing myself in their eyes would be far too painful. So I need to step out of my own head and put myself in their shoes. I need to feel something of the hurt that I have caused them. Then it will be possible for me to feel remorse for what I did to them. That will be a powerful motivation for me to 'come out of hiding' and do what I can to repair the harm that I have caused.

In sum, if I have wronged someone, and find myself driven by the *Flight* reaction of 'Avoidance', I can only escape by shifting to the *Fight* reaction of 'Attack Self'. First, I need to own up to what I have done. Then I need to engage in the kind of 'outward-directed' repair-work that will enable me to experience remorse.

7. Attack Other

A third response to shame that we can use when we have been harmed is to 'kick back' against the culprit. This is the 'Attack Other' shame-reaction, designed to shield us from the humiliation or guilt that others are making us feel. It works by 'turning the tables back on them'. We drum up evidence that it is *they* who should be feeling shame, not *us*. We throw out insults and counter-accusations that are calculated to make them feel the very emotions that they are making us feel.

We are greatly assisted in this strategy by the emotions of anger, rage and resentment.[1] These feelings are so powerfully self-affirming that they effectively push the shame out of our conscious awareness and block it from reappearing. We angrily dismiss the credibility of people who judge us. We lash out when they criticise us. We yell at them when they make us feel stupid or inadequate. We well up with resentment when they accuse us of something, and we instinctively try to put the blame back on them. We are outraged when we are treated unfairly. These are all 'Attack Other' reactions to shame.[2]

This kind of reaction—like all the others—can be employed by either those who have been harmed or those responsible for causing harm. There are similarities in how this reaction will appear in both. But in terms of the work of moral repair, there are a number of important differences. So we will examine them separately. We begin with the way in which those who have been harmed use the 'Attack Other' reaction.

The role of anger

Like the 'Fight' response to the threat of physical danger, anger can perform several important functions when we have been harmed.

1. Anger tells us that we have been wronged: Suppose you find yourself feeling resentful when someone speaks to you in a patronising tone of voice. This emotion reveals to you that you are being treated with disrespect. A cold intellectual analysis of the situation, on its own, is unlikely to have given you this understanding—at least not with the forcefulness or immediacy provided by your emotional response.[3]

2. Anger tells others that they have wronged us: Sometimes it is only when we get angry with someone that they come to realise they have wronged us. By contrast, when we respond calmly and dispassionately, it may seem to them that they have not hurt us at all. So expressing anger can reveal to the person responsible the fact and the severity of their violation.[4]

3. Anger affirms our own value and worth: The failure to experience *any* anger or resentment when we are wronged may indicate a tenuous grasp of our own intrinsic value and worth. It suggests that we suspect we may have actually deserved this treatment.[5] By contrast, if we do respond with anger, that indicates our refusal to be thought of as less than human. It shows that we care about the fact that we have not been treated with dignity and respect. The reaction of anger is therefore a crucial expression of self-respect and a powerful affirmation of our value and worth.[6]

4. Anger protects us from unsympathetic observers: Anger can also be important for surviving the treatment of observers in the aftermath of a victimisation experience. It is not uncommon for our friends, colleagues and family to respond badly to us when we are harmed. They ignore us, blame us for what happened, distance themselves, and feel exasperated when we do not just 'get over it and move on'. This is largely because they are protecting themselves. For example, they may want to avoid feeling inadequate in the face of our neediness; or they may fear that, if they accept that what happened to us was genuinely random or unpreventable, then it could also happen to them or their loved ones.[7] Feeling anger about what happened will provide us with an internal source of strength and affirmation with which to resist the fears, accusations and lack of compassion displayed by those around us.[8]

5. Anger gives us the strength and the motivation to seek justice: If it were not for this emotion, most wrongdoers would never be brought to justice. It is only when we feel sufficiently outraged that we are moved to hold them accountable for what they did. Anger is powerful enough to overcome our natural reticence to do something—especially when there is no guarantee that justice will be done. This emotion can provide us with the strength, energy and drive needed to endure the personal costs and risks that such a journey will require of us.[9]

6. *Anger is a pre-requisite to forgiveness:* As we have seen in earlier sections, forgiveness will not be compatible with self-respect unless we first allow ourselves to feel anger or resentment about the wrong we have suffered. To give a useful example of this: Gandhi was a renowned advocate for non-violent resistance. But when he was leading his country to independence, he insisted that no one join him who was not willing to take up arms to fight for independence. His argument was that they could not freely renounce what they had not entertained. In other words, he felt that we could not pass directly from passive submission to non-violent resistance. We need to discover first our own inner strength and capacity for violence. We do not actually need to become violent, but we do need to own our fury at the injustice. We need to care enough to be willing to fight and, if necessary, die for its eradication. Only then can we renounce violence and embrace active non-violence.[10] Likewise, if we have been harmed, the work of moral repair will not get off the ground until we have moved from the shame-reactions of 'Avoidance' and 'Withdrawal' to the reaction of 'Attack Other'. It is only then that our decision to forgive will be compatible with self-respect.

Defensive vs. offensive anger

As we have seen, there can be immense value in the outward-directed 'Fight' reaction of anger. But this emotion can also do considerable harm. It can easily transform into a permanent background temperament of bitterness, cynicism and distrust. Anger can also lead to acts of vengeance or retaliatory violence. In either case, this emotion is no longer serving a positive function. How is it that our anger can turn negative in this way?

We have seen that anger or resentment is evoked in us when someone does or says something that conveys the underlying message: 'You are lower than me on the scale of worth'. We have also seen that anger is a healthy and useful response when it serves to resist or defy this message. Its purpose is to defend us from the attack by vigorously reasserting our inherent equality of worth. It conveys the response:

'You are mistaken: we are both of *equal* worth'.[11]

But setting up a strong defence is not the only possible response. Another way of rejecting the message is to go on the offensive:

'You are mistaken: I am *higher* than you on the scale of worth'.

This message is conveyed whenever our anger degenerates into rage-filled revenge (e.g. returning the insult), seething indifference (e.g. 'you are not even worth the trouble of responding'), or vengeful rumination (e.g. imagining ways of humiliating them).[12] In other words, the focus of our anger moves from merely re-asserting *our own* worth to denying *their* worth. We return their message in kind. We reject our rejectors and oppress our oppressors.[13] Why would we take this approach? There seem to be three main explanations.

1. It is the only game in town: One reason is that we become caught up in the view of human worth that is presented to us by the person who has delivered the message of disrespect. This is particularly easy to do when the surrounding sub-culture or 'institutional norms' encourage or reward bullying, discrimination and other kinds of oppression.[14] In such a world, human worth is ranked according to position and status, relative to others. We are not equals: we are competitors, and there are only winners and losers. To survive and flourish in such an environment, we cannot merely assert our inherent, equal worth: we must instead fight to position ourselves on the scale that is presented to us. If someone tries to move us down a peg or two, relative to their position, then the only viable option is to 'return the favour'.[15]

This perhaps provides a deeper explanation for the phenomenon of revenge. On the face of it, it seems odd to want those who have harmed us to be hurt in return. How could their suffering possibly alleviate our own? It is not as if their pain can somehow replace ours. For one thing, it is too late. We have already endured the pain. What is done cannot be undone. So how could we gain from seeing them suffer in return? However, if we dig beneath the surface explanations (e.g. 'to teach them a lesson'), we will find a motive that has more to do with re-balancing the scales. In hurting us, they have sent the implicit message that we are inferior to them. They have 'put us down', quite literally. One way of defying this message is, as we have seen, to reject the notion that human worth can be unevenly distributed: in other words, we can dispute the assumption that there are any 'scales' to begin with. All humanity is equal. But this is not how revenge works. To seek vengeance is to run with the assumption that there are indeed scales that measure out human worth; and that justice will only be done when the scales that are used to compare our worth to that of the person who has wronged us are tipped in *our* favour.[16]

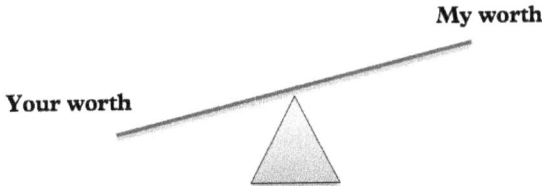

My worth

Your worth

2. If they don't count, then neither does their threat: We do not resent insects. When they bite us, we do not take it personally. They do not threaten our social self. We do not feel disrespected. They do not have the moral standing to make judgements about our worth. We do not see ourselves through the eyes of an insect. When we reflect on who we are, the perspective of an insect just does not count. It is not something we need to factor into the equation. It follows that one way of resisting a disrespectful message is to deny the humanity or moral standing of the one who sent it. If those who harm us are 'monsters', 'animals', 'evil', 'vermin', 'deranged', or 'filth', then their views about us do not count. We would not dream of seeing ourselves through their eyes. That would tell us nothing about ourselves that is worth knowing. Their opinion of us is not something we need to take seriously. Thus, by denying the humanity or the moral standing of the person who has hurt us, we defuse whatever threat their message might have posed to our self-worth.

This can perhaps be seen most vividly in the otherwise strange phenomenon of crime victims who remain unsatisfied by the most severe punishments available in Western society. For example, an individual sentenced to death in America is usually permitted to retain a semblance of humanity, even as they are being executed. They receive a last meal of their choosing. They have the opportunity to prepare themselves and speak to loved ones. Indeed, execution by lethal injection has evolved as 'a way of taking a life in the most humane and dignified manner possible'. The entire process is orientated around preserving a basic respect for the individual's humanity, even if at the same time it is designed to proclaim that this person is not worthy of life.[17]

However, for some victims or their families, this approach is *too* humane. It is too 'painless', too 'easy', and too 'respectful'. You cannot 'rid the world of a monster' in a manner that recognises their humanity. The act is a self-contradiction.[18] The crime that was committed by this individual poses an implicit threat to the worth and value of those who have been harmed. But this threat will not vanish just because the individual is no longer alive. So long as they retain moral standing, the threat will remain. If they are permitted to die in a dignified and humane way, the moral harm they have inflicted will remain undiminished. Hence, what some victims and family members are hoping for is not so much an end to the offender's existence, but rather the destruction of their humanity. The whole point of the execution, from their perspective, is that it gives official recognition to what they need to hear, namely:

'This life has no worth'.

But the exercise will be wasted if the officials then take it back by carrying out the execution in such a way as to imply that:

'This life *does* have worth'.

Prison creates much the same problem. Many crime victims vigorously object to any 'comforts', 'opportunities' and 'liberties' that might be given to prisoners. They demand instead conditions designed to inflict maximum suffering, misery, and degradation. This does not necessarily mean that they are inherently cruel or malevolent people. It is more likely that they are acting on the (tragically mistaken) assumption that they will somehow count for less, if the lives of prisoners count at all.

3. It is empowering: To defend ourselves against a message of disrespect, we must find some alternative source by which to buttress or reinforce our sense of dignity and self-worth. What better source than from within? Anger does all the work that is required. We do not need the person who hurt us to take back their degrading messages. It does not matter if they refuse to apologise or return the respect that they owed to us. We can secure our sense of self-worth independently.[19] Moreover, the sheer potency of anger as a prop for our sense of self-worth is such that this emotion can become highly addictive. For this reason, letting go of our anger may come to feel like a serious threat. So we sustain and nurture our rage. We constantly think about the wrong we have suffered. We pour over the details, nursing our wounds. We fantasise about the variety of ways in which the most severe humiliation and pain might be inflicted on the one who hurt us. We vent our spleen, again and again, to anyone who will listen. We seek out those who validate our cause, joining groups that keep alive the flames of bitterness, demonisation and hate.[20]

The problems with offensive anger

This general approach may 'work', insofar as it blocks or defuses the threat to our self-worth. But it also creates its own problems.

1. It chains us to the person responsible: It will be impossible to sustain our rage without thinking about the person who has hurt us. But in that case our sense of self-sufficiency and power is an illusion. Instead of the liberation and independence for which we long, our sense of worth is now shackled to the one figure we most detest.[21]

2. It can lock us into cycles of shame and revenge: When our anger goes on the offensive, it buries the shame even deeper—creating never-ending cycles of shame-reactions, both within ourselves and in our relationships with others. For example, suppose I feel angry about your insulting behaviour. I react by insulting you in response. Then I feel guilty about the way I responded to you. But I go on to deal with this guilt by doing something that causes me to feel ashamed of myself (e.g. getting blind drunk at a friend's party). So I have now placed myself in a closed loop of shame-reactions.[22]

Again, suppose I insult you. In your anger, you take revenge by insulting me back. I am incensed and attack you in return. Back and forth the tide of revenge will go, potentially sweeping up friends, relatives, communities and even entire nations in its wake. Or, what is perhaps more common, when I insult you, you take out your anger at me by instead attacking an innocent party. This will usually be someone who is less able to harm you in return, simply because they have less power, strength or status than you (e.g. your spouse or partner, a child, an employee, a student, etc.). But of course, since they are weaker than you, they are unlikely to retaliate against you. So they off-load their anger by instead attacking someone who is weaker than them. And on it goes.[23] Any of these reactions can easily create self-perpetuating shame-revenge cycles, examples of which can be found littered across human history.[24]

3. It lacks integrity: Responding with offensive anger inflicts the same wrong as the initial threat. By returning a message of disrespect, it fails to treat the recipient as having equal and intrinsic worth.[25]

4. It is ultimately futile: We suggested above one reason why some crime victims and their families are dissatisfied with the way in which our society currently operates the death penalty and imprisonment: namely, that these punishments are too humane. But even if we inflicted the most barbaric, cruel and malicious forms of retribution, this would not be enough to remove a person's humanity. Why? Because the worth and value of a human being is *intrinsic*. It cannot be diminished or destroyed, no matter how badly a person is treated. Even death cannot touch the equal, inherent worth of another human being. This is a principle that, at some level, we all recognise and accept. Perhaps the strongest evidence for this is that we would feel no shame, embarrassment, humiliation, anger or guilt if it were otherwise.

There are, of course, swathes of people who try to live as if human worth can be ranked in accordance with some arbitrary scale (such as wealth, intelligence, attractiveness, race, gender or power); and many of us are drawn into these hierarchical worlds. But the cost of living this way is extremely high. This is precisely the view of human worth that gives rise to acts of moral harm in the first place. It is hard to see how someone could use other people entirely for her own purposes *unless* she thought of them as being lower on the scale of worth. Again, how could someone treat another human being as a mere object *unless* he considered them to be his inferior, rather than his equal?

But as we have seen, most of us do not just submit and meekly accept our place in this kind of 'hierarchy of worth'. Even if we do not understand why, we still feel the disrespect and the humiliation. We instinctively react, usually with anger or resentment. Even those who know that they have harmed us will—unless they are psychopathic[26]—automatically feel ashamed of what they have done. Their shame may be deeply buried. They may show no signs of outward remorse or guilt. But if we know what to look for, we will see how this emotion is the driving force that lies behind their self-justifications, their excuses, their avoidance strategies, and their attempts to blame everyone except themselves. In other words, we need only observe how their reactions to what has happened reveal a concerted attempt to suppress their feelings of shame. In short, offensive anger assumes a view of human worth that will ultimately fail, given the kind of creatures we happen to be.

Perhaps most of us will, at times, long for the day when those who have betrayed us, used us and humiliated us are finally reduced to dust, recognised by all as no more significant than an insect. But this dream will never be realised. Neither the death penalty, prison, nor any other kind of punishment can ever be fully satisfying whilst we still carry this need within us. [27] In the meantime, we will be chained to the past, locked in prisons of bitterness and hatred. [28] Fortunately, there is a better way.

7.2 REPAIR-WORK FOR THE PERSON HARMED

Advocates of forgiveness often imply that we have only two options if we have been wronged: revenge or forgiveness. This not only forces upon us a false choice, it is also cruel. No one would ever choose to be consumed or trapped by hatred, bitterness and vengefulness. But if the only solution offered is forgiveness, then many will prefer to remain with 'the devil they know'. To make the leap from one extreme to the other will seem to them not only inconceivable, but also unconscionable. [29] They are right. If I am currently 'stuck' in *offensive* anger, then my first step should not be to move directly to forgiveness. For both psychological and moral reasons, there is a bridge I must take to get from revenge to forgiveness: first I need to feel *defensive* anger.

To explain: as mentioned earlier, I do not regard myself as having been wronged by an insect that bites me. That is because I do not see myself through the eyes of an insect. What it thinks of me is not something that I need to take into account. It poses no threat to my social self. It follows that if I want to forgive a wrong, then I must *first* consciously recognise and accept the moral standing—that is, the humanity—of the person I wish to forgive. Without this initial step, I could not even regard them as having *wronged* me; and in that case, there would be nothing to forgive. But to believe that someone has 'moral standing' in this sense is to accept that they have *equal* worth. This means that it is not possible to move from offensive anger to forgiveness without first undergoing a profound change in how I view the worth of the person who has harmed me. Forgiving someone is not just another kind of revenge, a way of 'putting someone in their place', demonstrating my 'moral superiority', or 'bringing them down a notch or two'. True forgiveness cannot, by definition, get off the ground unless it recognises and affirms the equal worth of the person who has caused harm.[30]

So from a psychological and a moral point of view, the gap between offensive anger and forgiveness could hardly be wider. What we need, therefore, is an *intermediate stage* between these two states: a transitionary step that retains our legitimate stand against the wrong that was done to us, but that also recognises our common and inviolable humanity. That stage is defensive anger. [31]

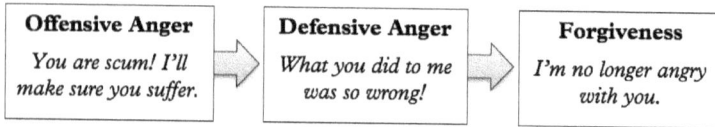

Offensive Anger	**Defensive Anger**	**Forgiveness**
You are scum! I'll make sure you suffer.	*What you did to me was so wrong!*	*I'm no longer angry with you.*

It should be noted that there is still a vast chasm between defensive anger and forgiveness. In Chapter 10, we will see how it is possible for a person who has been harmed to bridge this final gap in their journey of moral repair.

7.3 AS USED BY THE PERSON RESPONSIBLE

The category 'Attack Other' does not only capture the responses of those who have been harmed. People who are responsible for causing harm can also attempt to suppress their shame by using this outward-directed 'Fight' reaction: that is, by turning against others, angrily blaming them for the situation in which they find themselves. In one sense, this seems counter-intuitive. Shame indicates that there is a threat to our social self: we are facing the rejection of our social group. So it hardly makes sense to resolve this situation by attacking those who are making the threat. Surely this would do nothing to bring about the twin social goals of 'getting along' and 'getting ahead'. It will only compound the rejection. Hence, on the face of it, 'Attack Other' for a person responsible seems to be an entirely self-defeating reaction.

Yet if we look at the wider context, the pieces of the puzzle soon fall into place. This reaction is most likely to occur when the person responsible is faced with an explicit accusation; and even more so when the allegation has been proven in a public manner—such as in court or a disciplinary hearing. At this point, there is no place to hide. The wrong that was done is out in the open, for all to see. If the facts are all known and the sentence has already been delivered, then there is little point in trying to justify our actions or minimise the harm that was done. Who would believe us?

Some will, of course, continue to resist the public censure by defending their actions, claiming innocence, appealing the sentence, and so on. Others will see the writing on the wall, and give up these strategies of avoidance and withdrawal as a lost cause. But this does not necessarily mean that they will automatically admit fault and take responsibility. There is one remaining shame reaction left open to them: they can attack their attackers or reject their rejectors. This kind of 'Fight' reaction is one reason why the practice of punishment is so ineffective in bringing about moral repair.

The problem with punishment

Numerous philosophers and legal theorists have argued that punishment differs from revenge insofar as it is intended to respect the humanity of the offender. But in practice, those who are punished rarely 'hear' this distinction. When people experience the harsh realities of punishment—such as incarceration, fines, naming and shaming, or exclusion from school—the messages they hear are far more likely to be the following:

- 'We do not respect you.'

- 'We do not trust you.'

- 'You are a bad person.'

- 'We have power over you and can hurt you at any time.'[32]

These messages are all powerful shame triggers. It is of no surprise, then, that those who are punished react by suppressing or displacing their shame. And 'Attack Other', in the context of public censure, may be the only reaction that can achieve this aim. So they will 'kick back' at anyone who is, to their mind, conveying these messages.

Given the social nature of shame, this 'Attack Other' approach is extraordinarily difficult to sustain on our own. Like all self-conscious emotions, shame only arises as a result of seeing ourselves in the mirror presented to us by others. So to sustain this strategy, we will eventually need to find an alternative mirror in which to see ourselves. For example, suppose I am caught selling drugs. If I see myself through the eyes of my victim, the police, the judge and society at large, then this public exposure of my 'bad self' will bring about the most intense shame and guilt.[33] But suppose I see myself as belonging to a group of people for whom a successful drug sale is regarded as a matter of immense pride. In that case, I will see myself through the eyes of those who both approve of my actions and disapprove of the way in which everyone else has responded. As a result, I can overwhelm any shame that still lurks in the back of my mind with the pride generated by the criminal subculture into which I have immersed myself. This would, of course, be the worst possible outcome for any 'justice system'. My sense of self, my very identity, has now become deeply linked to an inverted sense of right and wrong. I will continue to break the law *as a matter of self-respect*. In other words, by entering a subculture that rejects the norms and expectations of law-abiding society, I can effectively disarm the threat that it posed to my social self.[34]

It is important to note that this approach presumes that I have the capacity for shame, guilt and empathy: I am not a psychopath. It is simply that what causes me to feel shame is out of sync with mainstream morality.[35] I have aligned myself with a quite different set of norms and expectations. For example, I will now feel pride when I get away with a significant drug sale, but guilty if I do not share the proceeds with my collaborators. It follows that if I am caught, punished and named and shamed by mainstream society, I will not even 'hear' the censure that these responses are designed to communicate. Instead, what I will 'hear' is a powerful *affirmation* of who I am. For me, punishment will be a badge of honour, a mark of respect. Far from being a deterrent, punishment is likely to encourage my recidivism.[36]

7.4 REPAIR-WORK FOR THE PERSON RESPONSIBLE

The only viable alternative, then, is the adage to 'hate the sin, love the sinner'. This can be translated as meaning: 'We cannot condone what you have done, but we respect you as a human being.' If I were a person responsible, then this message is precisely what I would need to hear in order to take the first step toward moral repair. If I feel that I am being treated as a human being with intrinsic worth, then this will help me to feel safe and respected—in spite of what I have done. As a result, I am less likely to resort to the self-protecting strategies of blaming and rejecting others.

Best of all, this recognition of my humanity allows me to admit that I have done the wrong thing. The reason is this: if I know that my humanity will be upheld, then I no longer have any reason to fear being dehumanised, rejected, humiliated and outcast as a 'monster'. I will still feel the shame of a guilty conscience. But this is precisely the kind of shame that any human being in my situation ought to feel. In other words, it is the kind of shame that *affirms* my humanity. It also re-connects me to those who hold the moral values that I have violated. Having admitted to my wrongdoing, I can now do something to remove the cause of my shame. I can repudiate my actions, apologise and make amends. I can make sure that I do not repeat such behaviour.[37]

Suppose, then, that I have done the wrong thing and I am 'stuck' in the shame reaction of rejecting or blaming others ('Attack Other'). We have seen how being censured and punished would, on its own, be very unlikely to result in my admitting fault and taking responsibility. On the contrary, I am more likely to maintain my sense of self-respect by retreating into a subculture that affirms my wrongdoing. This is also why forcing someone to apologise is so counter-productive. If I was required to offer an apology in an 'Attack Other' state of mind, I would invariably find some way to blame the victim (e.g. 'I'm sorry you feel that way'). The insincerity would be heard a mile away.

The only way I will admit fault and offer a genuine apology is by making the transition to self-blame ('Attack Self'). I will only do this if I feel safe: I need to know that I will not be rejected or dehumanised if I admit to wrongdoing. And I am far more likely to maintain this path of moral repair if those around me affirm what I am doing and trust me to deliver on my promise that I have changed.

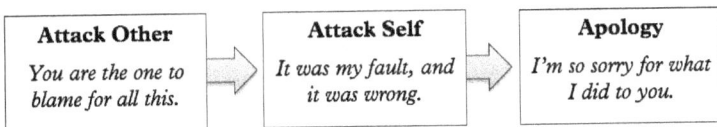

Attack Other	**Attack Self**	**Apology**
You are the one to blame for all this.	*It was my fault, and it was wrong.*	*I'm so sorry for what I did to you.*

Like the gap between defensive anger and forgiveness, there is more work to be done before a person responsible can move from self-blame to an apology. In Chapter 12, we will see what this involves.

8. Attack Self

The second type of 'Fight' reaction is inward-directed, in the sense that it involves *attacking ourselves*.[1] Like the outward-directed 'Fight' strategy ('Attack Other'), this approach is an attempt to take back control. The main difference is that this strategy does not defy the negative underlying message. Nor does it try to suppress or displace the shame we feel. Rather it tries to avoid an even greater potential threat to our social self. How? By accepting the current threat. We *embrace* the shame we already feel as a way of escaping an even greater degree of shame. It is, in this sense, a kind of trade-off. For example, suppose you say something to me that tells me you think I am inferior, stupid, incompetent, or evil. Unlikely as it may seem, one possible reaction I might have is to accept that you are right. I might even then start to treat myself accordingly. For instance, I might ridicule or denigrate myself for being so stupid. I might castigate or condemn myself for being so incompetent. I could even 'punish' myself for being such a bad person.

Why would anyone use such a strange, self-destructive tactic? There are three possible reasons, all of which have to do with the avoidance of an even greater shame. First, if I accept your view of me and treat myself accordingly, this will actually preserve a connection with you. We will be 'on the same wavelength'. We both agree about who was to blame, and what needs to be done to 'the person responsible', namely myself. We both perceive how useless and worthless I am. To me, this is a price worth paying. I am prepared to engage in this kind of self-blame simply because it would cause me far greater shame if I lost my connection with you.[2] And you have made it very clear to me that if I try to stand up to you and hold you responsible, that is precisely what will happen. So I choose to accept the blame and the punishment for something I did not do, in order to avoid the far more terrifying and painful humiliation of being abandoned and rejected.[3]

Second, if I am attacked for no apparent reason, many of my old certainties can become 'unstuck'. I thought that I had the capacity to protect myself. I thought I could predict how people are likely to behave. I assumed that I could gauge who was reliable and who was untrustworthy. But this capacity has now been seriously challenged. That is not only a cause for severe anxiety and fear, but also shame. I have become vividly aware that my social self is far more vulnerable than I had assumed. But there is a ready solution to hand. If I blame myself for what happened, then I can immediately re-gain a sense of control. If the threat to my social self comes from within, then it is not nearly as vulnerable to 'outside' threats. In other words, this is, again, a price worth paying. What I desperately want to do is avoid the even greater shame of being susceptible to forces that I did not predict and cannot explain. So I fill in the predictive and explanatory gap with my own agency. I say to myself: 'The reason that X happened to me is because of something that I did or said.' If the harm that I experienced was my own fault, that means I will know how to prevent this sort of thing from happening again. But if there is no explanation, then I will feel small, weak and helpless—subject to the inexplicable whim of other people or sheer chance.[4]

Third, if I blame myself, then I will not have to take the risk of standing up to the person who really was responsible. When there is a significant power imbalance—as between children and parents, wives and husbands, employees and employers—then the trade-off can become a matter of survival. We blame ourselves as a way of avoiding the even greater shame of being attacked, demeaned, humiliated or even destroyed.[5]

8.2 REPAIR-WORK FOR THE PERSON HARMED

Clearly there is much that is flawed and dangerous about the self-blame strategy. Even so, it is not uncommon for people who have been harmed to use this approach. We frequently blame ourselves for the actions of others. We take on the guilt and shame for things that were not our fault. But this solution is patently incompatible with our self-respect and dignity. It is also a falsehood that cannot be maintained without causing severe damage not only to our self-esteem, but also our grasp on reality.[6]

For a person harmed who is 'stuck' in the inward-directed 'Fight' reaction of *self-blame*, the work of moral repair cannot begin until they are willing and able to move to the outward-directed 'Fight' reaction of *defensive anger*. They must lay the blame at the feet of those who were actually responsible. They need to feel the outrage that comes with realising that, not only have they been wronged, but they have also taken the blame for something that was ultimately not their fault.

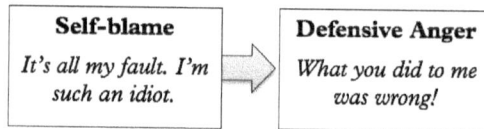

Self-blame	Defensive Anger
It's all my fault. I'm such an idiot.	*What you did to me was wrong!*

8.3 REPAIR-WORK FOR THE PERSON RESPONSIBLE

As we have seen, 'Attack Self' is also a strategy that can be used by those who have caused harm. Here it seems evident that, at least initially, this is the right response. Like anger, it is an essential first step in the work of moral repair. For example, suppose I do something bad, and, for this reason, come to believe that 'I am a bad person'. If this is true, then I need to be honest to myself about what I have done. This will not be easy. Facing up to the truth will bring the intense pain of shame or guilt into the forefront of my consciousness. I will feel terrible about myself because of what I have done.[7] But this kind of self-blame or self-incrimination is entirely appropriate when I really have done something wrong. Put another way, if I have caused harm to someone, then I cannot embark on the work of moral repair until I have moved from the 'Flight' reactions of 'Avoidance' and 'Withdrawal' to this kind of inward-directed 'Fight' reaction.

Nevertheless, even for those who really are responsible, self-blame is not a viable long-term strategy. It can easily degenerate into the extreme self-punishment or self-condemnation mentioned earlier. What I need to do instead is move from self-blame to making an apology to those I have wronged. In Chapter 12, we will see how it is possible to make this transition.

9. Compassion

We have seen how the work of moral repair cannot get off the ground until people have made the transition from the shame-reactions in which they are 'stuck' to one of two other reactions. Specifically, to begin the work of moral repair, the person harmed needs to move to the 'Attack Other' reaction we have called defensive anger. Meanwhile, the person responsible will need to move to the 'Attack Self' reactions of self-blame and remorse.

We have also noted along the way that this is not the end point. There is a transition that each will need to make if they are to complete this journey: namely, the move to offering a genuine *apology* (for the person responsible) and the response of *forgiveness* or other ways of 'letting go' (for the person harmed). But how does this work? How can these transitions be made? In each case, there is one emotion that is central to answering this question: compassion. So before we look more closely at each side of the equation, we will need to understand, in general terms, the nature and role of compassion.

9.2 THE ROLE OF COMPASSION

One of the most remarkable features that we have as human beings is the capacity to care about the suffering of others. But this capacity will lie dormant unless the fires of emotion are sparked. We all know what it is like to suffer. We have all experienced, to greater or lesser degrees, the torment and anguish of unrelieved pain. When we were in that state, we desperately wanted those around us to do everything they could to remove our pain. Yet we have also experienced situations in which we have failed to act to alleviate the suffering of others—even when we knew there was something we could have done. How can this be? How is it that we failed to act?

What seems to have been lacking is the emotion of compassion. As we have seen, the motivation to act, the thing that propels us to do something springs from our feelings, rather than mere intellectual understanding. It is only when we *feel for ourselves* something of the pain that others are feeling—imagining what it is like to be in their shoes—that we become motivated to alleviate their suffering. Compassion is the engine that drives altruism.[1]

Is compassion even possible?

It is worth considering at this point an objection to the possibility of compassion. One might argue that when we are motivated to help others, our ultimate goal is to relieve the empathetic pain that *we* feel, rather than the pain of others. Helping others to recover from their suffering is simply the means, not the end. But then it follows that acting out of compassion (as distinct from mere self-interest) is a psychological impossibility.

There are a number of confusions in this objection, but sorting them out will help us to clarify how compassion works. Seeing other people who are in pain, and feeling something of what they are going through, *can* be very distressing. Indeed, there are times when our own distress is so overwhelming that our attention becomes focused almost entirely on the pain we are feeling. The pain of the other person is pushed into the margins of our awareness. We are instinctively driven to concentrate on removing whatever pain is in the forefront of our consciousness. And since, in this situation, that will be the pain *we* are feeling, alleviating our own distress will become our priority.

It must be said that this self-interested motivation could (and often does) lead us to try and remove the suffering of the other person. But when *our own* distress is the focus, we will usually do so in a way that is insensitive to what they actually need. For example, we bluntly tell them to 'get over it'. We accuse them of being 'too sensitive' or of 'over-exaggerating' their pain. We might even pressure them to 'cut their losses' and forgive.[2] Another way of alleviating our distress is to walk away. For example, we might try to find some entertaining distraction to help us forget about the suffering we have witnessed. Out of sight, out of mind. And it's not difficult to come up with any number of rationalisations to justify our lack of action. For example:

- 'It is none of my business.'

- 'I've worked hard for my money. It's not my fault they are poor.'

- 'They brought it on themselves—it will teach them a lesson.'

- 'He must have known it was a dangerous line of work.'

What is interesting about these examples is that most of us can easily distinguish them from what we would ordinarily call 'compassion'. So we must have some experience of a reality with which to compare these pretenders—even if they are relatively rare. If so, the objection above is not so much a question about whether compassion is possible. We know that it is because we have experienced it (along with its absence). Rather the question is: How can we become *more* compassionate? More precisely, how is it possible for us to regulate the focus that we place on our own distress? How can we shift the balance of our attention from ourselves to others? What makes it possible for us to move our own pain to the margins of our consciousness, so that the pain of others can take centre stage?

Increasing our capacity for compassion

It is an important point to note that, for most of us, this shift in the balance of attention will not come naturally or easily. Aside from the occasional 'moral hero', we are more inclined to focus on ourselves, even at the best of times. So this outward focus will require a great deal of effort and determination. In particular, it will mean adopting the strategies below:

1. Separate their pain from your own: We need to differentiate between our own feelings of distress and the pain that is being experienced by the person for whom we feel empathy. Confusing the two is partly what leads us to focus on our own pain and forget that someone else is hurting. It's as if we imagine that we are the only one suffering in this situation. The person for whom we feel empathy is no more than an obstacle in the way of our own pain relief. We might even think of them as the cause of our suffering. Were it not   for their suffering, we would not feel so distressed!

2. Focus on the disparity between your feelings and theirs: It is crucial to remember that, when we experience empathy, we are only a mirror—not the reality. What we are feeling is only a reflection of *someone else's* lived experience, not our own.[3] Yes, these 'mirror feelings' are uncomfortable and disturbing. But they are usually not a patch on the real thing. Empathy does not replicate every detail or dimension of another person's thoughts and feelings. When we witness another person in pain, we do not experience exactly the same quality or degree of suffering. If we can keep our minds fixed on this disparity, it will be harder to prioritise the alleviation of our own distress.

3. *Where necessary, tend to your own wounds first:* It is likely that we can feel empathy when we see others in pain only because this triggers memories of our own painful experiences. The problem is that, in some cases, witnessing the suffering of another person may evoke memories of pain that, while similar, are even more severe than the pain we are observing. For example, we might see a parent lightly smacking a child; but then find ourselves overwhelmed by emotions that spring from the far more violent and cruel beatings we experienced in our own childhood. In such a case, there are two things we can do: First, we need to follow the first strategy above and separate our own pain from the pain of the other person, so that the two are not confused. Second, we need to be honest with ourselves. If our own remembered pain is so intense that we cannot focus on anything else, then we must tend to our own wounds first. Otherwise, we will be driven to relieve their pain as a means of relieving our own, which is likely to do them more harm than good.[4]

These three strategies should help us to regulate our own distress so that it does not absorb all our attention. They will also make it far more likely that our experience of empathy gives rise to other-directed emotions, such as sympathy and altruistic concern. Put another way, these strategies will tend to elicit feelings of compassion. And it is this emotion that will motivate us to relieve the suffering of others for their own sake.[5]

9.3 THE BENEFITS OF ACTING FROM COMPASSION

Acting out of compassion is not merely the right thing to do. It is also far more satisfying. First, the alternative, as we have seen, is to walk away from the suffering of others; or to offer assistance merely as a way of making ourselves feel better. But to sustain this distance from reality requires that we immerse ourselves into a world of self-deception, cognitive distortions, blaming-the-victim, callousness, and so on. This is a terrible price to pay.[6]

Second, the benefits of acting from compassion are so much greater for everyone involved. Empathy is not limited to feeling the pain of others. We can also feel the happiness that others experience. This means that, if we can ease the suffering of others, not only will our sympathy and concern for them dissipate—we will also experience something of the joy and relief that they feel as a consequence.

Third, if I act from compassion, then I will not need to resort to any self-destructive hiding from reality: I will be able to see myself through the eyes of those whose suffering I have helped to relieve, and feel the pride of being a good person. Likewise, those who I have helped can see themselves through my eyes, and feel the pride of being recognised as someone of equal worth, just as deserving of happiness and well-being as anyone else.

10. Moral Repair for Persons Harmed

10.1 THE ROLE OF DEFENSIVE ANGER

If I have been harmed, what needs to happen in order for me to make the transition from defensive anger to forgiveness or other ways of 'letting go'? How can I complete my journey of moral repair? To answer this question we need to take a closer look at how anger works.

How offensive anger arises

The 'Attack Other' shame reaction arises as a result of the following sequence of events:

Stage 1. *Trigger:* We hear a shame trigger (e.g. someone insults us, we are unexpectedly ignored, we are treated with contempt).

Stage 2. *Shame:* There is a period—lasting from microseconds to days, or even years—when we feel humiliated or inferior.

Stage 3. *Reaction:* Feelings of offensive or defensive anger burst to the surface of our consciousness, shunting aside our shame with the protective armour of emotional defiance.

One question that this sequence raises is this: why would *offensive* anger arise instead of *defensive* anger? Most researchers have suggested that the kind of blind rage that leads to violent revenge (which is what I have called 'offensive anger') is driven by a failure to *acknowledge* that it is shame we are feeling.[1] In other words, offensive anger requires that our feelings of shame somehow take place outside of our conscious awareness. If someone insults us, we react instinctively by returning the attack in kind, a tit-for-tat response.

This direct route from trigger to reaction 'bypasses' the awareness of shame, thereby avoiding the full force of this painful feeling. Shame must still be there, working away in the margins of our consciousness. But it remains behind the scenes, pulling the strings. Otherwise we would not be reacting at all against the shame-trigger.

So why does this process elicit the kind of rage that leads to revenge? Why would 'bypassing' the awareness of shame result in offensive anger? The reason seems to be this: As we have seen, shame does not merely alert us to the fact that our social self is under threat. It also reveals to us what it is that we value. It tells us what we care about. Most importantly, shame is the psychological mechanism by which we discover or re-affirm that we see ourselves and others as having equal and inherent worth. When someone treats us as an inferior being, or as a mere means to an end, it is shame that alerts us to the fact that we have not been treated as we ought to have been. But this fact would make no sense unless we see not only ourselves, but also the person who has attacked us as being of equal and intrinsic worth. So if we 'bypass' the awareness of shame and go straight to anger, it follows that we will have missed out this moral constraint on our actions. The purpose of revenge is, as we have seen, to 're-balance the scales' by bringing down the opponent, even to the point of destroying their very humanity. For the reasons given above, taking revenge could not be carried out by someone who is aware of their shame.

Put another way: when we say that someone 'has no shame', we mean that they are acting in a way that does not acknowledge the humanity of others, instead only seeming to care about themselves. In actual fact, such a person is indeed experiencing shame. But their shame reaction has suppressed this feeling to such an extent that it plays virtually no role in determining how they then treat others in response.[2]

How defensive anger arises

Defensive anger is quite different. It does involve an acknowledgement or awareness of shame. In other words, there is a moment—in between Stages 2 and 3 above—where we think to ourselves something like this:

'Why am I feeling bad about myself? This wasn't my fault. I have nothing to be ashamed of here.'

As these thoughts emerge, our defensive anger will kick in. Because of this intermediate stage, in which our shame is acknowledged, the 'Attack Other' reaction will serve a very different purpose. Rather than motivating revenge, it will instead defy the threat. The function of our anger will be to reject the negative messages that are being conveyed, rather than the messenger.

Defensive anger is an emotional buttress against messages that threaten to undermine my self-worth. When I experience this kind of anger, I feel in myself that I really do matter, that you cannot just use me for your own purposes, that I am not inferior to you, that I am as much a human being as you.[3] What this kind of anger does not do is compel me to return these messages in kind. It does not set out to affirm my humanity by destroying yours. And it takes this alternative path primarily because it springs from an awareness or acknowledgement of shame.

This is not to suggest that defensive anger is without its own problems. Defensive anger is still a reaction against shame. It does not, in itself, release or discharge shame. Rather its function is to suppress or displace this painful attack on our self-worth, shunting it aside in favour of the more empowering and affirming feelings of anger. But what this means is that, even as our anger is defying the attack against us, there will still be some part of us that remains in doubt about whether or not the negative message is true. Otherwise this message would not be heard as a threat from which we need to defend ourselves.[4]

Put another way, my defensive anger cannot *disarm* the threat to my social self, posed by the person who has harmed me: it only puts up a *defence*. As long as this person stands by their original message, I will need to continue defending myself against the mirror that they are holding up to me. Each time I remember what they did to me, my anger will need to kick in, re-affirming my self-worth and displacing the shame that threatens to flood my consciousness. Defensive anger does not eliminate the threat. It only protects us from its destructiveness.[5]

10.2 THE EFFECT OF AN APOLOGY

Suppose the person who hurt me decided to take back their original negative message about me: in other words, they withdraw their threat to my social self. And suppose they replaced this original message with positive, affirming messages instead. This would be extremely powerful. I would no longer need to maintain a defensive stance against how they see me. Thanks to my angry defiance, I have, until now, been able to resist the evidence against me that was presented in their message. But the evidence was still out there, causing enough doubt in me to warrant my continued anger. So if they take back their message, then they will have withdrawn this evidence completely and I would no longer be under threat. But how can they do this? How can a person who has caused harm remove the threat that they are posing? The answer is this: *they can engage in the work of moral repair.* They can apologise and make amends for the wrong that they did to me.

There is a catch, however. First, I will only be persuaded that they have withdrawn their message if I am convinced that their apology is sincere. I need to see that their words are motivated by remorse, rather than self-interest. Second, I will only allow myself to be persuaded of this if I can sense something of what it is like to be in their shoes. Both conditions require the same thing: the capacity to empathise. The problem is that, in my current state of mind, experiencing empathy for you is the last thing I feel like doing. My defences are still up. You may feel utterly mortified by what you have done to me, apologising repeatedly. But I will be unable to hear you while I am feeling the full force of my defensive anger. So far as my emotions are concerned, you are the enemy—the one who attacked my self-worth. I cannot yet accept the fact that you have withdrawn your disrespectful message. I first need to remove the wall of angry defiance I have put up to protect myself against how you see me. Until then, I will not be able to hear that you no longer stand by what you said about me.

This looks like a 'Catch-22' scenario. On the one hand, hearing that you no longer stand by your message would enable me to let go of my defensive anger. Yet I first need to let my guard down in order to hear you. Fortunately, there is a way to break this stalemate. It involves the person responsible for causing harm taking the initiative—as indeed they should, given their obligation to try and make things right.[6]

The humble admission of guilt

Suppose that you have harmed me. As we have seen, this means that you pose a threat, and so my guard is up. But suppose you admit to what you have done. You acknowledge to me that it was your fault, and that what you did was wrong. Would this not give me reason to lower my guard? Not on its own. The admission of fault can be done in a way that is belligerent, callous, aggressive and even mocking (e.g. 'Yeah, I did it. So what are you going to do about it?'). If this happens, then my defensive anger will remain firmly in place, as it should. You still pose a threat. There is no indication you have changed your views about me.

But suppose that your tone of voice, your words and your general demeanour communicates authentic signs of humility and remorse for the pain you have caused. In this situation, I would find it very difficult to maintain my wall of defiance. There would be no need. It would be clear to me that you are in 'Attack Self' mode, 'wearing your shame on your sleeve', as we say. The threat that you pose to me will have decreased significantly. Indeed, the fact that you have accepted blame in this self-effacing way creates a connection between us: we both agree that this is exactly the right self-appraisal for you to have in this situation. So, as this connection is made, I can begin to let down my guard. You have not yet explicitly taken back your message in an apology. So I still have cause to feel defensive anger. But now, my emotional barriers are not so overwhelming that I am unable to hear your apology. Your humble acceptance of blame and underlying remorse has created the safety and assurance that I need. I am now willing to allow myself to be persuaded that you have withdrawn your message.[7]

The role of empathy in accepting an apology

Suppose you then offer your apology. If I had still been feeling the full strength of my defensive anger, I would only have been able to hear your words and observe your outward expressions of emotion. My understanding would only have been skin deep. However, your opening admission of fault has cleared the way. It has allowed me to look behind the scenes, as it were. Not only can I hear the surface words and gestures that you are making. I can start to enter into your emotional world and feel something of what it is like to be in your shoes in this moment.[8] So as I hear your words of apology, I will begin to feel what this moment must be like for you. I can only do this, of course, by drawing upon my own life-experiences. I too have felt remorse for the wrongs that I have done, and I know how painful that can be. This will enable me to grasp something of the shame and sorrow that you are feeling.[9]

On the other hand, I have also offered apologies that were less than fully sincere. So I know the signs, intimately. I can tell the difference between an apology that is motivated by genuine remorse, and one that is self-interested or begrudging. I know how to lace an apology with subtle excuses, minimisations, and justifications. I know what it feels like to see the person I have harmed with distracted or glazed eyes—not really seeing them, not registering that this is a fellow human being whom I have hurt. I too have sighed, fidgeted and slumped down in a way that communicates annoyance, self-pity and surrender, rather than a heartfelt desire to do the right thing. So I will carefully observe the way in which you apologise: your body language, your tone of voice, and the words you use. But it will not be the surface impressions that ultimately persuade me of your sincerity. Rather it will be the 'mirror emotions' they trigger within me. I need to feel for myself something of what you are feeling as you apologise. I need to sense that your emotions match up with my own experience of what it feels like to offer a sincere apology. If there is enough similarity, I will be convinced that you no longer stand by your message. Only empathy can persuade me that your apology is giving voice to authentic feelings of remorse.

An objection

Some might argue that experiencing empathy for the person who has wronged us is unrealistic, even offensive. For example, the wrong against us may be so violent or repulsive that we could not possibly imagine what it might be like to be in their shoes. We have never done anything like this ourselves. Alternatively, in trying to imagine their 'point of view', we may find ourselves realising, in a far more vivid way, just how inexcusably brutal and malicious they were, which may simply increase our anger toward them.[10] But there are three points here that need to be clarified.

1. Our empathetic focus is not primarily directed toward gaining a better understanding of what it was like for them *to commit the wrongdoing*. Rather it is focused on what it is like for them *to feel the pain of remorse*, not only for what they did, but also the selfishness and cruelty of their motives and thoughts at the time.

2. As noted in a previous section, empathy does not entail being able to replicate *exactly* what someone is feeling. It only works because we can draw upon our own life experience and find *some* degree of commonality. And all of us know what it is like to do something wrong. We have all hurt someone else, at one time or another. We know what it is like to feel ashamed because of what we have done to others. We have all offered apologies, both sincere

and insincere. So we are all capable of being persuaded, in this way, by an apology.[11]

Having said this, it might be argued that the more dissimilar someone's wrongdoing is to anything we have done ourselves, the harder it is for us to be persuaded by their apology. For instance, I would find it very difficult to grasp what it is like to feel remorse for having committed a murder. On the other hand, it could also be argued that the hardest apology to accept is one in which the wrong done is almost exactly the same as something we have done ourselves. It may cut too close to the bone, particularly if we have not yet apologised for our own wrongdoing.

Yet these cases are not counter-examples: they both make perfect sense on the account above. It is harder to be persuaded where the wrongdoing is dissimilar to our own because it is more difficult for us to draw upon our life experiences, and so empathise with their situation. Again, if the wrongdoing is too similar to our own, then we may resist 'hearing' the apology because we do not want to feel what it is like to be in their shoes: that would only expose our own moral failings. In other words, in both cases, it is our capacity to empathise with the wrongdoer that governs our ability to be persuaded by their apology.

10.3 EXPERIENCING FORGIVENESS

Up to this point, we have only considered what needs to happen in order for me to be persuaded by your apology. But surely the work of moral repair is not so one-sided. Thanks to your apology, I now know that you think differently about me. But doesn't moral repair include a change in how I think about you? If so, how does this work? On what basis can I revise my views about you?

The moral barrier to forgiveness

Suppose that you have seriously wronged me. I cannot simply ignore what you did to me. It was deeply hurtful and completely unjustified. Also, what you have done tells me something about the kind of person you are. If it made no difference, I would be condoning or somehow excusing what you did. I would be, in effect, assuming that what you did was 'okay'; or that you were somehow not responsible for what happened, and so it does not reflect on your moral character. But I cannot do this. Not only would it be a lie: it would also be utterly disrespectful to myself. Whatever I do, I need to make sure that I reject and denounce the unfair and false messages that you sent when you hurt me. I need to stand up for myself and proclaim the truth about my own inherent worth.[12]

So what are the options? How can I change my views about the kind of person you are, in a way that is compatible with my self-respect? The answer is this: I need some evidence that will block the inference from 'you did a bad thing' to 'you are a bad person'. I need to be able to separate *what you have done* from *who you are*.[13]

It is important to be clear about what is needed here. To get to this point, I must have already recognised that, regardless of what you have done, you have intrinsic and equal worth as a human being. At some point, I would have acknowledged that, even though you did a monstrous thing, you are not literally a monster. If I thought that of you, I could not have moved from offensive to defensive anger. But none of this is equivalent to believing that, regardless of what you have done, you are still a good person. When we hurt other people, that reflects on our character. It says something about the kind of person we are. We can 'hate the sin and love the sinner'. But that does not erase the moral distinction between (a) someone who has committed a terrible crime and (b) someone who has, say, devoted their lives to alleviating poverty. Both have intrinsic worth. But this does not mean they are both just as morally good or virtuous as each other.[14] So to change my views about you, I need evidence that *the wrong that you have done to me* no longer reflects on your character, on the kind of person you are.

The evidence needed for forgiveness

Only you can provide this evidence: I need to hear you take back the messages that you sent me. You need to condemn the denigrating messages about me that you conveyed in your wrongful act. You need to return the dignity and respect that I was owed as a human being.[15] We have already seen how you can do this: you can offer me a sincere apology and make amends. These actions will block the inference from 'you have done a bad thing' to 'you are a 'bad person'. Why? Because you no longer stand by what you did. Your expression of remorse shows that the person you are *now* is not the person you were *then*. So if I am persuaded that your apology is sincere, I can legitimately revise my views about you. Doing so will be compatible with my self-respect: I am not thereby condoning, justifying or excusing what you did. It is simply that I no longer regard those actions as evidence of your character. What you did to me no longer reflects on who you are now.[16] I no longer see you through the darkened prism of your wrongdoing. It does not cloud my view of who you are. I no longer hold it against you.[17]

In short, I now see you as someone who is no longer a threat to my social self.[18] The evidence that supported my shame-belief, my suspicion that I might be inferior or worthless, has now been withdrawn.[19] Without this support, my shame-belief will vanish. That in turn will release my shame-feelings. As a consequence, I no longer have any reason to suppress or displace my shame. Nor do I need to block the threat that this painful emotion might again be triggered by you (or a memory of what you did). And so, my defensive anger will subside. It no longer has any role to play. I do not require its protection. This emotional release can happen very quickly or over a longer period of time.[20] But it is precisely what it means to experience forgiveness.

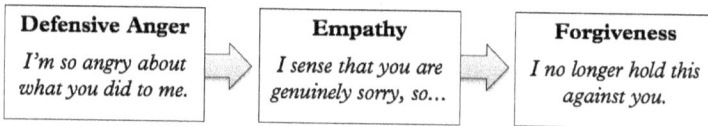

Defensive Anger	**Empathy**	**Forgiveness**
I'm so angry about what you did to me.	*I sense that you are genuinely sorry, so...*	*I no longer hold this against you.*

10.4 OFFERING FORGIVENESS

So far, we have looked at how a sincere apology is the means by which the person responsible can take back the message that triggered shame within the person harmed. We have also seen how 'hearing' a genuine apology can enable the person harmed to experience forgiveness. But there is one more step that could be taken toward moral repair.

The effect of responding to an apology

If someone has come to offer a sincere apology, this means that they will be immersed in feelings of guilt and remorse. The reason they feel this way is not merely because they have come to understand that they have violated some abstract moral code. Their shame has arisen primarily because they are seeing themselves through the eyes of those whom they have hurt and whose opinion of them matters. The message they are hearing, the trigger for their shame, is this: *The wrong that you have done reflects on your moral character: it changes how we think about you. There must be a character flaw or a badness within you that made it possible for you to do such an immoral, selfish and hurtful thing.*

It follows that the person whom they have hurt, as well as others who they care about, will have considerable control over whether or not their shame persists. The person harmed (and others) can decide whether or not to take back this message that they are conveying to the person responsible—and thereby contribute significantly to the alleviation of their shame. The person responsible can, perhaps, discharge a measure of shame by *imagining* how others would (or ought) to see them if they really knew how sincere they were. But imagination is no match for reality. Shame is a social emotion: it arises as a result of how *others* see us, not merely how we see ourselves. So shame-release largely depends upon those around us changing how they see us. That is why it matters so much to us how people respond to our efforts to redeem ourselves.

The motivation to offer forgiveness

Suppose that I have been persuaded that your apology is sincere. Your shame and remorse convince me that you are genuinely sorry. As a result of this, I no longer hold your wrongdoing against you, and so have experienced the liberation of forgiveness. Up to this point, I may still not have told you about any of this. Yet I know, from my own life experience, how painful it would be to offer an apology without hearing any response in return—or, even worse, to have it rejected. I too have wanted people not to hold my past actions against me—especially those who were hurt by them. So I know something of what it is like to be in your shoes. I can sense the pain of this unmet need within you. You are still feeling the shame triggered by how you think I feel about you. That message about the stain on your character remains hanging in the air. For all you know, I am still angry, and even contemptuous of you. So I can sense that you are waiting, hoping that I will accept your apology or offer you my forgiveness.[21]

But recall the previous Chapter on compassion. The fact that I can feel your pain empathetically is not enough to make me want to alleviate it—at least not for your sake. If I am feeling too distressed or anxious myself, then I may not be able to focus on what *you* are feeling. It would be of no help to you if I accepted your apology merely to relieve my own distress, rather than yours—even if my distress is primarily due to seeing you so desperate for me to forgive you. Any such offer of forgiveness is likely to come across as superficial, insincere, or condescending (e.g. 'I guess I should put you out of your misery and accept your apology'.) You will hear the lack of authenticity, and remain unconvinced. So I may need to wait until I have separated out my feelings from yours and tended to my own wounds. I need to be ready in myself, so that I can respond to you for the right reasons. In other words, if we really want to alleviate the shame of someone who has apologised to us, then we need to be motivated by compassion.[22] If we tell them that we accept their apology, or that we have forgiven them, this needs to be primarily for *their* sake, rather than merely our own.[23]

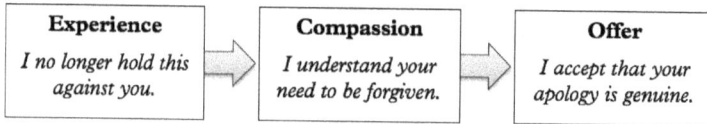

Experience		**Compassion**		**Offer**
I no longer hold this against you.	⇨	*I understand your need to be forgiven.*	⇨	*I accept that your apology is genuine.*

How offering forgiveness can release shame

When I let you know that I have accepted your apology or offered my forgiveness, I am telling you that I take back my view that what you did to me counts against you.[24] In doing so, you will have received powerful evidence against the shame-belief that you are a bad person. If this is sufficient to defeat your belief, then your own shame will be released. As a result, you are likely to feel immense relief—a relief that I will share, empathetically, with you. I will have already experienced the liberation from my own anger by forgiving you. But in taking the additional step of *offering* you forgiveness, I can also share in what it feels like for you to have the burden of shame lifted from your shoulders.[25]

11. Forgiveness

11.1 WHAT FORGIVENESS IS

The previous Chapter set out to explain the role of forgiveness in the work of moral repair. However, any perspective taken on forgiveness will invariably be controversial. There is a great deal of common ground in the literature on forgiveness, but also significant disagreement. Part of this is due to the disparate motives for advocating forgiveness, such as 'self-help', religious duty, political reconciliation, or, as in our case, moral repair. But there are also important conceptual and moral issues that any view of forgiveness will need to consider. Since forgiveness plays such a central role in *this* account of moral repair—and so, of restorative justice—we will need to work through at least some of these concerns. This will also help us to gain more clarity about what forgiveness means, and what it does not mean.

The components of forgiveness

There are four distinct components that make up the phenomenon of forgiveness: being willing to forgive, experiencing forgiveness, offering forgiveness and declaring forgiveness.

Willingness to forgive	Experience of forgiveness	Offer of forgiveness	Declaration of forgiveness

Much of the disagreement about the role of forgiveness can be traced to the fact that the word 'forgiveness' is very often used without specifying whether it is referring to one or more of these components. The problem is that each of these four components has a different function, some of which we have already identified. Moreover, each has a different set of moral pre-requisites: depending on the context, one component may be morally justified, whilst another may not (yet) be. This is partly why each component ought to follow the sequence above, especially given the problems that can arise when they do not. So our first step will be to tease apart these four components, with a particular focus on those we have not yet discussed in detail: namely, the willingness to forgive and declarations of forgiveness.

Willingness to forgive

We have seen that one crucial part of the work of forgiveness is that we feel some empathy for the pain that the person responsible is going through in expressing their remorse. But there is another role for empathy in this context, one that focuses on the circumstances that may have led to their offending behaviour. As we will see, this kind of empathy does not, on its own, provide us with an adequate reason for forgiving someone. But it can bring about a *willingness* to forgive them: and this openness can, of course, make it more likely that we come to experience forgiveness.

Before we go any further, it will be useful to distinguish between the willingness to forgive *in general*, and the willingness to forgive *a particular individual*. The former is a long-standing disposition or inclination that we will have inculcated over many years of empathetic reflection. The latter will only arise as we learn more about a particular individual who has caused us harm. We can, of course, have both the general and specific types at the same time; and each will have a significant influence on our decisions. For instance, we might already have a general willingness to forgive those who harm us. Indeed, this may have been one of the reasons why we were prepared to take part in the process of moral repair with a particular person. Then, as we learn more about their circumstances, we find that we are increasingly open to the possibility of forgiving them. An example may help to make this concrete.

Suppose I put myself in the shoes of the person who has wronged me. I soon begin to realise that, if I had been in their circumstances—with their upbringing, education, financial resources, life-opportunities, and so on—I might well have become the kind of person who would have committed the same wrong that they have just done to me. But in that case, it is largely a matter of 'moral luck' that I am not sitting exactly where they are right now.[1] On the other hand, it may be that I can't even imagine causing the kind of suffering that they have inflicted, even if I *had* been placed in their life-circumstances. So much about me would need to have changed, that I can't make any sense of *that* person still being 'me'.[2] Nevertheless, I do recognise that I too have hurt people terribly in the past—or, with enough temptation, could potentially do so in the future. I am no saint, after all. I just haven't been 'tested' in the way that many people have. The point, either way, is that I do not want to live in the kind of world in which my wrongs will *always* be held against me, regardless of how remorseful I am, and no matter how much I have sought to make amends and change my ways. So I feel as if I share a kind of 'moral solidarity' with the person responsible, in the sense that I would want to be forgiven if I were in their shoes.[3] This makes me far more open to forgiving them.

But we need to be clear here. Experiencing this kind of 'common ground' with the person responsible does not, on its own, give us a sound basis for actually forgiving them. It can only give us a good reason to be willing to forgive them, should the opportunity present itself. And that opportunity will only arise if they apologise for the harm they have caused, and we are persuaded that their remorse is genuine. That, as we have seen, is the only morally adequate reason for forgiveness.[4]

Declarations of forgiveness

We have seen how we can feel forgiveness for someone, without telling them about this change within us.[5] In other words, the experience of forgiveness is not the same as offering forgiveness. But there is another distinction that we need to make here. I can say the words 'I forgive you', and yet still feel just as much anger over the hurt you have caused me: I can still hold it against you. But then, my declaration of forgiveness will be false, since I have not actually forgiven you.[6]

Now, strictly speaking, I cannot 'offer' you something if it is not mine to give: I can't offer you a cup of coffee if it is not within my power to get you one. Likewise, I cannot offer you forgiveness unless I have first experienced it. Declarations are different: I can merely declare that I have forgiven you, without in fact offering you any forgiveness.[7] Of course, I can say the words 'I forgive you' as a *way* of offering you my forgiveness. But I don't need to use these words. I can offer you forgiveness nonverbally, through my facial expressions, tone of voice, how I treat you, and so on. Indeed, just like moral harm, any offer of my forgiveness will be most effectively communicated not by *what* I say, but by *how* I say it—that is, by the 'underlying messages' that are conveyed through my words and actions.

There are three practical implications that we can draw from the fact that declarations of forgiveness can be 'empty': First, declarations of forgiveness should not be seen as a kind of 'end-goal' in the journey of moral repair. We may think that we cannot move on from what has happened until the words 'I forgive you' have been said out loud or put down in writing, regardless of how people are really feeling. But just saying 'I forgive' doesn't make it so.[8]

Second, the offer of forgiveness, as we have seen, comes from a good heart: it is an honourable and compassionate thing to do. Unfortunately, for that very reason, declarations of forgiveness can be used as a 'badge of virtue'. The way in which the words 'I forgive you' are said can often betray an underlying attitude of self-congratulation or condescending moral superiority. In such cases, it is a near certainty that these words are not conveying a genuine offer of forgiveness. Sadly, as a consequence of this, declarations of forgiveness need to be treated with some degree of caution, and perhaps avoided altogether. It is, in any case, far more effective to offer forgiveness by means of nonverbal expressions—that is, in *how* we talk to and treat the person we have forgiven.

Third, there may be situations in which we not only falsely declare that we have forgiven the person responsible, but also follow this up by acting *as if* we no longer harbour any resentment toward them. Why would we do this? Here are two possibilities: First, we think it is in our best interest to give the impression that we are willing to 'let bygones be bygones'. For instance, we might be in a situation where any sign of unforgiveness is likely to be met with retaliation, social disapproval or other consequences that we could well live without. Second, we might feel that we really *should* forgive the person responsible: they have made a genuine apology, after all. But what they did was so terrible and has had such a profound impact on our lives, that we can't bring ourselves to change how we feel about them just yet. So in the meantime, we decide to 'fake it until we make it'.

Pretending to forgive might seem like a feasible strategy when we find ourselves in these predicaments. But there are three serious consequences that need to be taken into account. First, even the best actors 'leak'. Our suppressed anger will eventually surface: perhaps not in our choice of words or actions, but in our tone of voice or gestures. And then our 'fake' declaration of forgiveness will come back to bite us ('What's this all about? You said you had forgiven me!').[9] Second, our 'leakage' is likely to be indiscriminate. Instead of directing our anger against the person who deserves it, we unleash our rage upon the innocent: we lash out at a friend, we engage in malicious gossip, or much worse. Third, by taking this path, we are effectively choosing to give in to our fears, rather than be true to ourselves. The cost of this self-betrayal will, in the end, far outweigh whatever risks we were trying to avoid. In short, it is always better *not* to tell someone that we have forgiven them—let alone try to behave as if we have—merely for the sake of short-term expediency. We need to wait until we mean it.[10]

11.2 WHAT FORGIVENESS IS NOT

Some views about forgiveness give the impression that it is a great deal harder (or easier) than it really is. Others even suggest that it is morally questionable. One unfortunate impact of this is that people will be 'put off' moral repair as a viable option. So this section aims to look more closely at these views, in the hope of both clarifying and supporting the perspective that is offered here.

Forgiveness does not wipe clean a person's entire 'moral slate'

You might have apologised to me for a particular act that caused me harm. But that apology does not entail that you are also sorry for all the *other* wrong-doings you have committed over your lifetime. Likewise, when I forgive you, I am not making a judgment about your overall moral character. For one thing, I do not have enough evidence. I may think I know you well. But you could easily have wronged dozens of other people to whom you have not yet apologised, and I know nothing about this. Also, I may have no way of knowing whether your apology can be taken as representative of the kind of person you are, or whether your remorse in this case is a 'one-off'. There may be unique reasons why you felt ashamed for having committed this particular kind of offence, or why you were willing to apologise specifically to me. These reasons may or may not apply to other types of offences or other victims.[11]

In short, we need to stick to the evidence available to us at the time. We need to be very clear about the limitations of what we are doing when we forgive someone. All we are saying when we offer our forgiveness is this: 'So far as I am concerned, the wrong for which you have apologised no longer counts as evidence of the kind of person you are'.

Forgiveness is not satisfied vengeance

Suppose I am persuaded that you have experienced the pain of genuine remorse, and I find that this relieves me of my anger towards you. So far this
looks very much like forgiveness, as we have defined it. But in some cases, it
might be the very opposite. What could instead be happening is that the pain
I am witnessing has merely satisfied my desire for vengeance, and *that* is why
I am no longer angry at you.[12] How could this be?

In offering me an apology, your aim was to show me two things: first, that
you no longer stand by the shame-triggering message that you conveyed to
me in and through your wrongdoing: namely, that 'you are of lesser worth
than me'; and second, that you want to replace that message with the truth:
'you are of equal worth'. This is why you made your apology with both humility (to deny your superiority) and respect (to affirm our equality). But this
is not how I have 'read' your apology. I happen to hold the view that human
worth is not equal and inherent, but is instead determined by our relative
position or status. This means that I will only have heard one part of what
you wanted to convey in your apology: the denial of your superiority. In other
words, I took your expression of remorse to be a demonstration that you are
inferior to me: you deliberately 'put yourself down' or 'lowered yourself' on
the scales of worth, relative to me. That is why the pain of your remorse
enabled me to 'let go' of my anger. I no longer needed revenge. I didn't need
to ensure your worth was lower than mine. You did that for me.[13]

This 'solution' is deeply problematic for two reasons. First, revenge is
nothing more than the attempt to 'undo' the original wrong by returning it
in kind. Your original wrongdoing conveyed the message that 'you are of
lesser worth than I'. I have done nothing more than send precisely the same
message back. Second, human worth is not ranked by position or status. Any
strategy that assumes otherwise will never succeed in the long run. For instance, I may have 'read' your apology as evidence of your 'inferior worth'.
But what happens when you feel that you have done the right thing by apologising, and so begin to talk to me with your head held high? Given the way
that I think, would I not have to take this to mean that you have now reas-
serted your equality, or perhaps even your 'superiority' over me—thus
undoing your earlier message (as I understood it), and re-igniting my anger?
If so, my revenge would also have been extremely short-lived.

There is only one way that hearing your apology can relieve my anger in both a morally legitimate and enduring way. I need to accept the *full* message that it conveys: 'I am not superior to you: we are of equal, inherent worth'.

Forgiveness is not a never-ending journey

Just because we have forgiven someone does not guarantee that we will never feel angry or bitter about what happened to us, or never have another resentful thought toward the person we have forgiven. There are too many variables that can tug at our emotions: we might experience a sudden reminder of how much they hurt us, or a moment of self-doubt, or days when we are feeling especially fragile, and so on. We might be tempted to infer, as some have, that forgiveness is best seen as a process, not a one-off event. We might even want to say that forgiveness must be a kind of journey, except that no one can ever say that they have 'arrived'. Along the way, there may be peaks of inner peace, but also troughs of vengeful rumination—with everything imaginable in between. [14]

But there is a serious problem with this view of forgiveness. It means that we can never know whether we have actually forgiven someone. This places the possibility of moral repair forever out of reach. We may think we have drawn a line under what happened, but it can always, at any time, be erased *depending on how we feel at any given moment*. And then we have to doubleback and start the process of trying to forgive all over again. On this view, we will always feel tied to the person who harmed us. And yet it was the promise of being freed from this chain that motivated us to begin the work of moral repair in the first place. How do we resolve this?

As a first step, we need to accept that it is normal to experience ups and downs after any major life-change. The emotional vacillations that can be experienced after forgiveness are real. However, this does not mean that we have not yet forgiven; or worse, that forgiveness is, by definition, an unobtainable goal. Here is why:

First, forgiveness is not a spontaneous, inexplicable change in how we happen to feel about the person who has wronged us. There is no magic at work here. The change of heart that we experience is brought about by a real change in the person who has wronged us: they have expressed genuine remorse for what they did to us. In other words, forgiveness is anchored in reality: it is a rational response to evidence of a real change 'out there', in the world. The remorse of the person who hurt us really did remove their threat to our social self. It persuaded us that what they did no longer counts as evidence of who they are. As a consequence, there is no need for us to protect ourselves with defensive anger, or to hold what they did against them. In short, we have forgiven them *because we have good reason to do so*. This means that, even if our feelings waver from time to time, we can always return to the evidence that grounded our original response of forgiveness.

Of course, this evidence could change: the person responsible may take back or somehow undermine their original apology. We may have been mistaken about their sincerity, and only discover this later. That would be a good reason to withdraw our forgiveness, since their threat has not, in actual fact, been removed. And we are very likely to find ourselves responding to this new evidence with anger. But it does not follow that forgiveness depends entirely on *how we happen to feel at any moment*. What it means is that our feelings of forgiveness are, in this case, tracking the evidence. Since the evidence has changed, so have our feelings. This is the way it ought to be.

Take another scenario: Suppose that the evidence has *not* changed—in other words, we have no good reason to think that the original apology was faked or insincere. And yet we find ourselves suddenly experiencing the old feelings of anger about what they did. Again, this does not mean that we haven't forgiven them. All it means is that our feelings at this moment are, for whatever reason, not tracking the evidence to which our original response of forgiveness remains anchored. At such times, we need to be kind to ourselves and accept that it is normal for our feelings to fluctuate this way. It is not uncommon for our emotions to over-reach, not quite matching up to how things really are. But we generally make allowances for this kind of turbulence. We might feel intensely anxious about an upcoming flight, but then still get on the plane because we know the risk is miniscule. Only later do we realise that we were feeling especially vulnerable due to a sleepless night. Likewise, we might think we are still angry about what happened to us in the distant past. But, on reflection, it may have more to do with, say, a work colleague who has been condescending.

Second, it is crucial to distinguish between (a) overcoming our anger toward the person who hurt us, and (b) the ongoing impact of their actions. For instance, long after we have forgiven someone, we may still be grieving the loss of what they took from us: a loved one, our physical health, our financial security, our sense of feeling safe in the world, old friendships, and so on. Forgiveness cannot replace or restore these things; nor will it stop us from experiencing the normal emotions that accompany these losses. But again, to feel these things does not mean that we haven't forgiven the person. We can accept their apology as sincere and feel the liberation of our anger toward them being lifted *and still* weep over the people we have lost, the physical pain we are still in, or the life we used to have.

Third, we need to recall that forgiveness is *specific to the particular wrong for which an apology has been made*. So if someone commits a second offence against us, we might now feel justifiably angry at them; but that anger does not mean that we didn't forgive them for the first offence. It does not even mean that the forgiveness we experienced for the first offence has been withdrawn or 'undone'. After all, their remorse for the first offence was real, and that has not changed. Of course, given the second offence, it would not be unreasonable to question the sincerity of the initial apology, if only to protect ourselves from being the victim of a cycle of *faux* apologies.[15] But not necessarily. It may well be that the apology was genuine at the time, and we were right to be persuaded of this. We don't *need* to doubt a person's sincerity with respect to the first offence, in order to change our view about the kind of person they are. The second offence will be enough on its own. Without this kind of clarity, it will be very easy to muddy the waters when it comes to the question of whether we have forgiven someone.

Forgiveness is not unconditional

Some philosophers, theologians and psychologists have argued that it is possible to forgive without hearing an apology. This has been called 'unconditional forgiveness'.[16] This idea does have its attractions. For example, there will be many cases in which an apology is either not possible or not forthcoming. Surely we would not want to say that a person must remain 'stuck' in unforgiveness simply because the person who has wronged them is unrepentant or deceased.

But this extension of the concept of forgiveness is a serious mistake. It removes what is utterly essential to it. To forgive someone is not merely to overcome one's anger or resentment. That can be achieved by applying any number of therapeutic strategies. Forgiveness requires certain *moral* pre-conditions. It can only be evoked when the person who wronged us demonstrates—with a remorseful apology and the making of amends—that their past actions are no longer evidence of their character. If I have managed to let go of my anger in spite of the fact that you have not sincerely apologised to me, then this must be explained in some other way. Whatever it is that has allowed me to release my anger, it is not forgiveness. To allow the possibility of 'unconditional forgiveness' is to suggest that moral truth and self-respect are inconsequential.

It can also place an impossibly heavy burden to 'forgive' on those who have yet to hear an apology.[17] Research has found that the vast majority of people need to hear an apology before they can forgive.[18] One explanation might be that most of us are not as 'saintly' as the rare few who claim to have 'forgiven' the one who has wronged them, even when there is no evidence of remorse whatsoever.[19] But a more plausible reason is that most of us have an intuitive grasp of the moral pre-conditions for forgiveness. In short, those who claim to have 'forgiven' without hearing an apology are confused about what forgiveness entails; or they have been pressured into making a *faux* declaration of 'forgiveness' by the unrealistic expectations of others.

Forgiving does not mean being a 'walk over'

It could be that, prior to hearing your apology, I have already 'let go' of my anger toward you. For instance, it might be many months or even years since the original offence, and my anger toward you has dissipated over time. I am no longer mad at you: I have moved on with my life. Alternatively, I may have, over many years, dealt with your attack on me by independently strengthening my sense of self-worth: for instance, I may have concentrated on the affirmations of friends and family, rather than ruminating about what you did to me. By the time you come to apologise, I will have already gained so much confidence in my own worth that I no longer need to protect myself against your particular threat. Your apology might lead me to revise my views about who you are, in the sense that I will, as a result, no longer hold your wrongdoing against you. But it has come far too late to change how I feel about you: I had already 'let go' of my anger long before you decided to make things right.

In such a case, can I still say that I have 'forgiven' you? After all, according to the definition given in the previous Chapter, forgiveness involves the overcoming of our defensive anger *as a result of* hearing a sincere apology. But in this case, I 'let go' of my anger long before I heard your apology. So it would seem to follow that, even though I accept your apology and no longer hold your wrongdoing against you, I am unable to say that I have 'forgiven' you. This seems like an odd result.

One explanation might, of course, be that my forgiveness does not, in fact, strictly *require* the sequential process of: (A) first hearing a sincere apology from you, which then brings about the overcoming of my defensive anger against you (even if this might be the *normal* way in which forgiveness comes about). Perhaps in order to experience forgiveness, I only need: (B) to recognise or acknowledge that, in light of your sincere apology, your wrongdoing no longer counts against the kind of person you are; and to have 'let go' of my defensive anger toward you *at some time or other*.

Before we assess the definition of forgiveness given in (B), there are three implications that we need to note: First, according to (B), merely overcoming my anger toward you is not sufficient for forgiveness: I still need to hear your apology. So (B) is not advocating unconditional forgiveness as such. Second, if I had managed to overcome my anger *before* I heard your apology, then it follows from (B) that I can still forgive you. Your apology may not cause me to 'let go' of my anger, but it does enable me to *endorse* how I already feel about you. In other words, prior to your apology, I already felt that I did not need to protect myself against you with defensive anger. Your apology now assures me that I am right to feel this way. Third, (B) does not entail that your apology will have *no* causal effect on me: it will change my mind about the kind of person you are; and that in turn will give me a good reason to offer you forgiveness. Your apology can thus open up the way to releasing your shame, and even lead to a restored relationship.[20]

The definition of forgiveness in (B) has a ring of plausibility to it. But it has significant problems. Suppose a family member seriously hurt you many years ago. In the absence of any apology from them, together with your desire to keep the peace, you have suppressed your anger. You have 'put it on the back-burner', so to speak. But then, out of the blue, they come to you and express a genuine and heartfelt apology for how they treated you. Now, you have, for many years, not felt the kind of anger that was warranted in light of what they did to you—at least not consciously. But this is not a fact about your emotional history that you should endorse: instead, it is a problem you need to address. Otherwise, any offer of 'forgiveness' that you make in response to their apology will have been far too easily won. You will be left with a simmering resentment that they got off lightly. They never really understood just how hurtful and cruel their behaviour was; and that is largely because they did not have to face up to the kind of anger that their actions deserved. They didn't know the full extent of what they were apologising *for*. Just as importantly, you will be left with the sense that you have not taken yourself seriously enough: in offering them 'forgiveness' without having first felt or given voice to the anger that their actions deserved, you have not communicated, even to yourself, what you are owed as a human being of incalculable worth.[21]

In other words, we should be very suspicious about any account, such as (B), which implies that forgiveness can be 'easy', a kind of emotional *fait accompli*. Forgiveness is hard and demanding work, in part because we cannot simply take it on trust that how we currently feel about a wrong that was done to us is how we ought to feel; nor can we be entirely sure that we are aware of how we feel at rock bottom, underneath all the distractions and competing priorities. The work of forgiveness requires that we dig deep and carefully excavate our hearts. We need to uncover, perhaps for the first time, any unfelt pain and suppressed anger. And then we need to communicate these feelings to the person responsible, so that we can be assured that they have faced up to the pain and the justified anger that their actions have caused. Only then will they be capable of feeling the humility and remorse that will persuade us that they 'get it'. And only then will we be able to 'let go' of the protection that we needed: our defensive anger. In short, to 'accept' their apology without having felt or expressed the anger that they deserved is not forgiveness: it is acquiescence. It is to be little more than a 'walk over', and that is most emphatically *not* what it means to forgive.

Forgiveness is not a one-sided declaration

Many well-meaning people will advise us to write a letter of 'forgiveness' to the person who has hurt us—even when we have never received an apology from them, and have no idea whether they feel the slightest remorse. Some will even suggest that we send this letter. But is communicating a unilateral declaration of 'forgiveness' like this a good idea? Is it even really forgiveness?

To begin with, it has to be said that this kind of letter of 'forgiveness' can have a powerful impact on the sender. Some people claim that it has enabled them to draw a line that separates them from the past and from the person responsible for hurting them. It helped them to release their anger, and they felt free to move on with their lives. If this is true, and they really have found healing and peace, then who are we to quibble about how they are using the word 'forgiveness'? They are just doing the best they can, drawing on the advice that they find around them. Having said that, language *is* important. Using the wrong words can mislead us—and those with whom we are communicating—into thinking that we are doing one thing, when we are actually doing something quite different. And that can hurt people, including ourselves. So it will be instructive to explore why it is problematic for this kind of letter to use the word 'forgiveness' in the way that it does.

To begin, we need to be a little more precise about what we are *doing* when we offer forgiveness. First, this is not an isolated, autonomous act: offering someone forgiveness is not something that we can perform on our own, like shaking a stick or playing the piano. It is one part of a collective act—that is, the kind of action that can only be performed by two or more people acting together, such as shaking hands or playing a duet.[22] There is a bridge that must be built, and each side must do its own part if they are to 'connect': the person responsible contributes a sincere apology, and the person harmed contributes an offer of forgiveness.

Second, there is a particular sequence that these contributions must take: one must go before the other. Otherwise this collective act will not work or make any sense. The offer of a sincere apology must always come first: it plays the initiating role in this collective act. The offer of forgiveness can only be made in response: it must follow the apology. To offer forgiveness without first hearing an apology is like saying 'thank you' to someone before they have given you anything to be thankful for; or saying 'I'm fine', when no one has asked how you are; or again, it is like agreeing to a contract that you haven't seen.

We can now apply these clarifications to a hypothetical scenario. Suppose you write a letter to me, out of the blue, declaring that you 'forgive' me—even though you have not received any apology from me. For all you know, I may be deeply remorseful. But I could also be utterly indifferent. Or I may have simply pushed the whole shameful episode into the back of my mind. There are countless possibilities, but take just one: I receive your letter and, initially, feel hugely relieved. You could have written a vindictive and hateful letter. Instead, you are courteous and respectful. You say that you 'forgive' me, and you ask for nothing in return—not even an apology. And you close by wishing me well. But then, after a second read, I start to think how strange it is that you can say that you 'forgive' me without even wanting to know what I think or how I feel about what happened. It doesn't even seem to matter to you whether I have changed. It's like I don't exist. You have built one half of a bridge over to where I am standing, and then walked away. So far as I can tell, you don't even care whether I might have been working on my half of the bridge. You don't want to know. Of course, you have every right to do whatever you think will help you. But half a bridge is as good as no bridge: it leads to nothing and 'connects' with no one. And that is what your letter makes me feel like: a 'nobody'.

This scenario reveals something unexpected and troubling: a unilateral declaration of 'forgiveness' is, in significant ways, not unlike revenge—or at least it can feel that way to the recipient, whatever the sender's intentions may have been. We cannot help but communicate underlying messages, whether we want to or not. And when we say something like: 'I don't need your apology', the underlying message will be this: 'As far as I am concerned, you don't matter'. We might want to deny this, arguing that we wouldn't have sent the letter if they didn't matter to us. But if we dig deep and ask ourselves why we would want to send this kind of letter, we would have to acknowledge that we were only wanting a one-way exchange. This was something we needed to get off our chest: it was ultimately for us, not for them. But this means that this letter was a way of not 'seeing' them. That's why it would not be at all surprising if the recipient felt like a 'nobody'—and treating someone like this is obviously not a sign of forgiveness.

But why, then, can a unilateral declaration of 'forgiveness' have the effect of releasing our anger? Why does it help us to 'move on'? Why does it feel so much like forgiveness? Well, if the recipient doesn't matter to us, then their threat doesn't count; and so we don't need the protection of our defensive anger. We don't resent insects, and for the same reason. But like revenge, this approach does not work in the long run. Eventually, it will occur to us that they are just as human as we are; and so what they think of us and how they feel about what happened does matter after all. For instance, would we not always, at some level, wonder how they reacted to our letter? Could we really just walk away, and not care about what they thought?

In short, real forgiveness is far more demanding. We cannot forgive without acknowledging the inherent and equal worth of the person responsible. The two are inextricably bound up together. So if we want to engage in the work of forgiveness, then any communication with them must be done in a way that demonstrates—both to us and to them—that they count.

11.3 THERE *IS* A FUTURE WITHOUT FORGIVENESS

It is deeply unfair to pronounce that people cannot live good and fulfilling lives without forgiving those who have wronged them. It is possible to have a future without embracing the moral amnesia of 'unconditional forgiveness'. Indeed, the shoe is on the other foot. We have seen that those who have refused to apologise or make amends *ought* not to be forgiven. If living morally is part of what it means to live a 'Good Life', it follows that those who (try to) 'forgive' unconditionally are robbing themselves of a future that is worth having.

Suppose, then, that we find ourselves in a situation where forgiveness is not morally appropriate. What alternatives are open to us? What does a future *without* forgiveness look like? We might assume both that it is always possible to 'let go' of or overcome our anger and that it is always morally virtuous to do so. However, neither is necessarily true.

First, it is not always possible. Lowering our defensive stance against the threat posed by the wrongdoer is not something we can just decide to do. We are inherently social creatures. Hence, being susceptible to this kind of threat is part of what makes us human. We cannot simply eradicate this feature without doing serious damage to ourselves. Unless we are psychopaths, we will always be vulnerable to the person who has wronged us. It is in this sense that those who refuse to apologise for their wrongs against us continue to harm us. The memory of what they did is likely to re-surface from time to time. And when it does, we will almost invariably find ourselves experiencing varying degrees of defensive anger.

Second, this is not always a morally questionable stance. As we have seen, defensive anger is entirely appropriate when our self-worth has been threatened. If someone fails to experience anger at (or around) the time of the offence, we would have good reason to suspect that they lack self-respect. But why should the passage of time make a difference? If the messages of disrespect conveyed in the original act have not been withdrawn by the wrongdoer, then they remain. Indeed, the failure of the person responsible to admit their fault and denounce what they have done only compounds or amplifies the original disrespect.[23] Those who have been harmed will have even more reason to maintain their emotions of defiance against the threat posed by the wrongdoer. They have even greater justification for thinking that the wrong that was done to them reflects on the character of the person responsible.[24]

We all accept that the passing of time alone can neither undo nor diminish a wrong. But what we often fail to acknowledge is that the passing of time builds a stronger case against the moral character of the person responsible. The longer they leave their action unacknowledged and unrepaired, the more likely it is that this behaviour was not a mere aberration. We know that someone's behaviour reflects an established character trait not only when it is repeated, but also when there is no attempt to disavow or correct that behaviour. So the longer a person leaves their wrongdoing as it stands, the clearer it will be that this action was in line with who they really are. For this reason, it is a terrible mistake for us to censure or pathologise those who continue to experience defensive anger in cases where the person who wronged them has not yet apologised or made amends.[25] (On the other hand, we are also not entitled to judge those who feel that, if they are to regain their health and a measure of well-being, they have no choice but to forgo the strenuous demands of moral protest or the fight for justice.[26])

It must also be acknowledged that defensive anger is often only a hair's breadth away from degenerating into offensive anger. So it would be helpful if we could find other, more positive responses that can enable us to defy the threat of an unrepentant wrongdoer. Here are four possibilities, each of which is likely to ameliorate or defuse our defensive anger—whilst remaining compatible with moral truth and self-respect:[27]

1. Focus on other sources of self-worth: We can concentrate our attention on the 'social mirrors' around us that are positive and affirming. That is, we can deliberately adjust the balance of those about whom we think and with whom we associate. We can learn to see ourselves primarily through the eyes of those who love and care for us, thereby 'turning down the volume' of the negative messages sent by the one who has wronged us.[28] Another, powerful strategy is to engage in the practice of actively 'seeing' and honouring the intrinsic worth of *everyone* we encounter: friends, family, colleagues and strangers alike. As we develop this habit of 'seeing', we will find ourselves caught up in our own view of humanity. It will be almost impossible for us not to see ourselves through the same lens: we will see that, simply by virtue of our humanity, we too have incalculable, inherent worth.[29]

2. Acknowledge their equal worth: We can recognise that, regardless of what they have done, the person who wronged us has *equal* worth as a human being. This is not incompatible with seeing them as having a less-than-praiseworthy moral character; but it does prevent us from going down the endless, futile and unethical path of revenge. If there is anything that will put a stop to moving on, it is the business of seeking (or even just imagining) methods by which we can affirm our own worth by degrading or destroying theirs.

3. Be compassionate: We can try to gain a sense of what it might be like to be in their shoes. Again, this will not be easy, and it is not a path that everyone can take.[30] But there are clear benefits for us if we can manage it. If the person who has wronged us has not felt or expressed any remorse, then (unless they are a psychopath or genuinely unaware that they have hurt us) this means they will be suffering from the relentless need to suppress their shame; and so they will be 'stuck' in any number of shame-reactions. We know something of how negative and self-destructive this can be. So, as we put ourselves in their shoes, it is likely that we will begin to feel compassion for them. One benefit of this is that compassion has a similar quality to defensive anger: it can function as a powerful defence against attacks to our self-worth. It does not contain or convey the same messages as defensive anger (e.g. 'I did not deserve this'); and so it cannot—nor should it—be seen as a substitute for defensive anger. But there is something about the other-orientated goodness of compassion that can defuse an attack on our self-worth. Put simply, we are far less likely to feel that we need to protect ourselves from someone if we care about their suffering.

4. Confront them: A second benefit of feeling compassion for the person who has wronged us is that it will give us the motivation to alleviate the negative impact that suppressed shame is having on their lives. Rather than feeling helpless or apathetic about the situation, compassion can move us to do something constructive. We cannot forgive them, but we might confront them—respectfully challenging them to admit to their wrongdoing. Needless to say, confronting someone who has, to date, refused to accept any responsibility is a high-risk strategy. Doing so could just cement their denial. But we can at least say that we did what we could, in good faith and for the right (altruistic) reasons. Even if our endeavours do not bear fruit, the fact that we have tried could help us to turn the page.

12. Moral Repair for Persons Responsible

12.1 OFFERING AN APOLOGY

If I know I have done wrong, then I cannot show that the evidence supporting my shame-belief that 'I am a bad person' is false. Why? Because I cannot undo the past. So I need to find a way of undermining or over-riding this evidence, so that it is no longer the only evidence available. I need to find or create new evidence that is so strong it can outweigh the evidence in support of the belief that 'I am a bad person'. I can get this kind of evidence by demonstrating that I am a good person who has done a bad thing. In other words, I need to show that I no longer stand by what I did, and that I want to be seen as a different kind of person. I need to become someone who would not do such a thing again.[1]

It is one thing for me to prove this to myself. In some cases, this is all I can do. But the most effective way of overwhelming the negative evidence is to apologise to the very person that I have wronged. That is, I need to communicate to them that:

- I take responsibility for my part in what happened;
- I no longer stand by what I did;
- I believe that what I did was wrong;
- I feel terrible about the hurt and suffering that I have caused you;
- I want to repair this harm in any way that I can; and
- I won't do it again.

My apology should not attempt to deny the fact that negative underlying messages *were* conveyed to the person I harmed. This means that:

- the apology must not attempt to justify or rationalise what I did (e.g. 'I'm sorry, but I was drunk at the time');

- it should not try to make excuses (e.g. 'I'm sorry, but my friends told me to do it'); and

- it should not blame the person I have harmed for the way that they feel (e.g. 'I'm sorry, but isn't it time you moved on?').

None of these are authentic apologies: they are not genuine expressions of remorse. The reason for this is that they all refuse to embrace the shame of having wronged another person. Instead, they merely engage in fight-flight strategies that are designed either to suppress or displace this shame.[2] In other words, my apology needs to make explicit and thereby acknowledge responsibility for the messages that were conveyed by my actions (e.g. 'I am sorry that I hurt you by . . .'). In taking this approach, I am not attempting to change the past or pretend that it never happened. What I am aiming to do instead is to alter the effect that the wrongdoing has on the present. In this way, I can stand with the person I have harmed in denouncing and disavowing the shameful messages that were conveyed to them by my wrongdoing. I am removing the threat that I posed to their social self. I am restoring the acknowledgement and respect that I owed to them as a human being of equal worth.[3]

To offer an apology is therefore a way of saying that I want to be seen in a different light. I do not want this wrongdoing to define me. I want to reveal my commitment to the values that we share.[4] I don't want to feel ashamed of who I am anymore and what others think of me—particularly those whom I love and respect. I want to remove the threat to my own social self that this wrongdoing has created.[5]

12.2 THE MOTIVATION FOR AN APOLOGY

The role of empathy

Merely reciting an apology is not sufficient.[6] I can only be persuaded by the evidence that I am offering if my apology is genuine. And my apology will not be genuine if it is only motivated by a desire to alleviate my own shame. It needs to be an outward expression of remorse. In other words, I need to know what it is I am apologising *for*—and not just intellectually. I need to feel it. I need to pull myself out of my own self-absorbed world. I need to grasp, emotionally, what it is like to be in the shoes of the person I have harmed.[7] I need to *feel* what is reflected in the mirror that I held up to them when I humiliated and insulted them.[8]

This kind of emotional mirroring may, at first glance, seem like a tall order. After all, I cannot feel *exactly* what it was like to have suffered as they have. Yet, I do know what it feels like to be wronged. I may not have been hurt in precisely the way that they have. But I have been hurt myself. I know what it is like to feel humiliated, insulted and inferior because of how others have treated me. So it is not impossible for me to feel at least something of what they may be experiencing. If I can do this, then I will gain a far better understanding of the consequences of my actions. I will come to understand, at a deeper emotional level, why it is that what I did to them was wrong. Not only will I thereby gain a clearer sense of what it is that I am apologising for. I will also understand why apologising is the right thing to do.[9]

The role of compassion

Empathy is not enough, however. As we saw earlier, if I feel someone's pain, this can cause me to feel extremely distressed and uncomfortable. If these feelings of distress become overwhelming, then I can easily act from self-interested motives. My focus will be to remove my own distress, rather than the pain of the person for whom I feel empathy. This is even more likely to happen in a context where it is clear that *I* am the cause of their pain. But if I apologise simply to relieve my own distress, then the apology will be insincere. If it is to be genuine, it must ultimately be for their sake, and not merely for my own.[10] In other words, a genuine apology must spring from the humility of compassion, not mere self-interest.[11] Otherwise, the person harmed will have no reason to change their views about my moral character. An apology offered out of self-interest is consistent with the evidence of my past actions, and so will fail to repudiate the messages that were conveyed by my wrongdoing.[12]

The expression of remorse

What this means, in practice, is that no apology will count as sincere, unless it clearly expresses or 'gives voice to' underlying feelings of remorse. This emotion, as we have seen, is entirely 'outward-directed': it is, by definition, incompatible with conniving self-interest or a blank indifference to the pain of the person who was harmed. The essential 'building blocks' of remorse include the acknowledgement of responsibility, an empathetic understanding of the hurt and suffering that was caused, and a desire to alleviate the pain and suffering of the person who was wronged. In other words, compassion is 'built-into' remorse: so I cannot offer a sincere apology without it.[13]

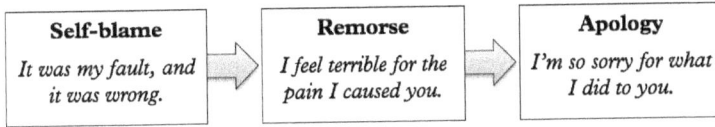

Self-blame	**Remorse**	**Apology**
It was my fault, and it was wrong.	*I feel terrible for the pain I caused you.*	*I'm so sorry for what I did to you.*

12.3 RESPONSES TO AN APOLOGY

The need for validation

The person harmed may, for whatever reason, not accept that my apology really is genuine. So I cannot measure the sincerity of my apology by how they happen to react. Rather, I need to examine my own motives with complete honesty. I need to be convinced that my apology really was an expression of remorse. If I know in myself that my apology was motivated instead by mere self-interest, then I will continue to see my wrongdoing as evidence of the kind of person I am. In other words, my apology will only be genuine if it counts as sufficient evidence *for me* that I am not a bad person.

Having said this, the response of the person I have harmed is not without consequence. I may be personally convinced that my apology was an authentic expression of my remorse. But if the person harmed angrily rejects my apology, I can find myself feeling even more shame for what I have done to them. This is because shame is a social emotion. So convincing *myself* that I am not a bad person is unlikely to be sufficient to release my shame. I need my apology to be accepted or validated by those around me. I need to hear them say that, because my apology seemed to them to be a genuine expression of remorse, they no longer hold my wrongdoing against me.

How a response of forgiveness can release shame

Fortunately, I do not need to be entirely dependent for this validation on the person harmed. Close friends and family—who know me and can see that I am being sincere—will be able to affirm that my remorse is real and that I have indeed changed and tried to do the right thing.[14]

On the other hand, if the person I have wronged accepts my apology as genuine and responds with forgiveness, then that will significantly strengthen the total evidence against my shame-belief that I am a bad person.[15] If this shame-belief is no longer fully supported by the evidence available to me, then that belief will evaporate—and with it will go my feelings of shame. Even better, this evidence will not merely remove my shame. It will also replace it with self-respect. I may even come to feel good about myself.[16]

Moving toward moral repair

The reciprocation that takes place in the exchanges of apology and for-giveness, as described above, thus provides a way of meeting the emotional and moral needs of both the person harmed and the person responsible.[17] It is a powerful way of releasing the shame and healing the hurt that both were feeling as a result of the wrongful act.[18] It enables them to restore the social bond that was broken.[19]

Of course, as we mentioned at the outset, there are no guarantees when it comes to the work of moral repair: people are far too complex for that. And what counts as 'success' will look quite different in each case. But if people come together in 'good faith', and are willing to engage in shared acts of hon-esty, respect and compassion, then moral repair will be within their reach.

PART 2.

Restorative Justice

1. Designing Restorative Justice Processes

1.1 MORAL REPAIR IN PRACTICE

At first glance, moral repair can seem like a complete mystery: one human being offers another a genuine apology for having caused them profound pain and suffering; and they receive forgiveness in response. That this kind of exchange could ever occur seems astonishing. Surely it only happens on the rarest of occasions. Even then it must be spontaneous and unpredictable. It doesn't seem to be the sort of thing that could be planned in advance. How could there be a set of procedures that, if followed, will make it more likely that the necessary 'magic' will appear?

The moral repair of serious wrongdoing is indeed complex, difficult, and all too rare. But it is not a 'black box' to which we have no access. As we have seen, a great deal is now known about the psychology of forgiveness and apologies. So it is not, in principle, beyond our capacity to design processes that will assist and enable those who wish to engage in the work of moral repair.[1] One useful way of explaining how this kind of process might work is by drawing an analogy with music, as Scheff does in the following:

> "An effective apology is . . . difficult because it depends upon a veritable symphony of verbal and nonverbal activities jointly enacted and felt by both parties. Each must coordinate their words, gestures, thoughts, and feelings with those of the other. It is a dance, a *pas de deux*, requiring not only the right lyrics but also the right music. That is, the timing (rhythm) of the moves of each party relative to the moves of the other is crucial, as are the emotions displayed (melody) and felt (harmony). . . . If the lyrics and the melody of the apologizing party are right, and the attitude of the apologized-to party is accepting, then a dramatic mood change can occur: the parties can go from a state of shared shame to one of shared pride in a matter of minutes, from fluster, awkwardness, and emotional pain to rapport and pleasure."[2]

The assumption here is that the work of moral repair follows a natural sequence of thoughts, emotions and behaviours. If this is so, then it should be possible to design a process that facilitates this very sequence. Scheff evokes the analogy of classical music ("symphony") in his description of an effective apology. But if such a process is possible, it seems far more likely to look like jazz.[3] Unlike classical music, jazz musicians do not follow a score in which every note they play is written down in advance. Instead, they follow a basic underlying sequence of chords (or 'chord progression')—usually one that supports a particular melody. The piece may start off with the melody played, in its pure form, over the chord progression. But after that, the musicians will begin to improvise over this same basic sequence of chords. In addition, jazz musicians will usually agree, in advance, on the order in which they take turns to do a solo improvisation, backed by the rest of the band. There are several advantages to this approach:

- *Safety:* The underlying chord progression provides the musicians with a common direction and a safety net. Even if it might seem that they have left the original melody far behind, the underlying chord progression enables them to know where they are heading, and how to get back on track.

- *Flow:* The sequence of chords they are following makes sense from a musical point of view. Each chord builds on what has gone before. The soloists are free to play what they want; but the chord progression allows them to do so without awkward and arbitrary lurches from one chord to another, confusing the musical flow.

- *Voice:* By agreeing to take turns as soloists, the musicians know that they will, at some point, be given an opportunity to 'say' what they want and be heard—without needing to worry about being interrupted or over-ridden by the others.

- *Individuality:* The freedom to improvise allows jazz musicians to express their own unique personalities, technical skills and musical styles. As a result, each time a jazz piece is played it will be recognisable, but it will also sound distinctive and original.

- *Uniqueness:* It would be impossible to repeat any jazz performance, down to the last note, tone, and volume. Doing so would also miss the point. It is the creative, spontaneous interaction between players and the unrehearsed expressions of emotion that distinguishes jazz from other musical styles.

Of course, when it comes to the work of moral repair, it is easy to see why some people might prefer a pre-scripted and fully rehearsed process, as in classical music. After all, it is difficult to imagine a group of people talking together, safely and respectfully, about a serious harm that one has inflicted upon another. Would it not be better if every word was written down in advance, and preferably spoken by emotionally detached third-parties? Surely, anything less controlled and predictable would, in this context, only result in a dissonant array of sound and fury, lacking any coherence or resolution.

However, human beings appear to have an instinctive capacity to 'perform' the kind of complex interactions that are required for moral repair.[4] They do not need every word and interaction to be written in advance. In fact, if this were attempted, the 'performance' would collapse. Like jazz, the work of moral repair *requires* a level of spontaneous interaction, individuality, creativity and flexibility. Moral repair cannot be mass-produced, out-sourced or performed by legal proxies. And particular thoughts, emotions and behaviours cannot be prescribed or forced (e.g. 'at this point in the proceeding, the person harmed must feel anger'). The participants in moral repair must 'perform their own music', however perilous and unpredictable that might appear.

1.2 DESIGNING A DIALOGUE STRUCTURE

It follows that, if we are to design a process that enables people to carry out the work of moral repair, we cannot try to 'nail everything down', scripting every word and action in advance. That may *seem* like the safest approach, but it will only undermine the process. What we can do instead is to create a *dialogue structure*: that is, a set of topics and speaking turns that, if followed, would be more likely than not to activate or elicit the relevant sequence of thoughts, emotions and behaviours.[5] To apply the analogy with jazz, if we (the musicians) want to carry out the work of moral repair (play jazz), then we will need to bring our own unique personalities, feelings, experiences, and communication skills to the conversation (improvisation). But that is not sufficient. To activate the sequence of thoughts, emotions and behaviours that are involved in moral repair, then we need to follow a particular dialogue structure (the chord progression).

1.3 CRITERIA FOR SUCCESS

If this kind of dialogue structure is possible, how will we know if the particular design we are using is successful? The ultimate test will be whether the participants feel that the moral harm that was done has been repaired, at least to whatever extent could be reasonably expected. But this test is not sufficient on its own.

For example, suppose we took the view that a restorative justice process should allow the participants to say whatever they like, whenever they feel like it. In other words, they should be given no preparation time, no pre-arranged sequence of topics and no agreed upon speaking turns. It should be an entirely spontaneous, unplanned and unstructured conversation. Now this approach could well result in *some* degree of moral repair. After all, there are cases in which participants have been able to reach a restorative outcome, even where the conversation has been confused, repetitive, chaotic, and disjointed. [6] However, the end doesn't justify the means. People are astonishingly resilient and resourceful. If they are all meeting with the intention of engaging in the work of moral repair, it is likely that they will eventually create, through trial and error, a path through the conversational jungle. But without either a compass or an experienced guide it will take them considerably longer to reach their destination. It may cause them unnecessary pain in the process. They will have wasted precious emotional and intellectual energy on doing the kind of basic 'navigation-work' that could so easily have been provided. All they required was someone who could guide them through a dialogue structure designed specifically for the purpose of facilitating moral repair. Had they received this guidance, they might well have found emotional healing at a deeper level, and more creative and satisfying ways of 'making things right'.

In other words, a well-designed restorative justice process should meet a range of other tests. Specifically, participants should have access to the same kind of benefits we presented earlier in the context of jazz:

- *Safety:* Even if people speak at great length and with emotional intensity, everyone should know where the conversation is going and what they hope to achieve by taking part.

- *Flow:* The conversation should feel instinctive and unobtrusive. One topic should lead naturally to the next, building on what came before. The order of the speaking turns should make sense: it should reflect the fact that, in this context, some things need to be said (and heard) before other things. Participants should not feel weighed down by misunderstandings, digressions, and confusing lurches from one topic to another.

- *Voice:* Every participant should know, in advance, that they will each be given a turn to say what they need to say. They need to know that they will be heard without interruption. They should not have to talk over each other, fight for their right to be heard, or feel that they were not given an opportunity to say all that they needed to say.

- *Individuality:* The participants should not feel that they are being manipulated or pressured into saying things that they do not mean. They should not feel that they cannot be themselves, or that they need to put on a show or play 'mind games' with other participants (or even the facilitator)—just so that they can be heard or avoid being humiliated. They should feel safe enough to be who they really are, to speak in a way that makes sense to them, and to express how they genuinely feel.

- *Uniqueness:* Every restorative justice process should be recognisable for what it is: its basic design should reflect the fact that its primary aim is *to facilitate moral repair*, rather than some other objective (such as reducing recidivism). This does not mean that restorative justice processes should 'sound' exactly the same. The process should free people up to interact in a way that is emotionally authentic, thoughtful, and in-the-moment. They should feel completely free to change how they think and feel as the conversation progresses.

With these criteria for success in mind, we can now begin to take a closer look at how the design of restorative justice processes can be optimised to facilitate moral repair. First, it will be argued that there are two key mechanisms required for activating shame-release, thus facilitating the work of moral repair: namely, *recall* and *compassionate listening*. Second, we will see how restorative justice processes can be designed so as to incorporate these two mechanisms in a way that meets the criteria for success above.

2. Mechanisms for Releasing Shame

2.1 INTRODUCTION

In Part 1, we established four interconnected points: First, moral repair depends crucially upon the release of our shame—whether we are the person harmed or the person responsible. Second, the four main types of shame reaction (Withdrawal, Avoidance, Attack Other, Attack Self) are each designed, in their own way, to suppress or displace feelings of shame: they do not, in themselves, release this emotion. Third, the only means by which we can release shame is to: (a) acknowledge its presence, which means bringing it to the forefront of our consciousness;[1] (b) identify the underlying shame-inducing messages that we now believe or suspect to be true;[2] and (c) take active steps to defeat those shame-beliefs by showing, in legitimate ways, that the evidence in their favour is absent, false or undermined by new evidence.[3] Finally, it follows that the work of moral repair depends upon our capacity to overcome our shame-reactions to such an extent that they do not prevent us from carrying out the three tasks listed above.

We also found that overcoming our shame-reactions is extremely difficult. There are two main obstacles that we face. First, shame makes us feel terrible about ourselves: it is so painful precisely because it is felt as a severe blow to our sense of self-worth. To bring our shame to the forefront of our conscious awareness would involve feeling the full force of this emotion. It would also mean having to face up to the self-deprecating messages that have triggered our shame (e.g. 'you are evil, 'you are worthless', 'you are stupid'). It is little wonder that we are so resistant to overcoming the protective shield of our shame-reactions.

The second obstacle is more practical: an entire shame experience can arise so quickly that we can be almost completely unaware of the underlying mechanics.[4] Someone insults us, we feel like we have been thrown a punch in the stomach, and we react angrily. But all of this happens so quickly that we do not have the time to put two and two together. We may not even be fully aware that we were insulted, let alone that this caused us to feel shame. We may simply find ourselves, strangely and unaccountably, feeling intensely angry.[5] Fortunately, we can overcome both obstacles: the first, by finding a compassionate listener; and the second, by our capacity for recall.

2.2 RECALL

We are the kind of creatures who can re-create a series of events in our minds, re-tracing our steps. We can recall an episode in our lives, playing it back in slow motion. It is this ability to replay what happened, frame by frame, that enables us, eventually, to reach a point in which the release of our shame becomes possible.

This is how it seems to work: as we re-trace *what happened*, we can begin to identify the incidents that triggered our shame. We may also start to re-member similar shameful incidents from the past. This will help to explain why our current shame experience has been more intense and prolonged than it might otherwise have been. As we recall *how we (and others) were affected*, we will begin to explore how we responded, as well as the responses of others. This will include not only behaviours, but also feelings. If we have been harmed, it is highly likely that, among these responses, there will be a series of shame-reactions (e.g. rage, blaming others, denial, and so on).[6] As we re-member these shame-reactions, it is likely that we will *re-experience the emotions involved*.[7]

For many of us, shutting down emotionally has become a coping strategy. This allows us to avoid being overwhelmed by our feelings. So getting to the point where we can re-experience these painful emotions may take time and perseverance. We may need to go over what happened, again and again, until we can push through the self-protecting barricades we have set up. It is cru-cial that we feel as safe as possible in order to let ourselves re-experience such threatening emotions.[8]

As we trace our way back through these shame-reactions, there will come a point at which we begin to uncover and re-experience the painful wound to our social self that has generated these reactions. In other words, we will be able to *access the feelings of shame that we felt at the time*, and perhaps also the shame we were unable to feel when we experienced a similar incident in the distant past.[9] Once we have brought this painful emotion into our conscious awareness, we should then be able to *identify the negative underlying messages* that triggered it in the first place. As these messages are exposed, we can then begin the process of moral repair: that is, finding ways in which it can be demonstrated (to ourselves and others) that *the messages are false*, which will re-affirm our self-worth and so *release our shame*.

2.3 COMPASSIONATE LISTENING

It is possible to re-call our experience on our own, perhaps using a private journal or by making a recording. But if we are able to describe our experience to another person, there can be enormous benefits—especially in terms of overcoming our intense resistance to feeling the full force of our shame. Who we choose, however, will make all the difference. The ideal person will be a 'compassionate witness', someone who can walk *with*—rather than *for*—us on our journey of repair.[10] In this respect, there are three main qualities we should look for:

1. Someone who can affirm our inherent and equal worth: Revealing our shame to another person is one of the most vulnerable things we can do. So we need to feel completely safe. One of the problems with talking about shame is that the very experience of this emotion is itself often seen as shameful. That is why it is so rarely discussed or brought out into the open. This means that we need to find someone who is not afraid of our shame, turning away or changing the subject when it arises.[11] Most of all, we need someone who does not add to our burden of shame by the way they treat us. We need someone who is not patronising, disapproving or condescending. They should not make us feel ashamed of our shame, by implying that we are strange, sick, crazy, or inferior in some way.[12] These responses will only confirm and amplify the self-denigrating messages with which we are already struggling.[13] Worse still, we are likely to react by withdrawing into ourselves,[14] or defiantly rejecting responsibility and blaming others.[15] In other words, we will protect ourselves by suppressing our shame and resorting to various 'Fight or Flight' shame-reactions. In short, what we need is someone who can, at all times, respect and affirm our inherent worth as a human being.[16] As Carl Rogers might have said, we need someone who can exhibit genuineness, unconditional positive regard and empathetic understanding.[17]

2. Someone who can separate the person from the act: We are more than the wrong that we have done. Likewise, we are more than the wrong that we have suffered. This is why labelling someone a 'victim' or an 'offender' is so un-helpful. It reduces them from the whole, complex, multi-faceted person that they are, to a single act. In doing this, we make it harder for them to change and to heal.[18] So we need someone who can help us to distinguish between *what has happened* and *who we are*. They can do this in two ways. First, they can enable us to see the evidence of goodness, virtue or other positive quali-ties in our lives. This means nurturing our self-esteem until such time as we can do this for ourselves.[19] Second, if we have been *harmed*, they can help us to see that we are not to be blamed for what someone else chose to do to us. If we have *caused harm*, then they can encourage and support us to take re-sponsibility, apologise and make amends.

3. Someone who can help us to release our shame: We need someone who can help us to acknowledge our shame, identify the negative underlying messages that caused it, and find ways to defeat those messages. These three precursors to shame-release are likely to arise naturally, as we talk through our experi-ence. A compassionate witness can facilitate this process by posing questions that are designed to elicit precisely these three elements, such as:

- 'What was it that made you react in that way?'
- 'By doing or saying_____, what were they saying about you?'
- 'How did/does that make you feel?'
- 'What can you do to show them that you are not like that?'

If the mechanisms for releasing shame suggested above are valid, then we have a well-grounded way of optimising the capacity of restorative justice to facilitate moral repair. So we will now consider how best to apply this method to each of the four stages of a restorative justice process: that is Commitment, Preparation, Communication and Action.

3. Commitment

3.1 AN INITIAL ASSESSMENT

In the initial meetings with each participant, the facilitator will need to decide whether or not the individual has already started the work of moral repair for themselves. In some cases, it will become clear that a participant has done a considerable amount of repair-work on their own. In other cases, a participant will still be consumed by destructive, self-defeating and out of control shame-reactions, such as retaliatory rage, self-harming, or cognitive distortions. However, it is unlikely that they will have even agreed to meet with a facilitator unless there was a spark of interest and a potential willingness to take part in the process.[1]

Regardless of where each participant is situated, the facilitator's role is to give them a genuine opportunity either to embark on or continue the journey of moral repair, if that is what they wish. This means that, prior to presenting a detailed explanation of what a restorative justice process involves, the facilitator needs to *listen compassionately* as they enable the participant to *recall their experience*, using the 'facts–consequences–future' sequence. As the participant begins to feel safe, listened to and respected, they are likely to find that they have less need to protect themselves with the more extreme shame-reactions. They may then feel more able to speak openly about their feelings and what they are needing.[2]

3.2 STARTING THE PROCESS

For the person harmed

If this transition occurs, then the process of moral repair will have begun. The person harmed may feel able to acknowledge, perhaps in small and fragmentary ways, that what happened made them feel shame. So they might say things like:

- 'They hurt me so much.'

- 'It was humiliating.'

- 'They put me down in front of everyone.'

- 'I felt so small.'

These words signify that they are *acknowledging their shame*. The person harmed may even, at this early stage, be able to *identify the underlying messages* that caused them to feel this way. For example, they might say:

- 'He treated me like I was garbage.'

- 'It was like I was nothing to him.'

- 'She told me I couldn't be trusted.'

- 'They made me feel totally incompetent.'

At this point, they will have started to accept that (or clarify how) they have been wronged. When they are asked to consider what they want to happen, they may be able to *identify things that will help them to defeat the negative messages* they have heard. For example, they may say:

- 'I just want him to take responsibility.'

- 'I need to hear her own up to what she did to me.'

- 'I want her to say that she is sorry.'

- 'I want him to take back what he said to me.'

For the person responsible

Likewise, the person responsible may feel safe enough, at some point, to put aside their defences and tell the facilitator that they did commit the crime or cause the harm that was alleged. When asked how they feel about what they did, they may begin to *acknowledge their shame* by saying things like:

- 'I feel terrible about it.'

- 'I feel so guilty about what I did.'

- 'I'm such an idiot.'

- 'I'm so angry with myself.'

If asked what has made them feel this way, they may begin to *identify the underlying messages* that triggered this shame. For example, they may say:

- 'I don't want to be thought of as a bad person.'
- 'She looked at me like I was this disgusting low-life.'
- 'They probably think I'm some kind of monster.'
- 'I know I shouldn't have done it.'

Finally, when asked what they can do to 'make things right', the person responsible may, to varying degrees, be able *to identify ways of defeating these negative messages*. So they might say, for example:

- 'I need to own up to what I did.'
- 'I'd like the chance to say I'm sorry.'
- 'I wish I could do something to repair what I've done.'
- 'I want them to know that I've changed.'

3.3 ASSESSING COMMITMENT

In either case, the extent to which each participant will be able to work through these thoughts and feelings will vary considerably. Some participants will still be vacillating between this kind of self-awareness and their shame-reactions. For example, the person responsible might angrily blame the person harmed, and a minute later freely admit that it was really their own fault; but then, in the next breath, return to blaming mode.

In some cases, this confusion and inconsistency may mean that the facilitator will need to meet with the participant several times before a decision can be made. But if the participant is saying, in a reasonably stable and convincing way, that they accept that the work of moral repair is what they need; and if it is clear that they have already taken the first few steps on that journey, then the invitation to take part in a restorative justice process can be offered to them. Once the participant fully understands what is involved, and feels able to commit themselves to seeing it through, then the process can begin.

4. Preparation

4.1 THE GOALS OF PREPARATION

There are two core goals for the preparation stage. The first is to enable the participants to get as close as they can to completing the work of moral repair on their own. This is so that by the time they meet, they are not completely dependent on the other participant(s) for the release of their shame and the affirmation of their self-worth (*independence*). The second goal is to enable the participants to communicate in a way that can be heard and absorbed by the other participants, whilst also preserving and affirming their own dignity and self-respect (*containment*). The following explains each of these two goals of independence and containment in turn.

4.2 INDEPENDENCE

Each participant can do a great deal of moral repair-work independently. For example, it is possible for the *person responsible* to feel remorse for what they have done and engage in redemptive activities entirely on their own initiative. They can distance themselves from their past behaviour by reforming their lives, not re-offending, giving back to the community, becoming a more productive citizen, and so on. It is also possible for a *person harmed* to re-affirm their self-worth, minimise their feelings of anger, and move on with their lives, without ever hearing an apology or receiving reparation.

Some might argue that, if this kind of repair-work has not yet been carried out by either participant, the facilitator should try to ensure that it is only done within the restorative justice meeting. Otherwise, what's the point of bringing people together? However, as we will see, the safety and effectiveness of a restorative justice meeting can be greatly enhanced if the participants do as much of this work as they can beforehand.

Independence for the person harmed

There are several reasons why the person harmed should carry out as much repair-work as they can *before* engaging with the person responsible. We can perhaps see these reasons most clearly by looking at two different scenarios.

Scenario 1.   The person harmed comes to a restorative justice meeting still blaming themselves for the wrong that was done to them. They feel that their ability to let go of this self-blame is completely reliant upon them hearing the person responsible admit that it was in fact their fault.

The problem with this scenario is that there is far too much power in the hands of the person responsible. This is the very person who has taken power and control away from the person harmed. So placing the person harmed in this position would merely add to their feelings of vulnerability. It could also prolong an unhealthy dependency on the person responsible, and create a dangerously unrealistic set of expectations for the restorative justice process. No matter how much preparation is done, no one can predict how the person responsible will behave on the day.

Scenario 2.   The person harmed comes to a restorative justice meeting full of unprocessed rage and bitterness. They simply want to off-load their pain and hatred onto the person responsible. The aim is to 'give them a piece of their minds' and 'put them in their place'.

In this scenario, it is very unlikely that this person harmed will experience the kind of healing that could have resulted from the encounter. They would be unable to hear any apology, no matter how sincere.[1] If the person harmed is not at least open to seeing the humanity of the person responsible, someone for whom they could potentially feel some empathy, then they will not be able to accept *any* evidence that this person has taken back the negative underlying messages conveyed in the wrongdoing.

Independence for the person responsible

There are several reasons why the repair-work of the person responsible also needs to be as independent as possible. Again, we can examine these reasons by looking at two possible scenarios.

Scenario 1. The person responsible feels they cannot accept that they are 'a good person who has done a bad thing' until the person harmed accepts their apology or offers them forgiveness.

The person responsible needs to come to a restorative justice meeting fully aware that they cannot control how the person harmed responds to them. They also need to accept that this is an ongoing consequence of their actions. The person harmed is not obligated to accept their apology or forgive them. Yet the person responsible also needs to know that if their apology is rejected, this will not in itself nullify all that they have done—and still plan to do—to redeem themselves.[2]

Again, the person responsible needs to offer an apology primarily for the sake of the person harmed, not merely to meet their own needs. Otherwise the apology will not be fully genuine.[3] But if the person responsible feels that the restoration of their self-worth is totally dependent on being forgiven by the person harmed, then this order of priority could easily become reversed. The person responsible would be far more likely to manipulate or pressure the person harmed into offering forgiveness—for example, by denigrating themselves, becoming overly distressed, or hinting at possible repercussions for the person harmed.[4] The person harmed should not feel that their role is to help the person responsible feel better about themselves, as if this individual's self-worth rests entirely upon their shoulders.

Scenario 2. The person responsible comes to the restorative justice meeting still wavering between wanting to justify their actions and admitting, without any excuses, that what they did was wrong. There is some part of them that has yet to accept that they were responsible for their part in what happened. In their own minds, they still feel that they were not entirely to blame for their own actions.

In such a case, it is highly likely that the person responsible would cause more harm than good and undermine the entire process.[5] When a person harmed is presented with various justifications, excuses and denials of responsibility, the underlying messages that they hear include: 'you are wrong to accuse me', 'it is your fault', and so on. The person harmed could respond to these messages with humiliated rage. The person responsible would then feel shamed in return, thus creating a shame-rage loop.[6]

There are, of course, cases in which the person harmed happens to be articulate, forceful and assertive—so much so that the person responsible eventually gives in and admits to their wrongdoing. But why should any person who has been harmed be placed in a situation where they have to defend themselves or argue their case? Why should it be their role to convince the person responsible to do the right thing? If this were the *modus operandi* of restorative justice, then it would only be suitable for the strongest, most confident and most persuasive of persons harmed. Worse still, the main purpose of including a person harmed would be to have them act as a kind of 'stage prop'. Their primary role would be to evoke remorse in an otherwise unrepentant offender. This is not a situation in which any person harmed should be placed. To do so would be a serious failure to honour the facilitator's duty of care to *all* participants.[7]

4.3 CONTAINMENT

If restorative justice participants have had little or no opportunity to process their feelings prior to the restorative justice meeting, then the encounter is very likely to open the floodgates. Their pent-up emotions and thoughts could tumble out all at once, without purpose or boundaries. Why is this a problem? Shouldn't restorative justice be a space in which participants can express exactly how they feel, no matter how messy, aggressive, confusing, overwhelming or unrestrained that might be? How can they achieve the catharsis they are looking for otherwise? But there are good reasons for rejecting this approach. This is perhaps best articulated by Jasmin Cori:

> "To contain something is to hold it, to create a place for it, in some way to *protect* it. When anger, for example, is not contained, it can result in impulsive acting-out behaviour that can cause real harm. Contained it can be channelled into assertion, direct action, self-defense, or carefully simmered until it becomes concentrated into a sense of power. With containment, instead of just

spitting out a feeling (and perhaps getting high off the rush associated with that), we learn to turn it over in our mouths and taste it. We learn to discriminate how much we can handle at any given moment without overload. We understand that the point is to keep the feelings from getting so intense that they burn us. We learn to contain a feeling so that it doesn't run roughshod over us but instead is given a place and listened to. [By contrast, not] only does catharsis sometimes prematurely release a feeling (before you've gotten the full learning from it), but it also becomes addictive and can retraumatize you. It can blow your circuits. . . . There is [also] evidence that the big emotions of catharsis actually strengthen traumatic memories. . . . When catharsis is serving you [i.e. when the emotional discharge is contained], it leaves you feeling more peaceful, feeling that some essential truth has now been accepted and expressed, and this helps you feel more complete with something [rather than fragmented]."[8]

It might be helpful to explain this further by using an analogy. Take the following three scenarios:

- a champagne bottle is vigorously shaken and popped, spraying the contents randomly and chaotically in the air (*mere catharsis*);

- the champagne is slowly, gently and accurately poured into glasses, and then served to the guests (*containment*);

- the champagne bottle is never opened, perhaps for fear or shame over how its contents might be received by the guests (*suppression*).

The *mere catharsis* scenario might be dramatic, loud and flashy. But the end result is a waste of precious and expensive champagne (i.e. the participants' emotions). It does not serve any long-term purpose; and the guests (the other participants) are left with empty glasses (not having heard what people wanted to say). In the *containment* scenario, the glass is carefully filled and presented so that the guests are able to receive (or hear) what is intended. Nothing is wasted. The (emotional) content is all there, but it is delivered in a dignified, protected and respectful manner (i.e. in saying how they feel, the participants do not feel overwhelmed, embarrassed, out of control, ashamed, or regretful).[9] In the *suppression* scenario, the bottle is never opened (i.e. the participants do not feel safe enough to share how they really feel, or even to experience these emotions themselves—and so they are hidden or silenced, continuing to cause them pain with no relief and possibly resulting in mental and physical illness).[10]

In short, there is a middle ground between suppression and mere catharsis. Participants should feel free to express how they feel. But the purpose of preparation is to make sure that they can do so in a way that can be heard and absorbed by the other participants. Otherwise, not only could they do themselves damage, but their efforts to communicate will have been wasted. In addition, the purpose of restorative justice is to enable the participants to *release* their shame, not to increase or further suppress it. So it is critical that the participants do not feel humiliated or embarrassed about what they say and how they say it. This is why the second core goal in preparing participants is to enable them to reach a point where they are able to communicate their thoughts and feelings in a way that is contained.

4.4 DEGREES OF INDEPENDENCE AND CONTAINMENT

We have seen that the aim of the preparation phase is to enable the participants to achieve *independence* and *containment*. But we need to be less 'black and white' about this. These qualities are on a continuum. For example, *complete* independence is an extremely difficult goal. Few, if any, participants will be able to achieve this kind of self-sufficiency. Likewise, we might all hope to express ourselves in a controlled, measured and respectful way. But no matter how much self-work we have done, there are few of us who can be that self-disciplined, particularly in the context of a face-to-face meeting. There will invariably be moments (or degrees) of uncontained communication.

In assessing whether or not the preparation phase has been completed, the facilitator, together with each participant, will therefore need to judge whether or not they have come as close as they can to the goals of independence and containment, in view of who they are and their life situations. This means that the assessment needs to take into account variables such as the seriousness of the incident, time-pressures, degrees of self-awareness, previous experiences, values, personality traits, how much social support they have, and so on.

In this respect, every participant will be different. Some will be able to achieve more independence and containment than others. This means that there will be some participants for whom a restorative justice meeting will be particularly confronting and emotionally challenging. For others, it may be less so. But if the preparation work is carried out effectively, then by the time they meet each other, each participant will be as independent and contained as they can be, given their life situations.

4.5 APPLYING THE MECHANISMS OF SHAME RELEASE

How can a facilitator enable participants to realise these two goals of independence and containment? Once again, the answer here involves the combination of *recall* and *compassionate listening* used in Stage 1. The facilitator will need to embody the qualities of a compassionate witness as they work with each participant separately. Their role is to help them:

- to recall what happened (the *facts*);

- to explore how people were affected (the *consequences*); and

- to think about how things can be made right (the *future*).

This will help the participants to move toward increased *independence* as they gradually release more of their shame. This progression will also help them to move toward greater *containment*. But how does this work? How does shame-release bring about more independence and containment?

Most of the destructive, disrespectful and overwhelming emotions are, in fact, shame-reactions. As the facilitator listens respectfully and compassionately, participants who remain 'stuck' in these reactions will find that they are able, over time, to discharge or abandon these negative emotions and cognitive strategies. This does not mean that they will have dispensed with their shame-reactions altogether. As we have seen, some shame-reactions (like defensive anger) are healthy and constructive. So to the extent that they have yet to release their shame entirely, there will be a transition from the negative shame-reactions to the more positive.

This transition is equivalent to the shift from mere catharsis to containment. For example, the *person harmed* might still be using the 'Attack Other' strategy. But instead of retaliatory fury, they will now be feeling defensive anger. Before they may have been full of uncontrollable rage and bitterness, wanting nothing other than to see the person responsible suffer excruciating pain. But now they are feeling assertive, strong, confident and unambiguous about the fact that they were wronged and are therefore owed some form of recompense. Likewise, the *person responsible* may still be using the 'Attack Self' shame-reactions. But where they were initially engaging in self-denigration, they are now taking the blame that is due, feeling remorse, and wanting to demonstrate that they have changed.[11]

4.6 ASSESSING PREPARATION

The movement toward independence and containment also explains why each participant is likely to require a different level and duration of preparation. For example, in the more serious or complex cases, it is unlikely that the participant will be able to discharge their more negative shame-reactions after only one or two sessions with a facilitator. It is more likely to take many hours of recall and compassionate listening, possibly over a period of several months, or even longer.

Because everyone is different, the preparation of participants in a restorative justice process cannot be rushed or allocated a pre-specified amount of time. To accommodate this level of unpredictability, the facilitator and/or restorative justice service will need to ensure that both the referral sources and participants are informed about and willing to accept the highly variable nature of a restorative justice process. For instance, referral sources need to know that timescales for completing a restorative justice process need to be highly flexible. Again, if the preparation of one participant is likely to take longer than the other, then the latter will need to be kept informed about the progress of the former, without breaching confidentiality.

5. Communication

5.1 THE PURPOSE OF COMMUNICATION

It might be argued that if the shame-release methods of recall and compassionate listening used in Stages 1 and 2 were entirely successful, then the more positive shame-reactions—like defensive anger—would have been overcome. After all, shame-reactions are, by definition, designed to suppress the feelings of shame. If the shame has been released, then no shame-reactions will be necessary. But then if the preparation for a restorative justice meeting brought about the full release of shame for the participants, what would be the purpose of arranging for them to communicate with each other?

One response to this question is that it poses an unrealistic scenario. Even the most thorough preparation is unlikely to achieve this kind of emotional 'clean slate'. Nevertheless, the concern is valid. The preparation stage is designed to bring about as much shame-release as possible; and the communication stage aims to release whatever shame remains. It follows that the better the preparation, the less need there is for communication, which seems like an odd result.

But there is a good answer to this conundrum. The primary reason for any communication is not merely to release whatever shame remains after the preparation phase. Rather it is this: *The goal of communication in a restorative justice process is to reinforce, extend and confirm whatever level of shame-release and affirmation of self-worth each participant has already achieved independently.*

5.2 ADDITIONAL BENEFITS OF COMMUNICATION

A well-prepared and well-facilitated restorative justice meeting can be extraordinarily powerful and healing for those who choose to take part in it. This is because communication can bring about two otherwise unobtainable benefits: that is, compassion and evidence.

Compassion

In the preparation phase, each participant will have reflected on how the other person might be feeling. This process will have generated some degree of empathy, and possibly even compassion. But the process of communication has the potential to enhance and deepen these feelings in a powerful way.

One of the problems with trying to feel empathy in isolation is that it is too easy to focus on our own feelings and needs. But if we are facing the other person 'in the flesh', looking in their eyes, and hearing the vulnerability in their voice, it will be a great deal harder to remain cloistered within our own emotional world, focused entirely on meeting our own needs. This movement toward *acting for the sake of the other* is precisely what is needed to bring about moral repair.[1]

Also, our capacity to empathise in isolation will be limited by our own imagination. We may think we have some idea about what the other person is going through. But we cannot really be sure until we hear it from them. Communication will correct, extend and reinforce whatever empathetic understanding we have gained on our own. For example, when the person responsible apologises in person, they will have a far better grasp of the hurt and suffering they have caused. This will almost invariably increase or deepen their feelings of remorse. When the person harmed considers whether there are grounds to change their views about the character of the person responsible, they will not have to guess. They can judge the sincerity of their remorse for themselves.

Evidence

It is one thing to find independent ways of defeating the underlying negative messages that cause our shame. But it is considerably more powerful to have those messages defeated by the very people who sent them to us in the first place. Why is this?

If we are left on our own to defeat the negative messages we have heard, then we are likely to find that this will not be a one-off task. With a great deal of self-work, the need to defeat these messages may eventually dissipate. But even so, it is likely to be an ongoing concern for some time. One reason for this is that we can often be unexpectedly reminded about how we were wronged. A familiar voice, a smell, a sudden movement—almost anything can trigger a memory of what happened. The original negative messages will then re-enter our consciousness, triggering renewed feelings of shame. For example, we may think we have independently moved on from a hurt we experienced long ago. But then a trigger arises, and we find ourselves suddenly consumed by the very feelings of anger we thought we had overcome. To defy the threat posed by these re-called messages, we need to stand up against them, again and again.[2]

But what would happen if the person who sent us those messages in the first place took them back? For example, *as a person harmed*, I may defy the threat posed to my self-worth by affirming to myself that:

'I did nothing to deserve the way I was treated'.

But suppose the very person who treated me in this way tells me, sincerely and to my face, that:

'You did nothing to deserve the way I treated you'.

Again, *as a person responsible*, I may try to convince myself that:

'I am a good person who did a bad thing'.

But suppose the very person who I harmed in effect tells me, sincerely and to my face, that:

'I can see that you are a good person who did a bad thing'.

In either case, the messages that I was hearing from the other person would be defeated once and for all. I would no longer need to guard myself from this threat to my social self, because it would have been removed. The moral harm will have been repaired.[3] The enormous relief, liberation and healing that can flow from the permanent removal of this threat is precisely the kind of benefit that a restorative justice process is uniquely designed to offer. It is what distinguishes restorative justice from any other type of process.

It is also a powerful reminder of how we are all interconnected. We are inherently social or relational beings. We cannot ultimately heal our social selves on our own. How others see us matters. Admitting that we have hurt someone in the privacy of our own minds (or to a friend or counsellor) is an important step forward in the work of moral repair. But it will never replace the act of offering an apology to the actual person we have harmed.[4] Likewise, through self-work and the compassionate support of others, it is possible to overcome, to a large degree, our anger against the person responsible for our pain. But there is nothing more powerful and healing than hearing a sincere apology directly from the very person who has hurt us.

5.3 APPLYING THE MECHANISMS OF SHAME RELEASE

We have seen that the purpose of communication between the person harmed and the person responsible is to confirm, extend or reinforce the release of shame and the affirmation of self-worth that has already started to occur in both. What does this mean in practice?

First, any communication should be designed to enable the participants to *listen compassionately* to each other. In other words, the facilitator should ensure that each person feels that:

- they are being treated equally and fairly, and with the utmost dignity and respect;

- this is a safe place, so that they will have less need to protect themselves with negative shame-reactions;

- they are being heard and understood; and

- they have the time and the space to feel, to reflect on what they have heard, and to become aware of any changes in themselves or in the other participants.

Second, the meeting should provide each participant with the opportunity to *recall* their respective experiences and speak openly about their feelings. Third, the meeting should provide opportunities for the participants to *defeat those negative underlying messages* that triggered feelings of shame in each other.

As with the preparation phase, these three objectives can be achieved by the facilitator guiding the participants through the same three topics of discussion: what happened (facts); how people have been affected (consequences); and how things can be made right (future).

6. Action

6.1 THE PROBLEM WITH APOLOGIES

The final stage of a restorative justice process involves carrying out any agreements or plans made in the communication stage. The importance of this phase in facilitating moral repair is often underestimated. We saw earlier that one of the main advantages of communication is that each participant takes back the negative underlying messages that were heard, thereby removing the threat once and for all. However, this finality assumes that each participant can be trusted to mean what they say. They might offer a full and unconditional apology in the meeting, but then laugh under their breath on their way home. The apology may even have been genuine at the time. Yet once the person responsible returns to that situation in which their harmful behaviour was enticing, they forget their remorse and re-offend.

Likewise, within the meeting, a person harmed might be moved with compassion for the person responsible, and so accept their apology or offer them forgiveness. But then, a few days later, they might question whether, in a moment of weakness, they were just 'taken for a ride'. Soon enough, they remember the wrong that was done to them, and the old anger and resentment wells up to the surface. Only this time it is magnified by the shame of feeling that they were manipulated into accepting a fake apology. It would be unwise to imagine that these thoughts and experiences do not occur to many participants in the aftermath of a restorative justice meeting.[1] It also seems clear that this could undermine much, if not all of the progress made in the previous three stages.

So if we want to design a restorative justice process that will maximise the likelihood of genuine and lasting moral repair, these are issues to which we need to devote some careful attention. How can we increase the probability that the person responsible will follow through on his or her promises? What can be done to inhibit the person harmed from slipping into damaging scepticism and bitter regret?

6.2 WHAT IT MEANS TO ACCEPT AN APOLOGY

An apology is never the final word. Its purpose is to persuade the person harmed that the individual before them no longer stands by their past actions. It takes back the hurtful, shame-inducing messages that were conveyed at that time. But an apology should also be read as a statement about the future.[2] An apology, in other words, is a kind of promise: it asks the person harmed to believe that this kind of behaviour will not be repeated.[3]

It follows that an apology is not a full and final payment of the moral debt that was owed to the person harmed. Instead, it is more like a down payment, with the remaining debt yet to be paid out. When the person harmed accepts the apology, they are not thereby handing over the keys to moral redemption. An apology is only the beginning. Like any promise, it can either be fulfilled or broken. So, what does this mean in practice? First, it means that the facilitator needs to clarify, with all participants, not only what it means to *offer* an apology, but also what the *acceptance* of that apology will mean. Specifically:

1. Unfinished work: The person harmed should not feel that they have given everything away if they accept the apology. They should expect that there is more to follow. The apology is a step in the right direction, rather than the end of the road.

2. Taken on trust: To accept an apology is not dissimilar to a business agreeing to take a deposit for a product, on the assumption that the full debt will be paid as agreed. In other words, accepting an apology is a way of saying 'I believe that you mean what you say, and I am willing to trust that you will keep your word'.[4]

3. Evidence-based: The acceptance of an apology should not be based upon blind trust. The person harmed will need to see evidence of reliability, good character and sincerity. This is why the behaviour of the person responsible within the entire restorative justice process is so critical. If they miss appointments with the facilitator, or arrive late to the restorative justice meeting, or come across as deceitful, manipulative, arrogant, impatient, bored or unremorseful, then they do not deserve to be trusted. The apology, if one is given, should be treated with suspicion, if not rejected outright.[5]

4. Properly motivated: In some cases, it will be clear to the facilitator that the person responsible has no intention of completing their agreements, or keeping their promise not to re-offend. For example, they might refuse to engage in rehabilitative programs that have been assessed as effective, available and suited to their needs. Or, it may become clear that they have agreed to take part in a restorative justice process for entirely self-interested motives (e.g. to avoid going to court, or a disciplinary hearing, or a tougher penalty).[6] It is extremely unhelpful when restorative justice is offered in such a context. Self-interest is more than likely to predominate, and so there will always be a question mark over the sincerity of the person responsible. The role of any facilitator is to ensure that the principles of restorative justice are not subverted by the self-interest of the person responsible. The person harmed should never be placed in a situation where the person responsible is only marginally concerned, if at all, with the moral harm they have caused.[7]

6.3 THE MEANING OF ACTION

The second practical implication of this account brings us to the action stage of a restorative justice process. If an apology is only a promissory note, then what happens *after* the restorative justice meeting takes on far more significance in relation to the work of moral repair. Specifically:

1. Keeping promises: It is not sufficient for a facilitator or a restorative justice service to offer a person harmed the opportunity to receive the moral debt that is owed to them, and yet do little or nothing to ensure that the person responsible can follow through on their promises to repay that debt in full. This would be like a bank that offers house loans to customers without doing any background checks on their ability to afford the repayments. It is irresponsible and irrational. Such a bank should expect to see a high rate of loan defaults (broken promises), with damaging consequences for all involved (undermining the repair-work already carried out).

2. Making Amends: If the person harmed has suffered physical or material harm, then they are entitled to ask for reparation or restitution. However, unless the damages are relatively minor, it is recommended that monetary restitution be handled through existing formal systems, so that the losses incurred can be fairly and accurately assessed. Restorative justice should not become a cheap civil court for processing restitution or compensation claims. It is not only ill equipped to do so, but the potential for inducing shame would be increased significantly. For example, there is almost always a perceived mismatch between the suffering endured and the amount of compensation offered. Likewise, the person responsible may feel humiliated by the fact that they are unable to pay enough, or on time. These scenarios will undermine, rather than facilitate the work of moral repair. Hence, in this context, the value or meaning of reparation should be regarded as primarily symbolic. It contributes to defeating the original negative underlying messages (e.g. 'you are a bad person') and affirming the self-worth and self-respect of all those involved.[8] Put another way, any reparative tasks should provide good evidence that the person responsible was sincere in his apology, and is committed to following through.[9]

3. Addressing recidivism: Any facilitator or restorative justice service should be able to ensure, as part of their remit, that the person responsible can take steps to abstain from re-offending. This will mean that the facilitator or the service should provide supplementary prevention programs as an integral part of the process and/or link up with external programs and services to which the person responsible can be referred and appropriately monitored.

4. Providing information: If an apology is a kind of promise, then the keeping of that promise is what sustains and confirms the message that an apology conveys. But how will the person harmed know that the promise has been kept unless they are told? There will, of course, be cases in which the participants have an ongoing connection (e.g. in a workplace or school); and so they will have more immediate access to how the person responsible behaves after the meeting. But in many other cases, they will never meet the person responsible again and so will have no independent way of finding out whether they have fulfilled their agreements. Without this information, the person harmed has little or no evidence, other than from the meeting itself, that the apology was genuine. In such cases, it is far more likely that they will, over time, question their own judgment and slip into a resentful scepticism.

It is therefore integral to the work of a facilitator that the person harmed is fully informed about the outcome of any agreement made in the meeting. Specifically, the facilitator's role is to ensure that any reparative tasks or rehabilitative activities agreed to are reliably monitored and completed. The person harmed must be informed when the tasks and activities have been successfully concluded. If there are legitimate reasons why the tasks or activities cannot be carried out, then the agreement should, if possible, be renegotiated with the involvement of the person harmed.

6.4 REALISTIC EXPECTATIONS

It is important to make a cautionary note at this point. The world is imperfect, and so expectations must be tailored to fit reality. For example, the *person responsible* may have serious mental health issues, a history of being abused or bullied themselves, a long-standing drug or alcohol addiction, and so on. It is essential that they at least make a commitment to take significant steps toward addressing these risk factors. But many will fail, and the person harmed will be invariably disappointed if the only goal on offer is perfection. The facilitator needs to make sure that, so far as possible, the person harmed has realistic expectations.

Likewise, the *person harmed* may have been severely wounded by the actions of the person responsible. But if they have lived for any length of time, they will be carrying a number of other wounds that are entirely unrelated to the person responsible. The problem is that it is often difficult to disentangle one wound from another. As we have seen, someone who has been wronged in the past may find their minds flooded with negative shame-inducing messages when they suffer a similar kind of wrong in the present. But if the two are not clearly distinguished, then the lack of resolution experienced in the past may leak into how they see the current situation.

What this means is that, no matter how sincere or remorseful the person responsible might be, no matter how hard they try to mend their ways, it may never be enough for the person harmed—simply because of unrelated wounds from the past. In their search for healing, a person harmed can then start to demand more and more. For example, they might contact the person responsible outside of the restorative justice process, check on them periodically, take them under their wing, become 'the parent they never had', try to 'fix' them, and so on.

Not all these actions are necessarily problematic, that is, if they are done for compassionate reasons and with adequate oversight, support and information. But they could also be unconsciously motivated by a need in the person harmed to heal from unrelated historical wounds. In that case, the person harmed will have moved beyond the boundaries of what is owed to them by the person responsible for the specific incident in question.

In short, the facilitator's role is to ensure that *all participants* are able to recognise the boundaries and inherent limitations of this particular journey of moral repair. Each participant needs to understand the purpose of this process and what it can realistically hope to achieve.

7. *Designing the Speaking Turns*

7.1 OPTIMISING THE DIALOGUE STRUCTURE

We have looked at how to optimise the four main stages of a restorative justice process for the purpose of facilitating moral repair: that is, commitment, preparation, communication, and action. But we also need to examine in more detail the internal structure of the dialogue that will occur in any direct communication between the participants.

To begin, we have seen that any such communication will cover the same three topics: the facts (what happened), the consequences (how people were affected) and the future (what needs to happen now). And that, as we will see, is also the most natural order in which these three topics will need to be covered. But is there an optimal sequence that the participants can use to discuss each topic? For instance, who should speak first? Who should follow? Is one sequence of speaking turns more likely to facilitate moral repair than another?

After years of careful reflection and observation, restorative justice practitioners have come to an (almost) uniform agreement on how best to answer these questions. Most practice guides and manuals will advocate a 'basic sequence' of speaking turns, with some variation depending on the type of process that is used and the range of participants who are attending. For example, in one widely used process ('conferencing'), there will be speaking turns assigned not only to the person responsible and the person harmed, but also to their respective 'support persons'.

The table below presents a 'basic sequence' for conferencing. This same dialogue structure can, of course, be used for meetings that do not involve support persons, simply by omitting their speaking turns. It should be noted here that this table includes a few important variations to the approach recommended by other practice guides and manuals. The aim of the sections that follow, then, will be to provide an explanation for key elements of this basic sequence, as well as for the variations.

Introduction	
1. Facts	• PR talks about what happened • PH can ask questions • Open dialogue
2. Consequences	• PH talks about impact • PH's support persons talk about impact • PR can offer apology • PR's support persons give their views • PH and support persons can respond
3. Future	• PH suggests how to make things right • PR makes further suggestions • Open dialogue • Finalise Action Plan
Refreshments	

7.2 FACTS

The person responsible opens the dialogue about the facts

The facilitator opens the first topic by asking the person responsible to talk about what happened. There are several reasons for this:[1] First, it gives the person responsible a chance to demonstrate that they are here to do the right thing by openly admitting what they did. This gesture can help to defuse any scepticism or suspicion that others might have felt about their motives. Second, it will help the person responsible to resist slipping into self-protecting shame-reactions, such as denying their role in what happened or blaming the person harmed. Third, the person harmed will not feel that they need to extract a confession from the person responsible. Fourth, if the person harmed speaks first, they may blame the person responsible for something that they didn't do. The person responsible (or their support persons) may feel affronted and react defensively. The group will then have to clear up the facts before moving on. This can cause unnecessary frustration and resentment. Finally, if the person responsible starts the conversation with humility and an admission of fault, this can assist everyone to start separating the person from their actions. Their humble demeanour will reduce the need for the person harmed to sustain an emotional defence, and so make it possible for them to hear the apology.

7.3 CONSEQUENCES

The person harmed opens the dialogue about the consequences

Some manuals recommend that, before moving on to the response of the person harmed, the facilitator should ask the person responsible to identify the impact that their action has had on the other people present at the conference. The rationale seems to be that this may help to show the other participants that the person responsible has given some thought to the effects of their behaviour. This sequence is not recommended here for two reasons:

First, the person responsible could—and, indeed, is very likely to—give an inaccurate or incomplete picture of who has been harmed or how they might have been impacted. Second, the person responsible is essentially pre-empting or speaking for the person harmed. However, the person harmed has come in order to explain precisely how they have been impacted. They do not need to hear attempts to guess at how they might be feeling.[2] In both cases, the person harmed could easily feel disrespected or devalued (i.e. shamed): in the first case, by the apparent lack of thought that the person responsible has given to how their actions have affected people; and in the second, by the person responsible's presumption that they could *already* know how the person harmed might have been affected before even listening to them. This disrespect is likely to result in shame-reactions such as anger; and that could quickly lead to shame-rage loops.

Support persons of the person harmed then talk about the consequences

There are several reasons why the support persons should be invited to talk about the impact of what happened *after* the person harmed:

First, this order is more likely to empower the person harmed. They will have had the opportunity to speak for themselves, using their own judgment about what they want to say and how they say it. If the support persons spoke first, it would be easy for the person harmed to feel that their voice or decisions had been taken over or pre-empted by their support persons.

Second, support persons often fill in some of the gaps left by the person harmed. Sometimes they can be more aware—or at least more articulate—about the effect of the incident on the person harmed than the person harmed themselves. It can be very affirming for the person harmed to hear how acutely conscious and empathetic others have been about their suffering, especially when they have not heard them talk about this before. However, in terms of empowering the person harmed, the perspective of the support persons should be heard as a supplement, rather than the primary voice. That status is best conveyed by placing them after the person harmed in the speaking sequence.

Third, placing the person harmed first can help to remind the support persons that their primary role is to provide support, rather than to focus on their own needs or agendas.

Finally, this sequence can, symbolically, help the person responsible to understand the ripple effect of their actions by making them aware of the harm and distress caused firstly to the person harmed, and then to a wider group of people.

The person responsible can then offer an apology

There are several reasons why the person responsible is given the opportunity to offer an apology *after* the person harmed and their support persons have spoken:

First, the person harmed has come to a meeting not just to hear the apology. They need to express how they feel. They want to be heard. They want the person responsible to learn about the human consequences of what they have done. Only then can they be assured that the person responsible knows what they are apologising *for*.[3]

Second, it is vital that, when support people are present, the group's moral sympathies are not one-sided. The final outcome should be a more or less equal moral regard for both participants. This is achieved by ensuring that the group has fully understood and empathised with the hurt and loss experienced by the person harmed *before* it hears the apology.

The group's moral sympathies will initially swing to the person harmed as they listen to how they have been harmed. They will then swing over to the person responsible when they hear the apology. But since the group will still feel compassion and empathy for the person harmed, they will not side with the person responsible. Since the person responsible has done the right thing and apologised, they will also not side with the person harmed. The effect of this sequence is to produce the sense that both are—at least with respect to the incident in question—moral equals.[4]

By contrast, suppose that the person responsible were to offer an apology in their opening statement (as they often do). And suppose that this apology was taken by the group to be the full and final apology. The person harmed could easily feel disinclined to say too much, if anything, about how they have been harmed. To do so, after an apology has already been given, might be interpreted as 'overkill' or 'harping on'.[5] Indeed, the person harmed may be concerned that the group's moral sympathies might swing over to the person responsible simply because they seem 'unable to accept the apology'. This is why—in addition to following the sequence suggested here—the facilitator must ensure that any such premature apology from the person responsible is not treated by the group as the final word.[6]

Third, the person responsible will have heard, for the first time, a personal account of how much they have hurt another human being. This is likely to increase their empathetic understanding, and thus the depth and sincerity of their remorse when they do offer their apology.

Finally, the person harmed has just poured out their pain and loss. It is crucial that this is immediately met with a response from the person responsible that is morally and psychologically fitting or appropriate. That response is a sincere apology.

Those supporting the person responsible give their views after the apology

Some manuals recommend that the support persons of the person responsible speak *before* the person responsible is given the opportunity to respond to all that has been said. The reason given for this order is so that, when the person responsible eventually does respond (e.g. with an apology), they can take into account the harm they may have also caused to their own support persons. But there are several reasons for reversing this order:

First, if the support persons of the person responsible speak first, and offer their own apology to the person harmed (as they often do), then the person responsible will have missed an opportunity to be seen as having *initiated* their own apology.[7] They will be seen as simply following the example of their own support persons—in which case, their apology may be regarded as less authentic or sincere.

Second, the support persons of the person responsible are usually connected to the person responsible in a way that the person harmed is not. For example, they may have been, to some degree, accountable for overseeing the behaviour of the person responsible (e.g. as their parent, probation officer, teacher, or manager). So their pain is more likely to be along the lines of disappointment, embarrassment or personal betrayal. These are serious harms. But they are of a different order to, say, a violent assault, a burglary, bullying, or the murder of a loved one. Yet if they are asked to speak about how they were harmed immediately after the person harmed and their support persons, then the implication is that all these harms are in the same moral category. This is likely to make the person harmed feel that their suffering has been somehow minimised or misunderstood. By contrast, if the support persons of the person responsible speak after the apology, then it will be very clear to everyone present that there is an important moral difference between these two types of harm. (The person responsible may still want to apologise to their own support persons for the harm that they have caused to them; but this should be done separately—for instance, immediately after their support persons have spoken. However, if significant repair-work is needed between the person responsible and their support persons, then this conversation should take place in an entirely separate meeting, and preferably prior to any meeting with the person harmed. This will ensure that the focus of the conference remains on what is owed to the person harmed.)

Third, the support persons of a person responsible often mean more to them, at a personal or relational level, than the person harmed—who is often a stranger they may never see again. Hence, if their apology follows the entire group's discussion about how the incident has affected each one of them, it is likely that the person responsible will, quite naturally, focus more on the remorse they feel for having hurt their own support persons, than how they feel about having hurt the person harmed. This will invariably result in the person harmed feeling that their pain has been sidelined.

Fourth, having virtually the entire group, one after the other, talk in detail about how the person responsible has hurt them is likely to overwhelm them with feelings of shame. To protect themselves, the person responsible may resort to various shame-reactions. For example, they may switch off or start defending themselves (Avoidance). Or they may retreat within themselves, looking down and not responding at all (Withdrawal). By contrast, if they are given a chance to apologise before their support persons speak, then the person responsible may be better able to maintain their self-respect, and so more able to hear everyone and respond appropriately.

Finally, the support persons will often be feeling shame themselves, simply by virtue of their connection with the person responsible. They may be hearing the message that, if they are associated with this person, then they too must be 'bad people'. To protect themselves from this threat to their self-worth, they are likely to use various shame-reactions—such as blaming the person harmed, defending the person responsible, or putting down or distancing themselves from the person responsible (e.g. 'He is totally useless'), and so on.[8]

These unhelpful reactions can be avoided by giving the support persons an alternative strategy. But this can only be done if the support persons follow the apology of the person responsible. It involves the facilitator inviting the support persons to speak by asking the following question: 'Would you like to add anything to what [the person responsible] has just said?'. Since the person responsible has just done the right thing by apologising, it is highly likely that the support persons will take this question as a cue to register their support for what the person responsible has just done. They may even take the opportunity to apologise for their part, if any, in what happened. In doing so, they will have communicated that they acknowledge the person responsible did the wrong thing, and that they do not stand by these actions—without needing to distance themselves from the person responsible.

The person harmed and their support persons can then respond

There are several reasons why the person harmed is given an opportunity to respond to the apology *after* the support persons of the person responsible have spoken. First, the immediate response from the person harmed to the apology will probably be a quick 'thank you' or a nod of their heads in polite acknowledgement. This is a natural and almost irresistible response to a verbal apology.[9] However, this should not be confused with accepting the apology or offering forgiveness. The person harmed and their support persons will have only recently finished explaining the impact of the incident on them. The act of recalling their experience is likely to have been emotionally painful and upsetting. It may have taken considerable time and energy for them to bring out the full impact. The problem is that the apology—even if sincere and remorseful—can seem relatively quick and easy by contrast. So in this context, it is perfectly understandable that the person harmed may feel able to respond with a spontaneous 'thanks' or a brief acknowledgement, but no more. The sequence has been too quick. Any substantive acceptance of the apology or gesture of forgiveness may, at this point, feel cheap or superficial.

In other words, they may need more time to reflect on what they have heard, and settle their emotions, before they can give their considered response to the apology.[10] Hence, if the facilitator opens up a space for the person harmed to respond to the apology immediately after it has been given, they may feel pressured into accepting the apology or offering forgiveness when they are not ready to do so. Indeed, they are more likely to avoid doing so by re-telling aspects of the harm they experienced. This in turn may make the person responsible feel like their apology has been rejected.

Second, the person harmed may not want to accept the apology immediately because they are sceptical about its sincerity. Hearing the views of the support persons for the person responsible can be a way of getting a 'reality check', as they are normally in a position to know whether the person responsible is being sincere or not.

It may, of course, turn out that, even with a little more space to consider how they want to respond to the apology, the person harmed or their support persons will still not feel right about accepting the apology at this point or offering forgiveness. In some cases, it will only be during the more informal conversations that occur over refreshments that a gesture of forgiveness will emerge.[11] For this reason, the facilitator should advise the person responsible, as part of their preparation, not to ask for forgiveness; nor should they feel entitled to expect it. Likewise, the person harmed should know beforehand that they will not be expected to offer forgiveness, nor should they feel in any way obligated to do so.[12] It may also be helpful to explore with them the differences between acknowledging an apology, being persuaded that an apology is genuine (or experiencing forgiveness), and accepting an apology (or offering forgiveness).[13]

7.4 FUTURE

The dialogue closes with the future

There are several reasons why the question of 'how things can be made right' is raised at this point in the meeting.

First, by the time the second topic ('Consequences') has come to a close, the participants will have, together, painted a picture of what happened and the impact that it has had. There will be a sense that they are now a community, all affected in some way by the incident. Second, there will also have been signs of change. An apology will have been offered. Remorse will have been expressed. And if this apology has been accepted as sincere or an offer of forgiveness has been made, then shame will have been released. Pride, self-respect and good will have been restored. There will now be a shared willingness to move forward. [14]

This is the perfect foundation upon which to base a discussion about what actions or plans need to be put in place. The work of moral repair has progressed to a significant extent. But, as discussed above, the apology is only a down payment. The full debt can only be paid by subsequent actions. Hence, this is the point where the person responsible can demonstrate their commitment to following through on their apology by making amends and taking steps to ensure that they do not repeat their actions.

7.5 REFRESHMENTS

The main rationale for offering refreshments after the meeting has been concluded is that this is the time when the repair of moral *relations* or 'reconciliation' is most likely to happen. The formal part of the meeting is over, the incident has been addressed, the issues dealt with, and the moral harm has been repaired. Participants can now begin to treat each other as moral equals, and this shift is often best confirmed or reinforced in an informal, relaxed setting.

Appendices

1. Shame vs. Guilt

1.1 ACTIONS IMPLICATE THE SELF

Many theorists in psychology and philosophy make a distinction between shame and guilt. Shame, they argue, is an emotion that carries with it a negative evaluation about what kind of *person* you are (e.g. 'I am a bad person'); whereas the feeling of guilt is focused on a negative evaluation of a particular *action* you have done ('I did a bad thing'). For example, Tangney, Stuewig and Mashek state the following:

> "Currently, the most dominant basis for distinguishing between shame and guilt centers on the object of negative evaluation and disapproval. Shame involves a negative evaluation of the global self; guilt involves a negative evaluation of a specific behaviour."[1]

But shame and guilt seem to be more intimately connected than this. If I have done a bad thing, then that has implications for what kind of person I am. We are not immune to feeling this implication. When I feel guilty, I will also feel shame ('If I did a bad thing, then I am a bad person'). Indeed, if I feel no shame over a wrong that I have done, this would suggest that I have yet to admit responsibility for my actions. There is something not quite right about someone who says: 'I agree that what I did was wrong. But that wasn't really me. I am not that kind of person'. Such a person has not yet come to terms with the fact that, logically, if they did commit the wrong, then they *must* have been the kind of person who could do such a thing.[2] The only way they can distinguish so neatly between what they have done and who they are is by resorting to the shame-reaction of *withdrawal from themselves* (i.e. by splitting their 'good self' from their 'bad self').[3]

For these reasons, it seems more accurate to say that guilt is a kind of shame.[4] It is the kind of shame that we feel *when we have done something wrong*. Thus guilt is distinct from, say, the kind of shame we feel when we are put down, disrespected or insulted, which we call 'humiliation'. It is also distinct from 'embarrassment', which is the kind of shame we experience when we feel socially out of place, for example, by a breach of etiquette.[5]

1.2 GUILT AND MORAL REPAIR

Guilt can only be legitimately relieved if it is a kind of shame

We can make a case for this taxonomy in another way. Theorists who distinguish between shame ('I am a bad person') and guilt ('I have done a bad thing') argue that we can relieve our guilt—but not our shame—by taking responsibility, apologising and making amends. Tangney et. al., for example, argue as follows:

> "Shame—and, shame-fused guilt—offers little opportunity for redemption. It is a daunting challenge to transform a self that is defective at its core. . . [But] there are typically a multitude of paths to redemption in the case of uncomplicated guilt focused on a specific behavior. A person *(a)* often has the option of changing the objectionable behavior; *(b)* or even better yet, has an opportunity to repair the negative consequences; *(c)* or at the very least, can extend a heartfelt apology. And when it is not possible to make these external amends, one can resolve to do better in the future."[6]

But if 'uncomplicated' guilt is merely about a specific behaviour ('my having done a bad thing'), then it is hard to see how an apology could free me from my feelings of guilt. To explain: My feeling of guilt depends upon my *belief* that I have done a bad thing. Now I cannot erase the past. It will always be true of me that I did something wrong. So if I cannot change *what I have done*, then the only way I can relieve my guilt is to change my *belief* about what I have done. I will need to somehow re-construe or re-think the morality of what I have done or just deny that I did anything at all. In short, to relieve my guilt I will need to find a reason for thinking that what I did was either morally acceptable, or that I was somehow not responsible for it, or that it didn't happen at all. There are, of course, well-known ways of achieving this end, none of which could be classified as morally praiseworthy or redemptive. They are called 'cognitive distortions', and include strategies such as denial, minimising, excusing, justifying, and so on.

But here is the point: what could never work—as a strategy to relieve my guilt—are the "paths to redemption" suggested by Tangney et. al.. If I offer an apology, take responsibility and make amends, I am thereby admitting to the fact that I was responsible for what happened, and that what I did was morally wrong. Far from divesting myself of the belief that 'I have done a bad thing', an apology would only affirm such a belief. It follows that if guilt is solely about *having done a bad thing*—without any implications for the kind of person that I am—there could be no morally legitimate way of relieving this emotion.

By contrast, if guilt is in fact a kind of shame, then an apology is the perfect solution. If I feel guilty over having done a bad thing, then the solution is not to try and get rid of the belief that what I did was wrong (e.g. by distorting the facts). I cannot undo the past, so I need to accept that this is a fact about my life history that will remain fixed. But what I can change is *how I now stand in relation to what I have done*. I can condemn what I did, withdraw the messages that it conveyed, express my remorse in a sincere apology, and commit to never doing that kind of thing again. I can, in other words, do the work that is required to repair my social self. This work effectively removes the legitimacy of the inference from 'I did a bad thing' to 'I am a bad person'. Since shame, in general, is about our social self, it follows that guilt can only be legitimately relieved if it is a kind of shame.

Another author who makes a similar distinction between how guilt and shame are respectively overcome is John Rawls:

"Feelings of guilt and shame have different settings and are overcome in different ways, and these variations reflect the defining principles with which they are connected and their peculiar psychological bases. Thus for example, guilt is relieved by reparation and the forgiveness that permits reconciliation; whereas shame is undone by proofs of defects made good, by a renewed confidence in the excellence of one's person."[7]

The mistake that Rawls makes here is to think that reparation is something other than a 'proof of [moral] defects made good'; or that forgiveness is something other than experiencing a 'renewed confidence in the [moral] excellence of the person' who has wronged you. In other words, reparation and forgiveness only relieve the feeling of guilt insofar as they 'undo' the shame of having done something wrong. And that connection only makes sense if guilt is conceived of as a kind of shame.

Rawls is right to say that shame *in general* can only be 'undone' by addressing apparent 'defects' and gaining a 'renewed confidence in the excellence of one's person'. But there are specific kinds of shame, each of which can be distinguished by the kind of 'defect' that we think others have seen in us; and each requires a different approach to 'undoing' this threat to our social self. Undoing the kind of shame we call 'guilt' requires that we apologise and make amends to those we have wronged. Undoing the kind of shame we call 'humiliation' may require that we stand up for ourselves and demand justice.

'Maladaptive guilt' is shame that requires release through moral repair

We can further reinforce this taxonomy by exploring why it is that the clinical literature has found that feelings of guilt often cause psychological distress. Tangney et. al. explain this phenomenon by arguing that:

> "... guilt is most likely to be maladaptive when it becomes fused with shame ... guilt with an overlay of shame is most likely the source of the painful self-castigation and rumination so often described in the clinical literature. . . . Ultimately, it's the shame component of this sequence—not the guilt component—that poses the problem, as the person becomes saddled with feelings of contempt and disgust for a bad, defective self."[8]

A better explanation for maladaptive guilt is not the presence of shame, which—as argued above—is inevitable in any case. Rather the problem is that a person who believes they have done wrong (and that they are therefore 'bad' or 'defective') has not yet carried out the work of moral repair. They have not accepted responsibility for their part in what happened, apologised to those they have harmed and made amends. Contrary to Tangney et. al., a 'bad, defective self' *can* be redeemed, repaired and healed.

'False guilt' is shame that can only be released by accepting the moral truth

Of course, this remedy only applies to those who truly are responsible for wrongdoing. False guilt requires a different solution. Tangney et. al. describes false guilt as arising:

> "... when people develop an exaggerated or distorted sense of responsibility for events beyond their control or for which they have no personal involvement. . . . Survivor guilt is a prime example of such a problematic guilt response that has been consistently linked to psychological maladjustment."[9]

If guilt is a kind of shame, then this explains why false guilt is so problematic. If the person is not truly responsible for doing something wrong, then it will be impossible for them to engage successfully in the work of moral repair. They will be unable, in any legitimate way, to take responsibility, apologise or make amends. It follows that their sense of being a 'bad' or 'defective' self will be extremely difficult to dislodge, at least while they are still feeling false guilt. The only remedy is to convince them that they were not responsible for any wrongdoing in the first place, and that their social self is therefore not in need of redemption or repair.

1.3 INTERPRETING THE RESEARCH

The research identifies distinct shame-reactions, not different emotions

Researchers in the field have defended the distinction between shame and guilt by appealing to a large body of empirical evidence—including:

> "experimental and correlational studies employing a range of methods, qualitative case studies analyses, content analyses of shame and guilt narratives, participants' quantitative ratings of personal shame and guilt experiences, analyses of attributions associated with shame and guilt, and analyses of participants' counterfactual thinking."[10]

It seems clear that these studies are indeed identifying distinct phenomena when they apply the terms 'shame' and 'guilt'. If not, it would be hard to account for the results. However, it is possible to explain this evidence without accepting the conclusion that 'shame' and 'guilt' refer to two different emotions. If one looks closely at the research findings, the terms 'shame' and 'guilt' are, in fact, used to distinguish two sets of (what we have called) *shame-reactions*. Take the finding below, for example:

> "Research shows that shame and guilt lead to contrasting motivations, or 'action tendencies' . . . . Shame often motivates efforts to deny, hide from, or escape the shame-inducing situation. Guilt often motivates reparative action (e.g. confession, apology, efforts to undo the harm done.)."[11]

The term 'shame' here evidently refers to those situations in which shame gives rise to the kind of shame-reactions we know as 'Avoidance' and

'Withdrawal'. The term 'guilt' (which would include false 'guilt') refers to those situations in which shame gives rise to the kind of behaviours that, if authentic, only emerge in the context of certain 'Attack Self' shame-reactions, namely, self-blame and remorse. A similar analysis can be applied to the following research:

> "In an effort to escape painful feelings of shame, shamed individuals are apt to defensively 'turn the tables,' externalizing blame and anger outward onto a convenient scapegoat. . . . Guilt-proneness, in contrast, is consistently associated with more constructive responses to anger (e.g., nonhostile discussion, direct corrective action and a disinclination toward aggression)."[12]

Here the term 'shame' refers to those situations in which shame gives rise to 'Attack Other' reactions that suppress or displace shame-feelings (anger, scapegoating, etc.). What is referred to as 'guilt' corresponds to situations in which shame gives rise to behaviours that are associated with morally appropriate 'Attack Self' shame-reactions (self-blame, remorse, etc.).

The feelings ascribed to 'shame' are identical with how guilt can feel

Perhaps the most common finding used to distinguish 'shame' from 'guilt' is the reported differences between how each 'feels':

> "On balance, shame is the more painful emotion because one's core self—not simply one's behaviour—is at stake. Feelings of shame are typically accompanied by a sense of shrinking or of feeling 'small,' and by a sense of worthlessness and powerlessness. Guilt, on the other hand, is typically a less devastating, less painful experience because the object of condemnation is a specific behaviour, not the entire self. Rather than needing to defend the exposed core of their identity, people in the throes of guilt are drawn to consider their behaviour and its consequences. This focus leads to tension, remorse, and regret over the 'bad thing done'."[13]

But as we will see, the feelings that are exclusively associated with 'shame' here can, in certain contexts, be appropriately ascribed to guilt as well—and *vice versa*. If so, this 'finding' can be explained without assuming that guilt and shame are distinct emotions.

To begin, we need some background. First, in Chapter 3, we set out a range of different shame-triggers (e.g. 'Performance', 'Attractiveness',

'Sexuality', etc.). Each of these triggers work because they attack or condemn something about us that has a bearing on our social self, or how people see us. This can include our behaviour, our appearance, our abilities, our character, and so on. In other words, virtually everything about us can be a source of shame. This means that *our core identity is always 'at stake'*—regardless of what it is about us that happens to be the target of a negative evaluation or condemnation.

Second, the painfulness of shame (when it is not being suppressed) *comes in degrees*: sometimes it will be utterly crushing, dramatically affecting our entire sense of the kind of person we thought we were. At the other extreme, a feeling of shame can be so slight as to make us merely wince or blush.

Third, the painfulness of any shame-trigger *depends on the social context from which it arises*. For instance, professional models will tend to feel far more devastated by a negative evaluation of their attractiveness, than, say, computer software programmers. Or again, suppose the underlying message 'you are stupid' is conveyed by something your partner or your parents say to you. This shame-trigger will be far more painful than it would have been if it had come from a complete stranger. The former will feel like an excruciating attack on your core identity; the latter will still hurt, but you won't feel quite so distressed. Shame-triggers that arise from people who matter to you will have a greater impact on the degree of shame that you feel.

To give a more pertinent example: different types of wrongdoing will tend to have a greater or lesser bearing on our social self. If you are found guilty of child abuse, for instance, you are likely to believe that most, if not all of the people around you will see your core identity—who you are as a person— as being profoundly flawed or defective. Unless you manage to suppress your shame entirely, it is very likely that you will, as a result, experience the most extreme or 'upper-level' degrees of this emotion. Wrongs that are seen as less serious will still be shameful, but the pain will not be nearly as devastating. In other words, the *painfulness* of being condemned for a specific wrongful behaviour is directly linked to *how badly it makes you feel about yourself*. And that, in turn, depends on how your wrongdoing is viewed by your social group and the people who matter to you the most.

What follows from the three points made above, is that there are significant problems with the way that the research above has interpreted its own findings. First, the feelings that are taken to be the distinguishing hallmark of 'shame' are in fact associated with only the most extreme or 'upper-level' degrees of shame. Second, what triggers off an experience of this higher level of shame *could* be a specific wrongful behaviour that we have committed. That depends on how negatively we think our behaviour has been (or will be) evaluated by the social group in which we are embedded and/or the individuals who matter to us the most. In other words, depending on our social context, engaging in a certain kind of wrongful behaviour can result in our experiencing exactly those feelings of 'devastation' that the research has identified as 'shame'. Now, even the research accepts that 'guilt' is the emotion we feel "when the object of condemnation is a specific [wrongful] behaviour". If that is true, then it follows that 'how guilt feels' *can*, in certain situations, be identical to 'how shame feels', according to the research. But then the research 'findings' can be explained without assuming that guilt and shame are distinct emotions.

How then do we explain the apparent finding that the experience of 'guilt' feels less painful than 'shame'? There are two possible reasons for this:

What the research identifies as 'guilt' is shame relieved by moral repair

First, the research reports that "people in the throes of guilt" were "drawn to consider their behaviour and its consequences"—a focus that lead to "tension, remorse, and regret over the 'bad thing done'." This suggests that what the researchers have identified are situations in which (a) people have done something wrong, but have (b) made significant progress toward successfully defeating the shame-inducing message of 'I am a bad person' by accepting responsibility, considering the impact of their behaviour, and feeling remorse. But if that is the case, then they will, as a consequence, have released much of their shame; and so, for that reason, they will feel better about themselves. In other words, what the researchers have identified as 'people in the throes of guilt' are, in fact, people who have significantly relieved their shame by having made good progress toward the goal of moral repair. If they had asked people to describe how they felt *prior* to these redemptive activities, then they are very likely to have heard responses like: 'I felt bad about myself', 'I felt like a monster', 'I just wanted to run and hide', and so on. In other words, they would have described the core elements of what it is like to feel the terrible pain of (un-released) shame. This would explain why the research found that the experience of 'guilt' felt less painful than 'shame'.

What the research identifies as 'guilt' is the shame of minor wrongdoing

Second, we know that it is shameful even to talk about, let alone admit to feeling shame—especially if it is caused by having done something wrong. We have also just seen how the painfulness of shame is determined by our social context. Putting these two points together, it seems likely that research participants will, in general, be more willing to talk about how they feel about wrongful behaviour that is seen as relatively minor by their social group or the people who matter to them most. But then it is no surprise to learn that most participants describe their feelings of 'guilt' as being less painful or devastating than their feelings of 'shame'. What they are most likely to be identifying here is the difference between the 'low-level' shame they felt after committing what their social group regarded as relatively minor wrongs (which is what the researchers then labelled as 'guilt'), and the far more 'devastating' degree of shame they felt as a result of some other kind of shame-trigger (which is what they called 'shame').

2. Terminology

The theory presented in this book involves several terms that are somewhat controversial. The most important of these are 'shame' and 'forgiveness'. Hence, it will be important to provide some explanation.

2.1 'SHAME'

Use of the terms 'shame' and its cognates in a restorative justice context is frequently criticised for the following reason: People who attend restorative justice processes are usually burdened with enough shame as it is. They already feel humiliated, betrayed, worthless, and demeaned. The last thing they need is to be shamed yet again, piling hurt upon hurt. Restorative justice should be about emotional healing and the removal of shame and stigma. Yet, by making 'shame' so central to the explanation of why restorative justice works, it is not inconceivable—in a culture dominated by shaming penalties[1]—that some will take this to legitimise the use of restorative justice processes as a means of shaming or humiliating those responsible for the wrongdoing.[2] Equally, participants who have been harmed may not take kindly to any suggestion that shame lies at the heart of their suffering. They might interpret such language as meaning that what happened to them, or how they are dealing with it, is shameful—which may intensify their suffering. As Susan Salasin puts it:

> "[M]ost victims are stigmatized by family, friends, and the public, who often blame the victim for his or her own plight, so that they do not have to confront the fact that it could happen to them. Victims learn to hide their status, not to speak of what occurred, not to share their feelings. These actions increase a sense of shame and rejection, compounding the victim trauma response."[3]

For all these reasons, it has been suggested that words such as 'shame' and 'shaming' should be avoided: they should be removed from any description or explanation of restorative justice processes.

The problem with this objection is that it gets the story only half right. First, restorative justice should never involve the shaming of any participant, in the sense of deliberately making them feel belittled, demeaned, humiliated or stigmatised. This would demonstrate a total failure to understand the purpose of restorative justice. Shaming, in this sense, is precisely what causes moral damage. It is the polar opposite of what would be required to bring about moral repair.

Second, the objection suggests that shame, as an emotion, is *always* bad. But this is not the case. Feeling ashamed (or guilty) about the harm that you have caused is precisely the kind of emotion that is essential to the work of moral repair. How would you respond to someone who hurt you, and yet felt no shame? [4]

Third, one might infer from the above that shaming—in the sense of deliberately inducing feelings of guilt—would be legitimate within a restorative justice process. However, this is not quite accurate. On the model defended here, the person responsible should have already started along the path of moral repair, prior to any communication with the person harmed. So they will *already* be feeling guilt by the time they attend the meeting. Moreover, when the person harmed recalls their experience in the meeting, this will, on its own, have the power to confirm and reinforce the guilt that is felt by the person responsible.

Fourth, the ultimate purpose of restorative justice is to *release* the shame that people are feeling, including guilt. It follows that there is no need to shame the person responsible, in the sense of calculating how best to induce or increase their feelings of guilt (e.g. by exaggerating the harm done, or blaming them for consequences that no reasonable person could have possibly foreseen or for which a causal link to their actions is extremely tenuous or implausible). That kind of 'guilt-stirring' is very likely to make the process of shame-release far more onerous.

Finally, the objection implies that it is possible to understand a restorative justice process without any reference to the emotion of shame. But, as we have seen, the behaviour, motivations, emotions and moral concepts at work in a restorative justice process are inexplicable without appealing to this emotion.[5] For this reason, the emotion of shame *must* be fully understood by restorative justice facilitators.

Having said all the above, the instinctive negative reaction that many people have to the term 'shame' cannot be dismissed. There is nothing to be gained by causing unnecessary confusion or adverse reactions—particularly in the contexts of advocating restorative justice policy or communicating with potential participants. Hence, the term 'shame' is best situated within an explanatory or theoretical context, where clarity about its application is more likely to be assured. For other purposes, there are equivalent terms that are more familiar, and less ambiguous or liable to misinterpretation. These include words like 'remorse', 'humiliation', 'hurt', 'betrayal', and so on. As Eliza Ahmed et. al. put it:

> "[S]hame and shaming are indispensable conceptual tools for understanding the effectiveness of restorative justice. This is because it is imperative to distinguish between good and bad shaming and harmful and helpful shame. This does not mean that social movement advocates should actually use the word shame as part of their reform rhetoric . . . responsibility and healing are likely to supply a more politically resonant, and a more prudent neo-liberal discourse than shame and reintegration."[6]

2.2 'FORGIVENESS'

The term 'forgiveness' is another very controversial word within a restorative justice context. There are several reasons for this.

Forgiveness excuses or condones

First, the concept of forgiveness is widely understood to involve condoning or excusing, as if the crime committed was 'okay' or understandable. This view is put forcefully by Cynthia Ozick:

> "We are asked to think that vengeance brutalizes, forgiveness refines. But the opposite can be true. Forgiveness can brutalize. Forgiveness can be pitiless. It forgets the victim. It negates the right of the victim to his own life. It blurs over suffering and death. It drowns the past. It cultivates sensitiveness toward the murderer at the price of insensitiveness toward the victim."[7]

While this construal of 'forgiveness' is not uncommon, it does not reflect the view of most psychologists and philosophers who have reflected on and studied the phenomenon. Genuine forgiveness, they argue, can and must be distinguished from condoning or excusing. We cannot forgive unless we believe that we were unjustifiably and inexcusably harmed. What would there be to forgive, after all, if we did not believe that wrong had been done to us?

In addition, forgiveness is not designed to serve the interests of the person responsible at the expense of the person harmed. As we have seen, it is possible to *experience* the healing of forgiveness without *offering* forgiveness to the one who hurt you. Nor does forgiveness mean that you must restore (or enter into) a relationship with the person responsible. That additional step requires that you actually *want* such a relationship, which is by no means a necessary part of what it means to forgive. We can forgive someone, knowing we will never meet them again. Even if the desire is there, issues of safety and trust must be considered; and this would, at the very least, involve obtaining clear evidence of consistent behavioural change over time.[8]

Finally, it is possible to forgive and yet also seek to have the offender held accountable by whatever justice systems are available. Forgiveness consists of a series of emotional, cognitive and behavioural changes. As such, it can only be undertaken and experienced by an individual person. Moreover, in order to remain free and properly motivated, forgiveness needs to be offered for personal reasons, for example to find healing and self-respect through the work of moral repair. It follows that forgiveness is not something that can be done by institutions, such as a court of law—partly because the court is not a person, but also because the primary role of a court is to further the wider interests of society, not the preferences or views of individuals. A court can perhaps show mercy, but it has no business forgiving offenders.[9] Likewise, a person who has been harmed may well forgive, but there are societal considerations that remain. Kathleen Moore gives a good example of this:

> "[When] a teenager injures her parents by stealing their pay-checks to support her drug habit, their resentment may quickly give way to sympathy and concern. They can forgive her, because they love her. Nevertheless, they may bring in the police and have their daughter prosecuted for theft, in a desperate attempt to change her behaviour."[10]

Talk of forgiveness creates expectations and obligations

A second reason for wanting to avoid the word 'forgiveness' is that it can trigger unhelpful pressures. For example, if the person harmed is a religious believer, they may feel obligated to forgive. The danger here is that someone might agree to participate in restorative justice merely as a means by which they can fulfil their religious duties. They seize the opportunity to offer forgiveness, not because this is how they actually feel, but so as to ensure that they are 'right with God' (e.g. "I forgive you, but only because God says that I have to.").[11]

A related problem lies in the fact that, by presenting restorative justice as 'a process that can help victims to forgive', an expectation is created that, if all goes to plan, forgiveness will *invariably* happen. But if this is the perception, then those who have caused harm may engage in restorative justice on the assumption that they will be forgiven: as long as they play their part, they have the right to expect it, and even to ask for it. Likewise, those participants who were harmed could feel that, at some point in the process, they will be expected or even required to offer forgiveness, whether they feel like it or not.

As we have seen, restorative justice is uniquely designed to facilitate the process of forgiveness. But that is not the same as saying that, 'if you take part in a restorative justice process, then you *must* forgive', or that 'forgiveness is an *inevitable* outcome of restorative justice'.[12] This assumes the falsehood that forgiveness can be called up 'on demand'. If forgiveness is not experienced freely and in one's own time, it is not forgiveness at all.[13] Likewise, if we have wronged someone, we cannot control how that person might respond. We cannot force them to change how they feel about us. Even if we offer an apology or make amends, they are under no obligation to accept it. We can no more expect or ask for forgiveness than we can expect or ask someone to fall in love with us. As Martha Minow puts it:

> "Forgiveness is a power held by the victimized, not a right to be claimed. The ability to dispense, but also to withhold, forgiveness is an ennobling capacity and part of the dignity to be reclaimed by those who survive the wrongdoing."[14]

The offer of 'forgiveness' can be mistaken or misunderstood

There may be situations in which a person harmed has offered 'forgiveness' because they *believed* the person responsible was genuinely remorseful; and yet, it turns out that they were mistaken. The person who hurt them was, for whatever reason, only faking their display of remorse—as becomes all too clear by their subsequent offending behaviour.

Perhaps even worse, there might be a situation in which the person responsible *was* experiencing genuine remorse; but then when they were offered 'forgiveness', they misunderstood this to imply that their actions were not so bad after all. They even come to think that they shouldn't have felt so remorseful in the first place.[15]

There are several things to say in response to these two possibilities: First, we need to accept that there are no guarantees when it comes to human communication: people can mis-read each other, for whatever reason. Second, this does not entail that we should never trust anyone enough to forgive them; or that we should never trust our own judgments about a person's sincerity. We do the best we can, knowing that, as in all things, there is always a risk; but also that, more often than not, we do get it right (or as 'right' as it is possible for human beings to get).

Third, these possibilities only confirm the importance of an in-depth and properly assessed preparation stage, before any communication takes place in a restorative justice process. It would be an utter failure of the facilitator's duty if the person responsible goes into a meeting without fully understanding: (a) that if the person harmed accepts their apology, they will do so only on the understanding that it is no more than a down-payment, requiring an ongoing commitment to pay out the moral debt in full; (b) that any offer of forgiveness does not mean that their wrongdoing wasn't so serious after all—far from it; (c) that they must not ask for, nor should they expect to receive forgiveness; and (d) the enormity of the gift that any offer of forgiveness would be.

Likewise, it is crucial, as we have seen, that a person harmed does not feel in any way pressured or manipulated into offering forgiveness. And if they appear to be overly eager to forgive, then they should be cautioned about the risks of doing so *before* they have heard the apology in the meeting. For one thing, they will not yet have assessed the sincerity of the apology, and so offering pre-emptive forgiveness may give the impression that they condone the wrong that was done to them, or perhaps even that they 'deserved' it in some way. It may also indicate that they are fearful of standing up for themselves. Either way, a pre-emptive offer of forgiveness is likely to prolong and intensify the threat to their social self, making it even harder for them to experience real forgiveness.[16]

In short, one of the main reasons for taking part in a restorative justice process—rather than simply 'going it alone'—is that, with all the preparation, guidance and oversight that is (or should be) provided, these possibilities and risks are far less likely to occur.

The centrality of forgiveness

Given all of the issues raised above, however, it might be thought that restorative justice practitioners should just avoid the idea of 'forgiveness' altogether. The problem is that, like the concept of shame, it is almost impossible to understand what is distinctive about restorative justice, what it is uniquely designed to achieve, without reference to the psychology of forgiveness—even if the term itself is not explicitly mentioned.

As we have seen, a core objective of restorative justice is to activate a dynamic that can enable a person who has been harmed, if they wish: (a) to recognise and treat the person responsible as a human being with inherent equal value and worth; (b) to accept that, in light of their sincere apology, the wrongdoing they committed no longer counts as evidence of the kind of person they are; (c) to thereby let go of their justified anger in a way that is compatible with their own self-respect; and (d) never to forget what happened, but to remember it now without the (same level of) hurt or anger. If this were not so, then it is hard to see how a restorative justice process would count as facilitating the work of moral repair. Yet, these four elements are precisely how most specialists define 'forgiveness'.[17] Put another way, if enabling the process of forgiveness is not a central objective of restorative justice, then it is unclear whether restorative justice has anything distinctive to offer in the aftermath of moral harm.

Having said this, the term 'forgiveness', like 'shame', does press red buttons for many people. It is the right concept, and so *must* be fully understood by facilitators—if for no other reason than to avoid placing subtle pressures upon the person harmed to forgive.[18] But the word itself is better employed in the context of a theoretical or explanatory framework, where its definition can be made clear. For similar reasons, publicly promoting restorative justice as a process that is designed to elicit 'forgiveness' or 'reconciliation' is likely to be counter-productive, and potentially abusive. Hence, it is recommended that restorative justice services and facilitators, in general, use alternative ways of describing the psychological and relational transformations that a restorative justice process can help to set in motion.

2.3 A CAUTIONARY NOTE

One problem with the suggestions above is that they might be read as advocating that facilitators or restorative justice services withhold key information about the process from participants. If the best explanation of why restorative justice works, or what it can offer, involves reference to concepts like shame or forgiveness, then should this not be explained up front? Are we not being overly protective or patronising, assuming that they will invariably take it the wrong way? Would this 'don't tell' principle not create a power imbalance between the facilitators and the participants?

The solution here lies in being clear about the problem. There is no question that participants should have access to a full and accurate explanation of what they can expect from a restorative justice process, how it works, what it can offer and why. So the issue is not one of *withholding* information, but rather of how best to *communicate* that information. Certain words are, in general, liable to be seriously misinterpreted or misunderstood. Moreover, it is likely that this kind of miscommunication could undermine the process or even put people off from taking part altogether. It is for this reason that the use of these words is, generally speaking, counter-productive.

Having said this, if the subjects of shame or forgiveness arise, or if a question is asked about these concepts, then facilitators should be equipped to provide a ready explanation and clarification, rather than side-step the issue—or, worse still, deny that these concepts have any relevance to restorative justice.

3. The Ethics of Shame

It may be thought that self-conscious emotions can arise due not only to *how we think others see us*, but also *what we think of ourselves*. For example, I can feel ashamed about having told a lie, even though no one knows but myself. However, there are two reasons to think that, in such a case, there is still a link to *how I think others see me*. First, I could be feeling shame because I am imagining what other people *would* think of me if only they knew. In other words, I have internalised the appraisals of others. This means that I can 'hear' their underlying messages (e.g. 'you are a bad person') even when there is no one around to communicate such a message. Second, I can feel shame because of how I think others see me *even if I am mistaken*. A good example of this is given by Raymond Crozier:

> "[A] fellow academic whom I did not know very well left me in charge of her bag. After a while I felt the need to go to the bathroom and I began to look through her bag to check if it contained anything valuable in order to decide whether or not it could safely be left, when she suddenly returned. Although she expressed neither surprise nor annoyance at my action I was immediately discomfited that she might think that I was looking for money or, perhaps even more shaming, taking a prurient interest in her private belongings."[1]

This suggests, again, that shame is not driven by *how I see myself*, but by *how I think others see me*.[2] There is only one sense in which my own evaluation is relevant to self-conscious emotions: *I* must come to believe that I am (or would be) seen by others in a certain way. It may well be that the academic who spotted Crozier going through her bag did not suspect anything untoward about his behaviour. Others may not be thinking badly of me at all. It may be that no one would think badly of me if they knew what I was doing. My assessment of how others are seeing me might be completely inaccurate. Yet, I can still feel shame.[3]

In short, the causes of self-conscious emotions, such as shame, would appear to be inherently social. Even so, some have questioned this—both on psychological and ethical grounds.

3.1 THE PSYCHOLOGICAL OBJECTION

Some have suggested an alternative reason for why we can feel shame or pride without an immediate audience. In such cases, the proximate cause of these emotions, they argue, is not *how we think others see us*. Rather the cause is *how we measure ourselves against our sense of the kind of person we would ideally like to be* (our 'ideal self-representation'). Put another way, we can feel shame even when others do not know what we are doing. But this is not because we imagine *them* thinking badly of us. Rather it is due to the fact that we believe we have failed to meet *our own* standard of morality or excellence.

One objection to this explanation is that it fails to take seriously the fact that our identity is formed in a social context. Our 'ideal self-representation' or 'internal standards of morality or excellence' do not appear out of nowhere. They reflect the (real or imagined) perceptions and evaluations of those around us—beginning with our parents, but extending to our peers, friends, work colleagues, and so on. But then it follows that what we call 'our moral standards' or 'the kind of person we would ideally like to be' is ultimately a reflection of how we think others would see us, and the possible social consequences for us.[4]

3.2 THE ETHICAL OBJECTION

There is, however, a serious ethical concern here. If the cause of shame can always be traced back to how we think others see us, then we would not be able to judge what is right or wrong for ourselves. We would just be slaves to the views of those around us. We would merely take on whatever moral standard our parents or peers happen to have. Yet it is surely a mark of moral maturity that our ethical decisions are based upon our own independent or autonomous judgments. Indeed, it would be difficult to understand how we could be morally responsible for our actions if our assessments about what is right and wrong were dependent upon the judgments of others.

It is for this reason that some moral philosophers have tried to find ways of making our experience of shame compatible with moral autonomy. To do this they make a distinction between 'mature (or rational) shame' and 'immature (or irrational) shame'. Those who feel shame merely because of how they think others see them are still in their 'moral infancy': they have not yet developed their own sense of who they are or what their own standards might be. Their shame is, for this reason, immature or irrational.

So what is 'mature' or 'rational' shame? Here there are two accounts. The first view is that mature moral agents will only feel shame in their own eyes, in the sense that they have fallen short of their own moral standards.[5] The problem with this view is that it is psychologically unrealistic. It might be compatible with those rare moments that we feel shame in private (assuming we ignore the evidence that 'our own standards' are ultimately derived from our social environment). But it is inconsistent with everything we know about the psychology of shame as an inherently social emotion: what is distinctive about the self-conscious emotions, like shame, is that they all arise as a consequence of how we think others see us.[6]

The second view tries to accommodate this fact by suggesting that mature moral agents will only feel shame *in the eyes of those whose moral standards they have independently come to respect.*[7] On this view, shame is still tied to how we think others see us, but that does not mean we have no say in the matter. A mature moral agent does not take everyone's view of them with equal weight. For example, suppose you walk into a den of thieves. Immediately, you know that you do not respect their moral standards, at least with respect to how they acquire the property of others. So when they insult you for not joining with them in their thieving exploits, you will not feel shame. That is because you are a mature moral agent who brings with you an independently formed sense of what is right and wrong.[8]

The problem with this strategy is that, as with the first one, it still fails to take sufficient account of the inherently social nature of shame. It also does not take account of the social nature of morality. When we are making moral judgments, it can be useful to imagine an ideal, perfectly rational individual who can take a 'God's-eye' view of the matter and is not swayed by any personal interest or emotional investment. We use this hypothetical abstract viewpoint to try and eliminate bias, and so make an objective assessment as to whether an action is morally right or wrong. But when we are making real life moral decisions, what counts for us is how we think others will (or might) see us and what the social consequences for us will (or might) be. These are the things to which we give weight in our day-to-day interactions, and that regulate how we treat each other.[9]

To give an example: Suppose you decided to take up work as a manager in an ordinary looking business enterprise. You are given status among the employees. You gain a measure of satisfaction and pride from your work. You earn good money, and this is keeping your children clothed and fed, and in a good school. You make friends with your colleagues, and you feel good about who you are. But then suppose you discover that, whilst on the surface, this business appears to be normal, it turns out that it is knowingly making and selling flawed products: it is ripping off its customers. As an employee, you are therefore indirectly contributing to this theft. You ask for an explanation, but no one else seems at all concerned. 'It's just business', they say. 'Everyone does it. If we don't, someone else will.' But this still does not feel right to you. So you start to object. Your colleagues respond by ridiculing you, saying: 'What are you now, Mother Theresa?' 'Who made you our judge and jury?' Then they start to exclude you from important meetings. People begin complaining about the quality of your work. The lunchroom goes quiet when you walk in. Your colleagues start to shun you. Someone spits at your feet as you walk past.

How would you feel? You have invested so much of yourself into this workplace. Yet now they have rejected you, questioned your abilities and insulted you. Would you not still feel humiliated? If so, then there is a problem with this second view. In this case, you have, independently, become convinced that what your colleagues are doing is morally wrong. You have worked out for yourself that you no longer respect their so-called 'moral standards'. So you are, technically, a mature, rational moral agent. Yet you still feel shame. This can only be due to the fact that what your colleagues think of you matters to you. Their assessment of what kind of person you are carries some kind of weight. Your emotional response suggests that, at some level, you still see yourself through the eyes of your colleagues.

How could this be? One response might be to argue that your shame is a sign that you are not, after all, a mature, rational moral agent. You have not yet 'grown up'. Since there is nothing you need to be ashamed of, the problem is your lack of self-esteem. You feel shame, not because you think that theft is morally acceptable, but because you half-believe that your colleagues are right about the kind of person you are: a loser, a self-righteous hypocrite, a bad person. Well, you need to 'pick yourself up', develop a 'thicker-skin' and be 'your own person'.

The problem with this response is that it is only half right. First, on the example above, you would not have had the courage to raise the objection and stick to it if you did not already possess a strong sense of self-esteem. But no one is invincible. It is one thing to stand up against a group of complete strangers. Without any personal investment or ongoing relationship, it is considerably easier to distance ourselves emotionally. But even in such cases, there is plenty of evidence to suggest that we will still feel shame, even when attacked by complete strangers. Why else would stranger-crimes cause so much hurt and humiliation? The reason for this is that we cannot help but feel shame when we hear underlying messages that attack our social self. Shame is an automatic 'in-built' response. So imagine how hard it would be to stand up against people whose opinion of us *matters*, people who we have come to like and respect, people who have given us a sense of who we are, and who have been a source of affirmation for our value and worth as a human being.[10] To think that we could somehow make ourselves immune to being rejected, humiliated and denounced by them is psychologically unrealistic.[11]

But then it looks like a mistake to suggest that a mature, moral agent would only feel shame in the eyes of those whose moral standards they already respect. That sets an impossible benchmark, given the nature of shame and the kind of creatures we happen to be.[12] The question instead should be this: how would a mature, moral agent *respond* to their feelings of shame? Would they collapse, capitulate, give up their moral protest, and apologise to their colleagues for having made such an outrageous accusation? Or would they 'pick themselves up', object furiously to how unfairly they are being treated, stand up for what they believe in, and do what they can to correct the injustice?

Second, in the example above, it may look as if your colleagues are not taking you seriously. In fact, their responses suggest that they have themselves been shamed by your accusation. But rather than take your side and admit to the wrongdoing, they have done everything possible to suppress the truth. Why else would they have rejected you? What this means is that, even where a subculture appears to be immune from moral criticism, it is still possible for one voice to make a difference. That is because we are social creatures. We all care about how others see us. Even the lone moral crusader will get our attention. If someone tells us that we are doing the wrong thing, particularly if they are embedded within our social network, then it is likely that we will notice the underlying messages—even if only in a faint and fleeting way. We will learn that, by contrast with everyone else in our social setting, this person sees us in a bad light. If we hear this message at all, then, because our sense of who we are is highly sensitive to how people see us, we are likely to experience shame.

The question is, what will we do about it? Will we deflect the shame by attacking the messenger? Will we find ways to minimise or rationalise the wrongdoing, or deny that it has anything to do with us? Will we see the way the wind is blowing, and protect ourselves by joining up with the majority view? Or will we take it seriously, and ask ourselves whether or not there might be something to it?[13]

There are several important lessons that we can draw from this. First, shame is a spontaneous and inherently social emotion. Once we hear an underlying message that threatens our social self, we cannot help but automatically respond with shame. Second, this feeling is intensified when the threat comes from someone who is from a social setting in which we are embedded—such as our family, friends, school, workplace, cultural subgroup, or even our country. Third, these social contexts will have their own set of standards or customs, most of which 'go without saying' to those embedded in those contexts. What counts as offensive or degrading is, to some degree, relative to each social context. Behaviour that might elicit a response that threatens one's social standing and relationships in one context would be perfectly acceptable in another. Fourth, there is nevertheless a bedrock standard that everyone can appeal to, namely the inherent equal worth and value that we all have as human beings, regardless of the social context we happen to inhabit. This makes it possible for us to stand up against or critique the conventions or authoritativeness of our social context—even when we are firmly embedded within it. However, this takes great moral courage and a strong grasp of one's own self-worth. It can be made significantly easier if there are others (or other groups) to which we also belong, wherein people agree with the standard we are trying to uphold and so see us in a good light—affirming our worth and value as we face insults and reprisals from the group we are attempting to challenge. In sum, the sign of ethical maturity is not whether or not we *feel* shame in appropriate contexts, but rather what we then *do* in response.

4. Preparing for an Apology

Some restorative justice manuals recommend that "apologies . . . [should] come from the offender spontaneously, or not at all."[1] But there are several reasons for letting the person responsible know, in advance, that there will be a specific place in the meeting for them to offer a full apology.

First, the fact that the apology is prepared does not make it any less sincere. Indeed, it can be more heartfelt, meaningful and genuine if the person responsible has spent some time thinking about what they want to say and how they want to say it beforehand.[2]

Second, unprepared apologies can be extremely counter-productive. As is frequently captured in videos of restorative justice meetings, a spontaneous apology is more likely to be little more than a mumbled 'sorry'. This kind of limited response is unlikely to be seen as adequate or meaningful to the person harmed.[3] Even worse, because there has been almost no thought given to what counts as a good apology, or what it is supposed to convey, a poorly-worded 'off the cuff' apology can easily damage, rather than facilitate the work of moral repair. This can happen, for example, where the apology blames the person harmed in some way (e.g. 'Sorry you feel that way'). Such *faux* apologies are likely to provoke a shame reaction (such as anger) in the person harmed, with shame-rage loops almost certain to follow.[4]

Third, as we have seen, an apology is so central to the work of moral repair that it cannot be left to chance. There is even empirical evidence that correlates higher recidivism rates with the failure to apologise.[5] This suggests that, without the down-payment of an apology, the remaining moral debt owed to the person harmed is far less likely to be paid. For this reason, if the facilitator discovers in advance that a person responsible has no intention of apologising, then they should not be permitted to participate in a restorative justice process. It would be like finding out that your prospective spouse is not intending to say the words 'I do' at the wedding. Would you still proceed?[6]

Finally, giving the person responsible the opportunity to *plan and prepare* for their apology is not the same as *coercing or forcing* them to apologise—which would, of course, be utterly incompatible with the goals of restorative justice.[7] Hence, in the meeting itself, if the person responsible does not apologise as planned, or in a way that seems genuine, then the facilitator should not step in to correct the situation or in any way demand that the apology be produced.

In practice, this means the facilitator should not ask a leading question, such as: 'Isn't there something you would like to say to [the person harmed]?' If the apology is extracted by this kind of question, then it will be less meaningful for everyone. It also means that facilitators need to be alert to the possibility that there may be an understandable reason why the person responsible does not feel able to apologise when they are given the space to do so. For example, they might be too nervous, or they cannot find the right words, or they are feeling too upset about what someone has said about them,[8] and so on.

In such circumstances, any perceived pressure from the facilitator will reduce the sincerity and meaningfulness of the apology. It would be far better to move on to the next stage of the meeting. The person responsible may feel more able to offer their apology later in the meeting, or even during refreshments. But if not, that is still their choice. The facilitator's role is only to prepare people to say what they want to say on the day. If they choose not to go through with it, then that is their responsibility, not the facilitator's—although, the facilitator will, of course, need to deal with the impact should an apology not be forthcoming, such as the disappointment felt by the person harmed.

5. Facilitator Scripts

The theoretical model presented here does not recommend the use of a 'facilitator script'—that is, where facilitators guide the conversation by presenting, in a particular sequence, pre-written statements and questions. The reason is this: facilitators need to be able to use their discretion—wording their contributions and questions in a way that closely reflects the particular dynamic, progression and tone of the conversation. In other words, the role of a facilitator is to listen and observe very carefully, speaking only when and as they sense that the moment is right. By contrast, following a set script can easily come across as wooden, intrusive and alienating.[1]

Having said this, there are many trainers who advocate a facilitator script, and yet advise that it be used with the kind of flexibility and discretion described above. This approach is perhaps the closest to the guidance offered here. Indeed, in my own training, I provide facilitators with examples of the kind of statements and questions that they might want to use at particular points; and most of these examples are similar to the statements and questions set out in standard facilitator scripts. Moreover, it could be argued that the main underlying purpose of a script is to ensure that facilitators lead the participants, in a respectful way, through a sequence of topics and speaking turns that is most likely to facilitate the work of moral repair. This general goal is, of course, consistent with the approach taken here. The key difference is the view that this objective can be better achieved by other means. Instead of a script, facilitators can be provided with: (a) a carefully designed sequence of topics and speaking turns, with an explanation of the moral psychology that underpins this sequence; (b) examples of questions and phrases they could use to guide participants through this sequence; (c) possible interventions they could make, if the need arises; and (d) key facilitation skills and techniques.

Endnotes

Preface

[1] Cf. "In every [restorative justice] conference, the emotional dynamics are different, due to the styles in which they are facilitated; the social positions, relationships, personalities and the roles of the participants (not only of the victim and the offender); the nature and circumstances of the offence and its consequences; and other favourable or unfavourable conditions." Harris, N., Walgrave, L. and Braithwaite, J. (2004). Emotional Dynamics in Restorative Conferences. *Theoretical Criminology*, 8, 191-210: p. 199.

[2] This means that facilitators will need to supplement their understanding of the material in this book with whatever specialist knowledge, skills and practice materials might be relevant to the particular contexts in which they are working.

[3] There are a number of (contested) ways in which the 'mechanics' of restorative justice can be explained. I have attempted to provide an account that is broadly consistent with empirical research and theoretical approaches that are widely accepted by restorative justice scholars and practitioners. To give some evidence of this, the endnotes provide references that affirm the same (or a 'comparable' = 'cf.') perspective. The model is also consistent with Section 3 of Brookes, D. (2009). *Restorative Justice and Work-Related Death: A Literature Review*. Melbourne, Victoria: Creative Ministries Network; and also with *Best Practice Standards for Restorative Justice Facilitators*. (2009). Victorian Association for Restorative Justice; *Best Practice Guidance for Restorative Practitioners and their Case Supervisors and Line Managers*. (2004). UK Home Office; or the 2008 Scottish adaptation of the original UK Guidance.

PART 1. Moral Repair

1. Introduction

[1] In suggesting that restorative justice (as I understand it) should be thought of as an answer to this kind of retrospective moral question, I am following Margaret Walker: "Moral philosophers following Immanuel Kant have often described ethics as answering the question: 'What ought I to do?' This seems to imply a set of choices on a fresh page. One of our recurrent ethical tasks, however, is better suggested by

the question 'What ought I – or, better, we – to do *now?*' after someone has blotted or torn the page by doing something wrong." Walker, M. U. (2006b). *Moral Repair*. Cambridge: Cambridge University Press: p. 6. See also the distinction between prospective and retrospective responsibility in Brookes (2009): p. 12.

[2] For more detail, see Brookes (2009): p. 41ff.

[3] See McCullough, M. (2008). *Beyond Revenge: The Evolution of the Forgiveness Instinct*. San Francisco, CA: Jossey-Bass: p. 19.

2. Moral Harm

[1] The terms 'moral harm' and 'moral injury' have been used in quite different senses to the way I am using them here. For instance, 'moral harm' has been used to refer to the harm that one does to oneself (or one's moral character) by engaging in a wrongful act. See, e.g., Feinberg, J. (1987). *The Moral Limits of the Criminal Law, Volume I: Harm to Others*. Oxford: Oxford University Press. This kind of 'self-harm' is certainly *one aspect* of what I mean by 'moral harm'. After all, if I have wronged another person, then at least part of what I am hoping, in offering them an apology, is that the wound I have inflicted on my own moral character will be repaired. But I mean much more than this when I use the term 'moral harm' in this book. For instance, I include the kind of harm that is experienced by those who have *suffered* a wrongdoing.

Again, the term 'moral injury' is often given a quite specific meaning, especially in the context of war. It refers to the kind of psychological harm that military personnel experience when they witness a moral atrocity or come to realise that they have themselves committed or are implicated in a wrongful act in the course of their service. This might include the post-hoc realization that the war in which they were engaged was itself morally unjustified. See, e.g., Nakashima, R. and Lettini, G. (2012). *Soul Repair: Recovering from Moral Injury After War*. Boston: Beacon Press. The term 'moral injury', as I use it in this book, does include this definition. For instance, someone might have committed a wrongful act, but only later come to *realise* that it was wrong—or that it was far worse, morally speaking, than they thought (e.g. after learning just how much suffering the action has caused from those directly affected). And in such an instance, the wrongdoer is likely to experience the kind of 'psychological injury' that can only be healed if they engage in the work of moral repair. Likewise, the term 'moral injury', as I use it, will include the kind of harm that is experienced by those who have *witnessed* a wrongful act or the *secondary* impact or trauma the act has had on other people. This is partly why, in any restorative justice process, there is a place for the friends and family of the person who was more 'directly' harmed—i.e. not merely to offer their support, but to experience some repair of the 'moral injury' they have 'indirectly' experienced themselves. In short, like 'moral harm', I use the term 'moral injury' to refer to *every* aspect of the harm that has been caused by a wrongful act.

² Cf. "One commonly thinks of a criminal victimization experience as involving the loss of personal property and/or bodily injury. Sometimes, even more important are the psychological losses, such as a feeling of a loss of control . . . or a sense of violation of the self. . . . Loss of identity and self-respect may also follow victimization. Feelings of loss, rejection by others, and humiliation are also common. Victims may experience erosion of trust and autonomy . . . ." Frieze, I. H., Hymer, S. and Greenberg, M. S. (1987). Describing the Crime Victim: Psychological Reactions to Victimization. *Professional Psychology: Research and Practice*, 18, 4, 299-315: pp. 300-1.

³ Underlying messages are also called 'meta-messages' or 'meta-communication'. See, e.g., Tyler, S. (1978). *Said and the Unsaid: Mind, Meaning and Culture*. New York, NY: Academic Press: p. 408. See also Thwaites, T., Davis L. and Mules, W. (1994). *Tools For Cultural Studies: An Introduction*. Melbourne, Victoria: Macmillan; and Grice's maxims of cooperation and his concept of conversational implicature in Grice, P. (1975). Logic and conversation. In *Syntax and Semantics, Vol. 3, Speech Acts*. ed. P. Cole and J. Morgan. New York, NY: Academic Press: pp. 41–58.

⁴ Cf. "In face-to-face quarrels between persons, the sources of irrational conflict seem to be located, for the most part, in nonverbal elements, in the paralinguistic and kinesic features of discourse." Scheff, T. (1994). *Bloody Revenge: Emotions, Nationalism, and War*. Oxford: Westview Press: p. 5.

⁵ Cf. Tyler (1978): p 408.

⁶ The following example is taken from research on the impact of non-verbal behaviour on romantic relationships: "Touch and proxemics also were reported to have [changed the way other participants thought about their relationships and to be the specific trigger for ending a relationship]: 'My ex-boyfriend had been drinking when we started to get into an argument. We were at a party and all of a sudden he started *yelling* at me. I walked up to him to just hug him and tell him that this is stupid when he *pushed me against the wall and walked away. This behavior obviously changed our relationship for the worse* and when he did this to me I felt as though he didn't give a care in the world about my feelings or hurting me'." Manusov, V., Docan-Morgan, T. and Harvey, J. (2015). Nonverbal Firsts: When Nonverbal Cues Are the Impetus of Relational and Personal Change in Romantic Relationships. In *The Social Psychology of Nonverbal Communication*. ed. A. Kostic and D. Chadee. Palgrave Macmillan: pp. 165-66.

⁷ "[M]etacommunication is an act of communication, between two or more persons, that communicates something about either the communication itself, either the relationship between them, or both. . . . Since a message is always tied to a particular context, it implies a relationship dimension, thus, every message contains an implicit metacommunication about the relationship between the communicators that classifies or frames the message." Mateus, S. (2017). Metacommunication as Second Order Communication. *KOME, An International Journal of Pure Communication Inquiry*, Vol. 5 Issue 1, 80-90: p. 88.

⁸ It may be that the underlying messages that we 'hear' from those around us are the primary means by which we develop our sense of self, our perception of who we are. See, e.g., "Numerous social theorists have established that an individual's sense of self is strongly grounded in social relationships and social processes." Parrott, W.

G. (2004). Appraisal, Emotion Words, and the Social Nature of Self-Conscious Emotions. *Psychological Inquiry*, 15, 136–138: p. 136. Again, the capacity to 'grasp' underlying messages is activated in our infancy, which may explain both their non-linguistic features and their function as 'mirrors' by which we find our sense of self or identity. Cf. "A child checks the facial expressions, body language, and tone of voice of people around her—particularly her parents—to determine what kind of person she is. The ones close to her become reflections of herself—her mirrors. If these mirrors are smiling, the child feels good about herself; if they are frowning, she may become frightened and not feel so good about herself." Engle, B. (2006). *Healing your Emotional Self*. New York, NY: John Wiley & Sons: p. 81.

[9] Cf. "[Someone] fails to treat me with respect if she makes no effort to hide her disinterest in, or contempt for, my feelings. When she treats me this way, she implies that my concerns, my feelings, my point of view do not matter, that is, that I have no intrinsic value, after all." Buss, S. (1999). Appearing Respectful: The Moral Significance of Manners. *Ethics*, 109, 4, 795-826: p. 804; "One reason we so deeply resent moral injuries done to us is not simply that they hurt us in some tangible or sensible way; it is because such injuries are also messages—symbolic communications. They are ways a wrongdoer has of saying to us, 'I count but you do not,' 'I can use you for my purposes,' or 'I am here up high and you are there down below.' Intentional wrongdoing insults us and attempts (sometimes successfully) to degrade us—and thus it involves a kind of injury that is not merely tangible and sensible. It is moral injury, and we care about such injuries." Murphy, J. G. (1988a). Forgiveness and Resentment. In J. G. Murphy and J. Hampton, *Forgiveness and Mercy*. New York, NY: Cambridge University Press: p. 25.

[10] Cf. "[S]hame will not be experienced if the individual simply reflects on his or her own actions, however adverse his judgment, unless the perspective of the other is adopted." Crozier, R. W. (1998). Self-Consciousness in Shame: The Role of the 'Other'. *Journal for the Theory of Social Behaviour*, 28, 3, 273-86: p. 278.

[11] Cf. "Self-conscious emotions are highly social in nature. Their social nature stems from the social nature of the self and from the social nature of the situations that elicit them." Parrott (2004): p. 136; "Self-conscious emotions arise only from the perception that something about the self may have implications for important social goals." Baldwin, M. W. and Baccus, J. R. (2004). Maintaining a Focus on the Social Goals Underlying Self-Conscious Emotions. *Psychological Inquiry*, 15, 2, 139-144: p. 140; "[T]he self-conscious emotions are characterized by a shift in perspective where the individual views his or her own behaviour as if through the eyes of another." Crozier (1998): p. 277; "Self-conscious emotions differ from basic emotions [like fear, joy and sadness] because they require self-awareness and self-representations . . . . Importantly, by self-representations, we do not mean simply the cognitive contents of the personal self, but also relational, social, and collective self-representations. We are social creatures, so our self-representations reflect how we see ourselves vis-a-vis close others (e.g., as a romantic partner), social groups (e.g., as a professor), and broader cultural collectives (e.g., as a woman, as an American)." Tracy, J. L. and Robins, R. W. (2007). The Self in Self-Conscious Emotions: A Cognitive Appraisal Approach. In *The Self-Conscious Emotions: Theory and Research*. ed. Tracy, J. L., Robins, R. W. and Tangney, J. P. NY and London: The Guilford Press: pp. 5-6.

¹² Cf. "[E]mbarrassment can occur only when attentional focus is directed toward the *public self*, activating corresponding public self-representations. . . . Importantly, activation of the public self does not require a public context. Rather, the public self is always present because it reflects the way we see ourselves through the (real or imagined) eyes of others." Tracy and Robins (2007): p. 14. For a list of sources that suggest a similar account of how embarrassment generally follows from (a) "a minor breach of codes of manners or loss of poise", (b) "faux pas and social transgressions", (c) "violations of social conventions" and (d) minor, specific breaches of norms", see Crozier, W. R. (2014). Differentiating Shame from Embarrassment. *Emotion Review*, 6(3), 269-276: p. 271. It should be noted that Crozier's review of the relevant literature found considerable disagreement about how, or to what extent, the terms 'embarrassment' and 'shame' are or should be distinguished. In my view, embarrassment is a species of shame. See also Appendix 1.

¹³ Since shame is often distinguished from guilt, an explanation for defining guilt as a species of shame is given in Appendix 1. The account of restorative justice presented here does not depend on whether this definition of guilt is accepted, however. Readers who prefer to define guilt as distinct from shame can simply take my use of the word 'shame' (to encompass guilt) as a term of art for the purposes of this book.

¹⁴ "[S]evere physical discipline, emotional abuse, neglect and abandonment . . . all send the message that the child is worthless, unacceptable, and bad. These acts also convey the message that the adult will treat you any way he or she wants because you are a worthless commodity." Engle (2006): p. 56.

¹⁵ Cf. "In primitive times, when one member [of a clan] offended another, it was essential that some mechanism for reconciling the injury was present. . . . No one could survive totally alone, and the group could not afford to lose any member." Flanigan, B. (1992). *Forgiving the Unforgivable*. New York, NY: MacMillan: p. 8.

¹⁶ Cf. "Emotions are assumed to have evolved through natural selection to facilitate survival and reproductive goals. It is easy to understand how a basic emotion might promote survival goals—for example, fear may cause an individual to run away from a predator, thereby enhancing his or her chances for survival in the face of threat. In contrast, we believe that self-conscious emotions evolved primarily to promote the attainment of specifically *social* goals, such as the maintenance of enhancement of status, or the prevention of group rejection. . . . Consistent with this account, self-conscious emotions seem to be present only in humans and other species (e.g., great apes) with highly complex and frequently shifting social hierarchies." Tracy and Robins (2007): p. 6.

¹⁷ Cf. "[T]he reason failures or transgressions elicit negative affect is because they signal the possibility of social exclusion, a threat to the 'need to belong' that evolution has designed into our nature as social animals. . . . When people evaluate themselves as inadequate or unworthy the expectation that others might have a similarly critical reaction resulting in social exclusion or loss of status is implicitly triggered, which implicates core, hardwired social motives. Research supports this formulation. For example, the things that make people feel bad about themselves tend to be precisely those things they feel would make important others reject them . . . . or derogate them." Baldwin and Baccus (2004): p. 139, 141.

[18] Cf. "Far from being rare or unusual, [the emotions of gratitude, respect, elevation, appreciation, and trust] are ubiquitous but generally fly below the radar of consciousness and are rarely noticed, evident for example in conventional displays of politeness and good manners. . . . [But] the ABSENCE of an expected display of politeness is noticed and responded to with remarkable strength and negativity as a sign of disrespect." Buck, R. and Miller, M. (2015). Beyond Facial Expression: Spatial Distance as a Factor in the Communication of Discrete Emotions. In *The Social Psychology of Nonverbal Communication*. ed. A. Kostic and D. Chadee. Palgrave Macmillan: pp. 187-88.

[19] The distinction between (a) what it is to respect a person's 'inherent value' and (b) respecting their 'acquired value' corresponds very closely to a distinction made by Stephen Darwall between (a) "recognition respect" and (b) "appraisal respect". As he puts it: "all persons are entitled to [recognition] respect just by virtue of their being persons and . . . deserving of more or less [appraisal] respect by virtue of their personal characteristics." Darwall, S. L. (1977). Two Kinds of Respect. *Ethics*, Vol. 88, No. 1 (Oct.), 36-49: p. 46.

[20] "[A]n insult, and presumably any disrespectful act, is experienced as unjust because it deprives people of something that they believe is rightfully theirs. When they are denied the respect to which they believe they are entitled, people feel as unjustly treated as when they are denied the material resources to which they believe they are entitled." Miller (2001): p. 533.

[21] "[S]hame, guilt, embarrassment, and pride function as an emotional moral barometer, providing immediate and salient feedback on our social and moral acceptability." Tangney, J. P., Stuewig, J. and Mashek, D. J. (2007b). What's Moral about the Self-Conscious Emotions? In Tracy, Robins and Tangney (2007): p. 22.

[22] "From our perspective, self-conscious emotions are experienced when a person's identity is threatened or elevated . . . as long as the eliciting event is relevant to the aspirations and ideals (as well as the fears) of the self. In fact, social evaluations will not elicit self-conscious emotions if the evaluated individual does not make the corresponding self-evaluative appraisals. For example, the public praise of others will not produce pride in individuals who discount the evaluations (e.g., if they have low self-esteem . . .), and negative evaluations will not produce shame if they pertain to non-self-relevant domains, as James (1890) noted: 'I, who for the time have staked my all on being a psychologist, am mortified if others know much more psychology than I. But I am contented to wallow in the grossest ignorance of Greek' (p. 310)." Tracy and Robins, 2007: p. 11.

[23] "[Egalitarian] theories of worth . . . insist that [human worth] does not and cannot diminish no matter what we do (so that even a wrongdoer is held to be valuable, and deserving of our respect)." Hampton, J. (1997). The Wisdom of the Egoist: The Moral and Political Implications of Valuing the Self. *Social Philosophy and Policy*, 14, 21-51: p. 28; "Our intrinsic worth is not tied to our level of performance on some moral scale, nor does it fluctuate with the character of our choices and attitudes." Holmgren, M. R. (1993). Forgiveness and the Intrinsic Value of Persons. *American Philosophical Quarterly*, 30, 4, 341-52: p. 349; "Instead of seeing yourself as an empty

vessel who is filled up, drop by drop, with your achievements, you need to begin to recognize your intrinsic worth as a human being." Engle (2006): p. 134.

²⁴ "[T]he equality of human worth [is the] justification, or ground, of equal human rights." Vlastos, G. (1969). Human Worth, Merit, and Equality. In *Moral Concepts*, ed. J. Feinberg. Oxford University Press: p. 149. "All human beings are born free and equal in dignity and rights". *The Universal Declaration of Human Rights*. 1948: Article 1.

²⁵ "[T]hink of the Jews of Europe in the hideous Nazi period, herded into cattle trucks and carried away to be gassed or worked to death, or machine-gunned into pits they had been forced to dig. Think of their teeth and hair and spectacles piled up for recycling, think of the emaciated and bewildered barely alive prisoners found by Allied soldiers in concentration camps in 1945. These were the bleak and desperate circumstances that prompted the adoption of the Universal Declaration of Human Rights three years later, a fact evidently forgotten by those in comfortable academic studies who employ the casuistries of their trade to prove that the concept of human rights is empty." Grayling, A. C. (2007). *Towards the Light: The Story of the Struggles for Liberty and Rights That Made the Modern West*. Great Britain: Bloomsbury Publishing: p. 12. See also: "It can be argued further against skeptics that a world with equal rights is a *more just* world, a way of organizing society for which we would all opt if we were designing our institutions afresh in ignorance of the roles we might one day have to play in them. It is also a *less dangerous* world generally, and one with a *more elevated and civilized* tone. If none of this convinces the skeptic, we should turn our backs on him to examine more important problems." Feinberg, J. (1973). *Social Philosophy*. Englewood Cliffs, New Jersey: Prentice-Hall: p. 94.

²⁶ "Most of us tend to care about what others (at least *some* others, some significant group whose good opinion we value) think about us—how much they think we matter. Our self-respect is *social* in at least this sense, and it is simply part of the human condition that we are weak and vulnerable in these ways. And thus when we are treated with contempt by others it attacks us in profound and deeply threatening ways." Murphy (1988a): p. 25; "[B]ehind the feeling of shame stands not the fear of hatred, but the fear of *contempt* which, on an even deeper level of the unconscious, spells fear of *abandonment*, the death by emotional starvation." Piers, G. (1953). Shame and Guilt: Part I. *Shame and Guilt: A Psychoanalytic Study*. ed. G. Piers and M. B. Singer. Springfield, Il.: Charles C. Thomas: p. 16.

²⁷ It may be, as Feinberg suggests, that 'human worth' is not a property or quality of human persons, but rather the "attitude of respect" that we take toward the "humanity" in each person. "That attitude", he thinks, "follows naturally from regarding everyone from the 'human point of view'"—that is, to see the world from another person's point of view, to sense what it might be like to put ourselves in their shoes. But this attitude of respect "is not grounded on anything more ultimate than itself, and it is not demonstrably justifiable." Feinberg (1973): p. 94.

²⁸ "[Shame] requires self-regard as its essential backdrop. It is only because one expects oneself to have worth or even perfection in some respect that one will shrink from or cover the evidence of one's nonworth or imperfection." Nussbaum, M. C. (2004). *Hiding from Humanity: Shame, Disgust and the Law*. Princeton, NJ: Princeton University Press: p. 184.

²⁹ Cf. "[B]ecause certain forms of anger—which can be generated only if the agent holds a hierarchical (and indeed competitive) theory of human worth—are very common, it may be that many of us are only paying lip service to the egalitarian theories of worth which we tend to commend as appropriate foundations for our moral theorizing." Hampton. J. (1988a). Forgiveness, Resentment and Hatred. In J. G. Murphy and J. Hampton, *Forgiveness and Mercy*. New York, NY: Cambridge University Press: p. 49.

³⁰ E.g. "[T]he indignation with which people respond to unfavorable outcomes (e.g. lower than expected salary offers) often reflects the fact that their prestige or status has been threatened more than the fact that their purchasing power has been diminished." Miller, D. T. (2001). Disrespect and the experience of injustice. *Annual Review of Psychology*, 52, 527-53: p. 530.

3. The Shame Experience

¹ Cf. "Analyses of the 'passions' (as the derivation of the word suggests) typically make them out to be entities with respect to which we are passive so that we cannot be held responsible for them." Hampton (1988a): p. 79.

² Shame can also arise in anticipation of a likely shame-trigger, not merely as a consequence. For obvious reasons, the anticipatory function is more relevant to how we arrive at moral decisions ('What ought I to do in this situation?'), as distinct from how we respond to moral failures ('What ought I to do *now*?')—the latter being the focus of restorative justice, and therefore this book. Cf. "People can *anticipate* their likely emotional reactions (e.g., guilt vs. pride/self-approval) as they consider behavioral alternatives. Thus, the 'self-conscious' moral emotions can exert a strong influence on moral choice and behavior by providing critical feedback regarding both anticipated behavior (feedback in the form of *anticipatory* shame, guilt or pride) and actual behavior (feedback in the form of *consequential* shame, guilt, or pride)." Tangney, Stuewig and Mashe (2007b): p. 22.

³ "[E]motions produce changes in parts of our brain that mobilize us to deal with what has set off the emotion, as well as changes in our autonomic nervous system, which regulates our heart rate, breathing, sweating, and many other bodily changes, preparing us for different actions. Emotions send out signals, changes in our expressions, face, voice, and bodily posture. We don't choose these changes; they simply happen." Ekman, P. (2003). *Emotions Revealed: Understanding Faces and Feelings*. Great Britain: Weidenfeld & Nicolson: p. 20.

⁴ "[E]mpirical studies have shown that shame and embarrassment can be communicated via a combination of facial actions, postural changes (e.g, head movements down), and gaze activity. . . . [These] nonverbal display of self-conscious emotions . . . lasted about 5 sec, and their actions occur in a coherent, coordinated pattern, similar to other evolved signals. . . . Furthermore, there is evidence that these displays are universally recognized. In particular, participants from rural India and the United States reliably identified displays of embarrassment and shame from

photographs at above-chance levels." Beer, J. S. and Keltner, D. (2004). What Is Unique about Self-Conscious Emotions? *Psychological Inquiry*, 15, 2, 126-129: p. 126. Cf. [R]esearchers have failed to identify distinct expressions for any self-conscious emotion. They have, however, found distinct expressions that include bodily posture or head movement combined with facial expression for embarrassment, pride, and shame. . . . Furthermore, recent research conducted among isolated tribal villagers in Burkina Faso suggests that at least two of these expressions—pride and shame—may be universally recognised." Tracy and Robins (2007): p. 7. This research was published in Tracy, J. L. and Robins, R. W. (2008). The nonverbal expression of pride: Evidence for cross-cultural recognition. *Journal of Personality and Social Psychology*, 94, 3, 516 –530.

[5] An excess of shame memories can lead to shame-prone personalities, that is, where shame becomes a dominant factor in a person's life. "Shame-[prone] people suffer from extremely low self-esteem, feelings of worthlessness, and self-hatred. . . . They were often taught that they were worthless or bad by hearing adults say such things to them as 'You are in my way', 'I wish you were never born', or 'You'll never amount to anything'." Engle (2006): p. 56.

[6] This reaction becomes more likely when the original shame has not yet been acknowledged and released. "Emotions that go unexpressed often lie dormant inside us until someone or something reminds us of our past and triggers a memory – and the feeling." Engle (2006): p. 89.

[7] This is particularly evident in 'street codes', where there is often an extraordinary hypersensitivity to discourteous behaviour: e.g. "Where I lived, stepping on someone's shoe was a capital offense punishable by death. This was not just in a few isolated instances, or as a result of one or two hotheads, but a recognized given for the crime of disrespect." Shakur, S. (1993). *Monster: The Autobiography of an L.A. Gang Member*. New York, NY: Penguin: p. 102 - quoted in Buss (1999): p. 814. One explanation for this 'hyper-sensitivity' is the weight of shame that people in this life-situation often feel, together with the fact that there are so few sources of affirmation and respect available to them. As Buss puts it, "Most adherents of the street code believe that they have been 'written off' by the larger society of which they are marginally a part. . . . Under these circumstances, they naturally attribute exaggerated significance to manners: some sort of acknowledgment is better than none." Buss (1999): p. 816. This is not to suggest that economic deprivation is invariably the cause. As Holmgren notes, "The millionaire who consistently received cruel words from her parents may have a much more difficult adjustment than someone who grew up in the ghetto with loving, nurturing parents." Holmgren (1993): p. 350.

[8] Adapted from Nathanson, D. L. (1992). *Shame and Pride*. NY and London: W.W. Norton & Co.: p. 312.

4. *Responding to Shame-Reactions*

[1] This view is called the cognitive theory of emotions. "[S]ome aspect of thought [is] central to the definition of the emotion itself. . . . emotions involve certain distinctive evaluative beliefs and desires which accompany any feelings or physiological changes in the person who experiences them." Hampton, J. (1988b). Forgiveness, Resentment and Hatred. In J. G. Murphy and J. Hampton, *Forgiveness and Mercy*. New York, NY: Cambridge University Press: p. 54, n. 14. See also: Lyons, W. (1980). *Emotions*. Cambridge: Cambridge University Press.

[2] "[E]ven if a certain physical feeling that goes along with [an emotion] is something which just afflicts us, these emotions also contain cognitive content over which we have control . . . . Hence they should be treated as voluntary and something for which we can be held responsible." Hampton (1988a): p. 79.

[3] Cf. "I [do not] have effective voluntary control over whether I do or do not believe that the tree has leaves on it when I see a tree with leaves on it just before me in broad daylight with my eyesight working perfectly." Alston, W. (1989). *Epistemic Justification*. Ithaca and London: Cornell University Press: p. 123; "[P]eople do not knowingly believe propositions for bad reasons. . . . A belief—to be actually believed— entails the corollary belief that we have accepted it *because* it seems to be true." Harris, S. (2010). *The Moral Landscape*. Great Britain: Simon & Schuster: p. 136.

[4] The view that 'how we think can change how we feel' is the basis for Cognitive Behavioural Therapy. Cf. "Suppose someone you respect criticizes you. How would you feel? You may feel guilty and inadequate if you tell yourself you're no good and the problem is all your fault. You will feel anxious and worried if you tell yourself that the other person is looking down on you and is going to reject you. You'll feel angry if you tell yourself that it's all their fault and they have no right to say such unfair things. If you have a good sense of self-esteem, you might feel curious and try to understand what the other person is thinking and feeling. In each case your reaction will depend on the way you think about the criticism. The messages you give yourself have an enormous impact on your emotions. And what's even more important, by learning to change your thoughts, you can change the way you feel." Burns, D. D. (1999). *The Feeling Good Handbook*. New York, NY: Penguin Books: p. 4.

[5] This analogy is from Thomas Scheff. "We are interdependent not only in the sense that our physical survival depends upon others to protect us from starvation and exposure but also in the emotional sense that we need to feel connected." Scheff (1994): p. 51.

[6] "[T]hreats to the social self, or situations which threaten to demean one's social image or standing . . . elicit increases in feelings of low social worth (eg, shame, humiliation), decrements in social self-esteem, and increases in cortisol, a hormone of the hypothalamic-pituitary-adrenal (HPA) system. . . . [which] is thought to be centrally involved in regulating physiological responses to stress." Gruenewald, T. L., Kemeny, M. E., Aziz, N. and Fahey, J. L. (2004). Acute Threat to the Social Self: Shame, Social Self-esteem, and Cortisol Activity. *Psychosomatic Medicine*, 66, 915-924: p. 915.

[7] Cf. "All efforts at therapy will cause initial pain because the therapist is asking the patient to give up a defensive system that prevents, or at least mitigates, the experience of shame. Yet this must be done in order to find and heal the pain that lurks beneath the surface." Nathanson (1992): p. 334.

5. Withdrawal

[1] Cf. "At the Withdrawal pole, the person acknowledges the experience as negative, accepts shame's message as valid, and tries to withdraw or hide from the situation." Elison, J., Lennon, R. and Pulos, S. (2006). Investigating the Compass of Shame: The development of the Compass of Shame Scale. *Social Behavior and Personality*, 34, 3, 221-238: p. 222.

[2] E.g. "In a family whose very style of operation involves the use of shame for each to achieve dominion over the intimate other, and in which there is no habit of solace for an injured other, the wounds of shame demand withdrawal to some deeply private space where they can be licked until the pain has decreased enough to permit reentry into the ever-dangerous social milieu. . . . Who among us has not witnessed the abject humiliation of one who could not escape the taunts of a far more powerful other? . . . [W]itnessing such a scene we tend to avert our own gaze and cry out our wish that the protagonist be shielded from view." Nathanson (1992): p. 318.

[3] Cf. "Wurmser said once that the eye is the organ of shame *par excellence*. When we withdraw, we escape the eyes of the other, the eyes before which we have been shamed." Nathanson (1992): p. 325.

[4] E.g. "One woman told me that in the four years of [experiencing biological depression] she did not leave her home for fear of meeting the eyes of any person outside her family. The withdrawal accompanying severe biological depression is not specific to the disease but rather a learned defense against intense and ensuring shame affect that has been produced by a defect in neurotransmitter mechanisms." Nathanson (1992): p. 31.

[5] Taylor gives a literary example of this: "Jonas, in Dickens' *Martin Chuzzlewit* . . . has just murdered a blackmailer and is now on his way home. He is terrified of entering his room. He is supposed to have been in his room all the time while in fact he was otherwise engaged. He knows perfectly well, of course, that at the moment he is on his way to London and not in his own room at all. But it seems as if he had left the 'good' self behind while the 'bad' self went about its business. He sees himself 'as it were, a part of the room', and he is afraid not so much *for* himself as *of* himself." Taylor, G. (1985). *Pride, Shame, and Guilt*. Oxford: Clarendon Press: p. 95.

[6] In the Chapters that follow, we will look at this question in far more detail. But it will be helpful to provide an outline here of what is needed to begin the journey toward moral repair.

[7] Cf. "True forgiveness occurs only when we allow ourselves to face the truth and to feel and release . . . our anger, about what was done to us." Engle (2006): p. 113-14.

"[T]he victim who attempts to cut off her [anger] in order to forgive her offender fails to respect herself." Holmgren (1993): p. 343.

[8] It will soon become clear in what follows that there are a number of key similarities between the kind of repair-work that the person responsible will need to undertake and the repair-work—described above—that the person harmed needs to engage in. One consequence of this is that they will both start to move onto 'the same page', in terms of how they see what happened and how they feel about it.

[9] Cf. "[Regret] describes a negative emotion elicited by knowledge of a rejected alternative's outcome for oneself; [remorse] entails an aversive state induced by information that a foregone alternative would have produced a better outcome for another." Baskin-Sommers, A., Stuppy-Sullivan, A. M. and Buckholtz, J. W. (2016). Psychopathic individuals exhibit but do not avoid regret during counterfactual decision making. *Proceedings of the National Academy of Sciences*, 113(50), 14438-43: p. 14443.

[10] Cf. "In remorse, the agent is responding not just to a wrong that she has committed; she is responding to a wrong that she has done *to another*." Pugh, J. and Maslen, H. (2017). 'Drugs That Make You Feel Bad'? Remorse-Based Mitigation and Neurointerventions. *Criminal Law and Philosophy*, 11(3), 499-522: p. 501.

[11] "Feelings of remorse or their absence are perceived as reflecting core attributes of the person who has offended. . . . How a person feels is perceived as revealing a truth that words alone cannot achieve. It is this crucial assumption, that a show of remorse reflects the essence of the person, that helps explain its use by judges and forensic psychologists as a predictor of future behavior . . . ." Weisman, R. (2014). *Showing Remorse*. London: Routledge: p. 11.

[12] Cf. "[Remorse produces] the desire to atone . . . [which] will most often involve the agent trying to apologise and to offer some sort of reparation to the victim." Pugh and Maslen (2017): p. 503; Cf. "In dealing with one's remorse, it is often felt necessary to bring one's remorse forward and articulate it. That can take the shape of apology, making amends through reparation, self-mortification, and so on. . . . Another aspect of [remorse] . . . is the desire to 'make things better' for the victim of my wrongdoing." Proeve, M. and Tudor, S. (2010). *Remorse*. London: Routledge: p. 44.

6. *Avoidance*

[1] "Hedonism, then, is usually a way of decreasing chronic shame and distress, rather than a search for pleasure. It represents an attempt to avoid whatever might be learned from an introspective study of the lessons to be learned from shame. . . . Joy-rides, thrill-seeking, dangerous pastimes of any sort, and a host of other activities form the macho system of defense in which excitement and anger substitute for shame. In many respects, the use of certain drugs, like cocaine and the amphetamines, can represent an attempt to escape shame through the pharmacologic instigation of excitement." Nathanson (1992): p. 356.

[2] Distractions *per se* are not necessarily a bad thing, e.g.: "There are number of foundations that minister to the needs of terminally ill children by granting some long-cherished wish . . . By infusing excitement and joy into the loves of those who have been living with fear, pain, and distress, by distracting them to this new focus of attention, these organizations bring the grace of temporary [distraction]." Nathanson (1992): p. 339.

[3] Cf. "There are, then, two types of shame avoidance related to [distraction]—the acquisition and display of trophies that define a wished-for self and that call to the attention of everybody this new gestalt; and the pressured pursuit of new levels of ability, competence, and wealth in order to prevent recognition of some deeply felt internal defect visible only to the struggling individual. Display and competition can become strategies undertaken to distract both the viewing other and the inner judge." Nathanson (1992): p. 345.

[4] Cf. "Unable to build into myself certain attributes and powers, I may adopt the self-enhancing fantasy that I share the traits of a cherished idol. . . The deficiencies of our personal identity are somewhat reduced by a fantasized immersion in the identity of someone without those particular defects." Nathanson (1992): p. 346.

[5] Cf. "[W]e may be aware of and empathetic toward someone else's embarrassment without feeling it ourselves (e.g, the vicarious embarrassment that occurs when we watch an actor in a play forget his lines), but if we identify with the individual such that his or her mishap feels like our own, where 'our own' is defined in the broader, collective sense, then the embarrassment we feel is likely to be direct, and not vicarious (e.g., if our romantic partner commits a social faux pas)." Tracy and Robins, (2007): p. 12.

[6] Cf. "Self-presentation strategies in these circumstances typically involve excuses and justifications, where the actor offers an explanation of his or her conduct that minimises the seriousness by deflecting interpretations away from the core self." Crozier (1998): p. 279; "[T]echniques for justifying and excusing wrongdoing [are] used [by offenders] as defense mechanisms to avoid facing consequences of actions . . . [and] neutralize their negative self-evaluation . . . [by] removing shame from wrongdoing . . . ." Ahmed, E. and Braithwaite, V. (2004). 'What, Me Ashamed?' Shame Management and School Bullying. *Journal of Research in Crime and Delinquency*, 41, 269-94: p. 271.

[7] Cf. "[B]ecause of the highly competitive nature of our culture, achieving and winning are valued far more than courtesy, kindness, and a concern for the consequences of our actions. Some people even believe that apologising is a sign of weakness, and not apologising is a recommended strategy for staying in control." Engle, B. (2001). *The Power of Apology*. New York, NY: John Wiley & Sons: p. 39-40.

[8] Cf. "If we choose to act contrary to the voice of our conscience in a particular instance, this can also lead to us no longer regarding the action as wrong. We therefore silence our conscience. A similar thought is expressed in the Jewish scripture, the Talmud: 'Commit a sin twice and it will not seem to thee a crime'." Einhorn, S. (2006). *The Art of Being Kind*. Great Britain: Sphere: pp. 24-25.

[9] Shakespeare's Macbeth is a well-known dramatic embodiment of this kind of progressive corruption. As Taylor describes it: "[Macbeth] does not try and dissociate

himself from the doer of the terrible deed; for this is now not what he sees as alien. He dissociates himself rather from the good and honourable." Taylor (1985): p. 96.

[10] "Rape victims have been found to note that they could have been killed or subjected to even more humiliating circumstances than did occur. . . . Victims may also compare themselves with others who have not coped as well with the victimization, and they thereby build their own self-esteem by believing that they have coped extremely well. . . . [O]ne can minimize victimization by reconstructing the event as leading to personal growth or some other benefit." Frieze Hymer and Greenberg (1987): p. 305; "Those with low self-esteem and those who were deeply shamed as children will have a far more difficult time shaking off a shame attack. . . . It is as if they are already so filled with shame that there is simply no more room for it. . . . [T]hey immediately construct an emotional wall of steel to protect themselves. This wall goes up so rapidly that . . . they themselves are unaware of how deeply they have been affected." Engle (2001): p. 48.

[11] Cf. "Scratch the surface of the desperately driven business tycoon, the philandering politician, the relentlessly busy surgeon who cannot afford to slow down for a moment, the empire builder, the famous lawyer known as well for his adulterous lifestyle as for his flamboyant courtroom tactics, the religious leader who seems more interested in his image than his message – drill an exploratory hole into the inner lives of any of these icons of our culture and you are likely to tap a gusher of shame handled by *avoidance*. 'Look at me,' they say, 'but look only where I tell you to look'." Nathanson (1992): p. 351.

[12] Cf. "In the past, I've tended to be somewhat oblivious that my behaviour hurt other people. At times, I took this to such an extreme that even when people told me I had hurt their feelings, I would minimize my behaviour and discount their feelings. I would sometimes go so far as to accuse the other person of being too sensitive or of misinterpreting my actions." Engle (2001): p. 42.

[13] Cf. "At the Avoidance pole, the person typically does not acknowledge the negative experience of self, typically does not accept shame's message as valid (denial), and attempts are made to distract the self and others from the painful feeling." Elison, Lennon and Pulos (2006): p. 223.

7. Attack Other

[1] "Desperate to escape painful feelings of shame, shamed individuals are apt to turn the tables defensively, externalizing blame and anger outward onto a convenient scapegoat." Tangney et. al. (2007): p. 351, 352. Cf. "Some people defend against shame by projecting it on others and by raging at them." Engle (2006): p. 223.

[2] "[A]t the Attack Other pole, the person may—or may not—acknowledge the negative experience of self, typically does not accept shame's message, and attempts are made to make someone else feel worse." Elison, Lennon and Pulos (2006): p. 223-24.

3 "Anger has [an] . . . important cue value to the individual who experiences it; it is a powerful signal to a person that he or she has been insulted." Miller (2001): p. 533. Cf. Engle (2006): p. 201.

4 "People routinely assume that the presence of anger in another person indicates that he or she feels insulted and, perhaps because of this, people routinely respond to the anger of another with an apology." Miller (2001): p. 533.

5 Cf. "Although you may *intellectually* understand that the abuse or neglect was not your fault, you may not know it *emotionally*. . . . Getting angry at your abuser will affirm your innocence, and the vital force of anger will be moving in the right direction: outward instead of inward." Engle (2006): p. 93.

6 Cf. "[T]he victim who attempts to cut off her [anger] in order to forgive her offender fails to respect herself." Holmgren (1993): p. 343; "[A]nger . . . establishes one's identity as a strong and determined person who demands respect and does not tolerate unjust treatment by others." Miller (2001): p. 541; "Just as physical pain tells us to take our hand off the hot stove, the pain of our anger preserves the very integrity of our self. Our anger can motivate us to say 'no' to the ways in which we are defined by others and 'yes' to the dictates of our inner self." Lerner, H. (2005). *The Dance of Anger*. New York, NY: Perennial Currents: p. 1

7 "Perceiving others as victims is threatening, particularly if the choice of a victim is believed to be random. If it could be anyone, it could also be oneself. In order to protect against concern over such a possibility, observers assume that something the victim did caused the victimization." Frieze Hymer and Greenberg (1987): p. 307.

8 "[The] concept of a second injury refers to the escalation in victimization as social supports and the larger community further blame the victim. As a result, the victim feels humiliated and begins to doubt the validity of his or her complaints. The victim may thereby perceive himself or herself as a nonperson who must deny or suppress feelings or choose to express his or her feelings at the risk of the second injury from others." Frieze, Hymer and Greenberg (1987): p. 307.

9 Cf. "The individual who forgives for psychological or spiritual reasons 'lets go' of useful anger and has less psychic energy to put forward toward obtaining justice. Although anger can be self-destructive and paralyzing, it can also motivate and engage victims in struggles for justice." Lamb, S. and Murphy, J. G. eds. (2002). *Before Forgiving*. New York, NY: Oxford University Press: p. 55.

10 Adapted from Wink, W. (1992). *Engaging the Powers: Discernment and Resistance in a World of Domination*. Minneapolis MN: Augsburg Fortress: p. 187.

11 Cf. "Non-malicious [victims who have won a court case] will wish wrongdoers to conclude not that 'this victim (or his government representative) is now my superior because he can force me to submit to his will' but, rather, that 'I am not more valuable than anyone else, and my loss to this person is a sign of that fact'." Hampton (1988b): p. 129, n. 26.

12 Cf. "Because you feel shamed by the other person's comment, you may spend hours making the other person feel horrible about himself by dumping shame back on him. . . . It's as if they are saying, 'I'll show you. I'll make you feel like shit because that's what you think of me'." Engle (2006): p. 56.

[13] Cf. "[W]hen we become outcasts we can reject our rejectors and the shame no longer matters to us." Braithwaite, J. (1989). *Crime, Shame and Reintegration.* New York, NY: Cambridge University Press: p. 101, 55.

[14] E.g. "Children who report that their school disapproves of bullying and looks after those who are victimized by bullying were more likely to acknowledge shame and were less likely to displace shame. Capacities to manage shame seem to be shaped at least in part by external signals about what is acceptable and how much authority figures care about those for whom they are responsible." Ahmed and Braithwaite, V. (2004): p. 287

[15] Cf. "[A]lmost always, during the initial stage of the struggle, the oppressed, instead of striving for liberation, tend themselves to become oppressors, or 'sub-oppressors.' The very structure of their thought has been conditioned by the contradictions of the concrete existential situation by which they were shaped. Their ideal is to be [human]; but for them, to be [human] is to be oppressors. This is their model of humanity." Freire, P. (1994). *Pedagogy of the Oppressed.* New York: Continuum: p. 27; "In most societies it is not acceptable for men to be perceived as victims. Because of this, boys [may] come to identify with the aggressor—that is, become like his abuser. The only way left for him to discharge his shame and aggression is to do to others what was done to him." Engle (2006): p. 57.

[16] Cf. "Someone must be made lower than I, says the denizen of the *attack other* pole. Every incident of domestic violence, of graffiti, of public vandalism, of schoolyard fighting, of put-down, ridicule, contempt, and intentional public humiliation can be traced to activity around this locus of reaction to shame affect." Nathanson (1992): pp. 313-14.

[17] Cf. "The rituals of execution are full of contradictions and irony. The execution process requires a recognition of humanity in the offender that the media and the criminal justice system have spent years trying to deny. A 'humane' killing requires that the offender understand what an execution means, recognise the difference between right and wrong, and specifically comprehend why they are being executed. Prior to execution an inmate lives in a subhuman world—he is a number who is fed through a slot in his cell door, who a jury and judge have determined does not deserve to live. Then, when the deathwatch begins, people affiliated with the state begin to acknowledge his humanity. He receives visits and is given a spiritual advisor who has a great deal of access to him and with whom he can spend considerable time. He is given a meal of his choice, sometimes one that would have been too expensive for his budget prior to incarceration. In exchange for this treatment, the state trusts that he will go to his death in a cooperative manner and appear as if he has merely fallen asleep." Beck, E., Britto, S. and Andrews, A. (2007). *In the Shadow of Death: Restorative Justice and Death Row Families.* Oxford: Oxford University Press: p. 90

[18] E.g. "Having a needle put into your arm and getting into a nice, peaceful sleep. That is nothing compared to putting a gun to our families' heads." (Family member of a murder victim) <http://pro-dp.appspot.com/init/ default/view/63011/Victims-families-waiting-for-justice-to-be-served> Accessed August 25, 2010; "After the court hearing Wednesday, James Young's brother, Danny, said he thought the death penalty was too easy for Wells. 'I think he should go to prison for 80 to 90 years. I

want all the days of his life to be miserable,' Young said." <http://www.firstcoastnews.com/news/news-article.aspx?storyid=4650> Accessed August 25, 2010.

[19] Cf. "[T]he thoughts that cause the most pain are those of weakness, smallness, incompetence, clumsiness and stupidity. If all else pales in significance alongside those issues, then any strategy that attenuates these painful thoughts will be acceptable . . . . In a burst of rage we prove our power, competence and size." Nathanson (1992): p. 365.

[20] Cf. "No doubt, picturing the offender humiliated and suffering produces a kind of narcissistic joy in whoever seeks vengeance. It spreads a temporary balm over their own suffering and humiliation." Monbourquette, J. (2000). *How to Forgive*. Canada: Novalis: p. 24; "By hating one's oppressor and nursing revenge fantasies, the shamed and wounded person can salvage something of his or her dignity. To do otherwise, to give in to the power of others, may feel to some like a relinquishing of integrity and, in doing so, a loss of self-respect." Engle (2006): p. 57.

[21] Cf. "When we remain angry with someone, we stay emotionally tied to them in a very negative way. We continue to feel victimized by them, investing a tremendous amount of energy in blaming them." Engle (2006): p. 110; "[I]f you don't confront those who have hurt you, you will always have an emotional connection to them even if you don't want it. Confronting will help you to *disconnect* from them, once and for all." Engle, B. (1989). *The Right to Innocence: Healing the Trauma of Childhood Sexual Abuse*. New York, NY: Random Publishing House: p. 136. As we will see in the next Chapter, there are some victims who, from fear of abandonment or rejection, *want* to remain 'chained' to the person who has hurt them, but they use a different approach: they blame themselves for the wrong that was done (i.e. the 'Attack Self' reaction): "Many people seem puzzled by sado-masochistic relationships, asking why anyone would enter such a system or accept the treatment it demands. . . . [The answer is that it] is only a person with a characteristic stance of *attack self* who can form a stable link with one whose approach to life favours the scripts of *attack other*. And it is obvious that one who lives within the code of *attack other* would be lonely indeed were it not for the ubiquity of people who agree to accept a somewhat reduced status in order to prevent insecurity or abandonment." Nathanson (1992): pp. 372-73.

[22] "We seem to get angry at someone who insults or rejects us as a way of *avoiding* the painful feeling of shame. . . . However, . . . we may then feel ashamed of becoming angry. Apparently the alternation between shame and anger, if it goes completely unacknowledged, can become a closed loop a self-perpetuating emotional 'upset' that refuses to subside." Scheff (1994): p. 25. Cf. "[S]hame about the body then often produces a vicious cycle, in which feelings of inadequacy produce an eating disorder, initially aimed at restoring control over the body and achieving the desired perfection. But the eating disorder itself (especially if it is bulimia with its messy and hidden vomiting and purging) becomes a new source of shame. The disorder is concealed, giving rise to still further shame." Nussbaum (2004): p. 202; "It is a tragic fact that parents beat their children in order to escape the emotions stemming from how they were treated by their own parents." Miller, A. (1987). *For your Own Good: The Roots of Violence in Child-Rearing*. Great Britain: Virago: pp. 281-82.

[23] "We tend to mimic our offender, as if we had somehow been contaminated by a contagious virus. . . . How many sexual aggressors and violent abusers do nothing but repeat the injuries perpetrated on them in their youth?" Monbourquette (2000): p. 20.

[24] "[People can react] to each other's insulting and rejecting words and manner. Like two hot coals placed close together, the heat of one further inflames the other." Scheff (1994): p. 25.

[25] Cf. "Any response to the wrongdoer that fails to incorporate respect and compassion also fails to recognize the wrongdoer's full worth as a person, and is therefore deficient. Thus resentment, hatred, and ill will are ultimately inappropriate responses to the wrongdoer, although the victim of wrongdoing does need to experience his grief and anger as he works towards a state of genuine forgiveness." Holmgren (1993): p. 349; "If something like Kant's theory of human worth is right, . . . [then] it is no more right when the victim tries to degrade or falsely diminish the wrongdoer than when the wrongdoer originally degraded or falsely diminished the victim." Hampton (1988b): p.145.

[26] "Psychopaths are without conscience and incapable of empathy, guilt, or loyalty to anyone but themselves." Babiak, P. and Hare, R. D. (2006). *Snakes in Suits: When Psychopaths Go to Work*. New York, NY: HarperCollins: p. 19. See also Millon, T., Simonsen, E., Birket-Smith, M. and Davis, R. D. (1998). *Psychopathy: Antisocial, Criminal, and Violent Behaviour*. New York, NY: Guildord Press. For this reason, restorative justice should not be used with people who have been clinically diagnosed as being psychopathic.

[27] For instance: a study conducted 6 months after the Oklahoma bombing reported that 85% of victims' families and survivors wanted the death penalty for McVeigh. Six years later, "[t]he figure had dropped to nearly half, and now most of those who supported his execution have come to believe it was a mistake. In other words, they didn't feel any better after Tim McVeigh was taken from his cell and killed." <http://www.murdervictimsfamilies.org> Accessed August 25, 2010.

[28] Cf. "People who will not or cannot [undertake the work of moral repair] . . . cling to the past and, in so doing, condemn themselves both to miss out on the present and to block off the future." Monbourquette (2000): pp. 22-23.

[29] Cf. "If the possibilities for addressing conflict are represented as 'vengeance or forgiveness,' victims may feel, or may actually be, pressed to take an undemanding, or even a forgiving stance, even where this frustrates their needs for vindication or forecloses any of the varieties of vindication that might satisfy their needs to have their dignity restored, their suffering acknowledged, or their losses compensated." Walker, M. (2006a). The Cycle of Violence. *Human Rights and Negative Emotions: Special Issue of Journal of Human Rights* 5 (1), 81-105: p. 99.

[30] Cf. "Some acts of forgiveness humiliate more than they liberate. In these cases, forgiveness can become a subtle gesture of moral grandstanding. . . . Overcome by shame and rejection, they try to protect themselves . . . by playing the wronged but generous and merciful lord. . . . Authentic forgiveness from the heart stems from humility, and opens the path to genuine reconciliation." Monbourquette (2000): p. 40. The view of forgiveness is explored in more detail in Chapter 11.

[31] On this account, the difference between offensive and defensive anger is not about the *intensity* of the emotion, but rather how the anger is being used by—or what it is doing for—the person who feels it. Cf. "Resentment [or 'defensive anger']. . . is distinguished not by how it feels, but by the way in which those who account for their feeling make reference to perceived injustice, injury, or violation Thus construed, resentment is not defined by a certain (low state) kind of emotional intensity, but can range from a momentary irritation to outrage." Brudholm (2008): p. 11.

[32] These messages are not necessarily a misunderstanding on the part of those who are punished. For example: "Coercion, the act of restraining or demanding compliance by the application of superior force, is another way of diminishing the self-respect of another person." Nathanson (1992): p. 372. Again, "[Our ideal of a legitimate state] requires seeing our fellow citizen as a moral subject, and there is a tendency to see the criminal only as a moral object. To put it another way, legitimacy requires us to ask, 'How should we behave toward our fellow citizens, and how should they behave toward us?' but when it comes to dealing with criminals, we often are tempted to drop the second half of the question. We ask only, 'What can we do with them?' or '. . . to them?' as if they were things to be manipulated." Alder, J. (1992). *The Urgings of Conscience*. Philadelphia: Temple University Press: p. 14—as quoted in Radzik, L. (2009). *Making Amends: Atonement in Morality, Law, and Politics*. Oxford: Oxford University Press: p. 13.

[33] "The famous witch trials of colonial Salem, the public stocks of colonial Williamsburg, arrest, trial and imprisonment of any sort, public spanking or reprimand, any form of punishment by exposure to public censure—all these are but the merest hint of the catalogue of punishments made all the worse because the culprit is denied the recourse of privacy." Nathanson (1992): p. 319.

[34] Cf. "[Many] criminals are not predisposed to repentance, being either dedicated zealots or revolutionaries, calculating amoral risk-takers paying the price, without regret, for their losing gamble, sullen prisoners of the class war (in their own eyes), or sociopathic personalities. Inflicting pain on these individuals by depriving them of their liberty may be socially necessary to protect others, but its most likely effects on the prisoners themselves will be to confirm their cynicism and hatred, or convince them to take greater precautions against discovery next time around—hardly 'moral messages'." Feinberg, J. (1988). *The Moral Limits of the Criminal Law, Volume IV: Harmless Wrongdoing*. Oxford: Oxford University Press: pp. 304-5. Cf. "Punishment erects barriers between the offender and punisher through transforming the relationship into one of power assertion and injury." Braithwaite (1989): p. 73.

[35] There will be mainstream societies that uphold unjust laws, punish the innocent, and encourage wide spread abuse and corruption. In such societies, good people will retreat into subcultures that seek to maintain a sense of right and wrong; and they will find their sense of self, their identity, in the mirror held up by members of these ethical subcultures. The kind of issue is explored in more detail in Appendix 3.

[36] "Sometimes punishment or the threat of punishment provokes defiant reactions that can make crime more likely, not less." Braithwaite, J. (2018). Minimally sufficient deterrence. *Crime and Justice*, 47(1), 69-118. This 'Attack Other' strategy might also be classified as sociopathy: "*Sociopathy* . . . refers to attitudes and behaviours that are

considered antisocial and criminal by society at large, but are seen as normal or necessary by the subculture or social environment in which they developed. Sociopaths may have a well-developed conscience and a normal capacity for empathy, guilt and loyalty, but their sense of right and wrong is based upon the norms and expectations of their subculture or group." Babiak and Hare (2006): p. 19.

[37] Cf. "[I[t has been suggested that people will act more virtuously when motivated to atone for their prior misdeeds . . . and that in order to maximize prosocial efforts, then, past good deeds should be highlighted in abstract terms (e.g., their implications for one's identity), whereas past failures to help or support others should be framed in concrete (e.g., behavioral) terms . . . . This approach would avoid the need to defend themselves because at some abstract point they are validated as moral persons." Vecina, M. L. and Marzana, D. (2016). Always looking for a moral identity: The moral licensing effect in men convicted of domestic violence. *New Ideas in Psychology*, 41, 33-38: pp. 36-37.

8. Attack Self

[1] Cf. "At the Attack Self pole, the person acknowledges the experience as negative, accepts shame's message as valid, and turns anger inward." Elison, Lennon and Pulos (2006): p. 223.

[2] Cf. "[T]here is a dark side to the system of *attack self*, for some people are so willing to accept shame in order to guarantee the stability of their link to others that they become quite masochistic. . . . What passes for delight in the suffering of the masochist is the anticipatory positive affect masking the pain experienced during an activity that is intended to assure bonding." Nathanson (1992): p. 333.

[3] Cf. "Being victimized causes us to feel helpless, and it is this helplessness that leads us to feel humiliated and ashamed. As a protection against these feelings we may take personal responsibility for our own victimization." Engle (2006): p. 55.

[4] This 'control' rationale also explains why we sometimes use the 'Attack Self' reaction in situations where we think someone is very likely to 'put us down' or get angry with us: Cf. "What is it that happens when, intentionally, we put ourselves down in a conversation with others, ridicule ourselves, describe our own actions with disgust . . . or exhibit anger toward our own self? Simply stated, such a maneuver permits us to accept a moment of shame during which we anticipate that all of those other affects and ideas will be totally under our control. We have, for instance, avoided the possibility that others *really* view us with . . . disgust because *we* gave them the idea in the first place. The much-feared unpleasant affects still exist in the interpersonal interaction, but they have been reduced vastly in significance." Nathanson (1992): p. 329.

[5] Cf. "Children [who are being abused by their parents] will adopt a sense of themselves as being personally defective in order to explain away parental failure. . . . [This] allows the child to trade unbearable fear—the terror of abandonment and death—for merely uncomfortable shame." Nathanson (1992): p. 341.

⁶ "You may try to defend against or block the feelings of worthlessness by attacking yourself, believing that if you beat yourself up enough you will finally correct your flaws . . . . This kind of self-flagellation can actually work temporarily. You are so focused on correcting your flaws that the deep feeling of not being okay gets masked for awhile. But over time you are further destroying your self-esteem and self-worth." Engle (2006): p. 199. Cf. Frieze, Hymer and Greenberg (1987): p. 304.

⁷ An important distinction should be made here. It is possible to feel shame over the fact that others think you did something wrong—even though you don't believe you did, or feel you were justified in some way. This kind of shame might be called embarrassment or even humiliation. But it is clearly not guilt. This is important, since restorative justice will fail as moral repair if the 'person responsible' is only participating in order to alleviate their *embarrassment* over having been caught. An apology will not be sincere unless it is driven by genuine feelings of *guilt*. Cf. "Shame is a painful emotion, and the willingness to correct one's shame-causing behaviour in order to avoid shame in the future seems reasonable. Still, it must be acknowledged that if the change in behaviour is motivated only by fear of how others perceive the self and does not reflect internalized morality, the change may be more superficial and temporary than a guilt-motivated change." Silver, M. (2007). Coping with guilt and shame: a narrative approach. *Journal of Moral Education*, 36, 2, 169–183: p. 179.

9. Compassion

¹ Cf. "[Compassion is a] social emotion elicited by witnessing the suffering of others and is rather associated with feelings of concern and warmth, linked to the motivation to help." Preckel, K., Kanske, P. and Singer, T. (2018). On the interaction of social affect and cognition: empathy, compassion and theory of mind. *Current Opinion in Behavioral Sciences*, 19, 1-6: p. 1; "If the hijackers had been able to imagine themselves into the thoughts and feelings of the passengers, they would have been unable to proceed. . . . Imagining what it is like to be someone other than yourself is at the core of our humanity. It is the essence of compassion and it is the beginning of morality." McEwan, I. (2001). *The Guardian*, September 13th.

² Cf. "There is considerable evidence that feeling distress at witnessing another person in distress can produce motivation to help that person. This motivation does not, however, appear to be directed toward the ultimate goal of relieving the other's distress (i.e. altruistic motivation); the motivation appears to be directed toward the ultimate goal of relieving one's own distress (i.e. egoistic motivation). As a result, this distress may not lead one to respond with sensitivity to the suffering of another, especially if there is an opportunity to relieve one's own distress without having to relieve the other's distress." Batson, C. D. (2009). These Things Called Empathy. In *The Social Neuroscience of Empathy*. ed. J. Decety and W. Ickes. Cambridge, Massachusetts: MIT: p. 9.

³ Cf. "Empathy describes the process of sharing feelings, that is, resonating with someone else's feelings, regardless of valence (positive/negative), but with the explicit

knowledge that the other person is the origin of this emotion. This socio-affective process results from neural network activations that resemble those activations observed when the same emotion is experienced first-hand." Preckel, Kanske, and Singer (2018): p. 1.

[4] Cf. "Before I saw the data, I thought that unhappy people—identifying with the suffering that they know so well—would be more altruistic. So I was taken aback when the findings on mood and helping others without exception revealed that happy people were more likely to demonstrate that trait. In the laboratory, children and adults who are made happy display more empathy and are willing to donate more money to others in need. When we are happy, we are less self-focused, we like others more, and we want to share our good fortune even with strangers. When we are down, though, we become distrustful, turn inward, and focus defensively on our own needs. Looking out for number one is more characteristic of sadness than of well-being." Seligman, M. E. (2002). *Authentic Happiness: Using the New Positive Psychology to Realize Your Potential for Lasting Fulfillment.* Australia: Random House: p. 43.

[5] Cf. "[E]mpathy, if above some minimal threshold, is likely to evolve into sympathy, personal distress, or both (perhaps alternating). *Sympathy* is an emotional response, stemming from the apprehension of another's emotional state or condition, that is not the same as the other's state or condition but consists of feelings of sorrow or concern for the other . . . . In contrast, *personal distress* is a self-focused, aversive reaction to the apprehension of another's emotion, associated with the desire to alleviate one's own but not the other's distress." Eisenberg, N. and Eggum, N. D. (2009). Empathetic Responding: Sympathy and Personal Distress. In *The Social Neuroscience of Empathy.* ed. J. Decety and W. Ickes. Cambridge, Massachusetts: MIT: pp. 71-72. See also: "The importance of this motivational distinction is underscored by evidence that parents at high risk of abusing a child are the ones who more frequently report distress at seeing an infant cry; those at low risk report increased other-orientated feelings—sympathy and compassion—rather than increased distress." Batson (2009): p. 9.

[6] Cf. "Personal distress [over witnessing another's pain] generally has been negatively related or unrelated to prosocial behaviour when the actor can escape contact with the person evoking the distress, whereas sympathy tends to be positively related." Eisenberg and Eggum (2009): p. 72.

10. Moral Repair for Persons Harmed

[1] "[A] particular sequence of emotions underlies all destructive aggression: shame is first evoked, which leads to rage and then violence. But shame leads to violence under only one condition—that it is hidden to the point that it is not acknowledged or resolved." Retzinger, S. and Scheff, T. (1991). *Emotions and Violence: Shame and Rage in Destructive Conflicts.* Mass: Lexington Books: p. 3.

[2] "[I]ndividuals high in narcissism do not respond to ego threats with withdrawal; instead, they typically become angry and aggressive . . . . One explanation for this

alternate response to failure is that narcissists invoke a defensive process, using anger and aggression to avoid feeling shame." Bushman, B. J., and Baumeister, R. F. (1998). Threatened egotism, narcissism, self-esteem, and direct and displaced aggression: Does self-love or self-hate lead to violence? *Journal of Personality and Social Psychology*, 75, 219-229. Quoted in Tracy and Robins (2007): p. 15.

[3] "[T]he victim must clarify for herself the claim implicit in the act of wrongdoing [e.g. 'Your needs and feelings don't count']. She must recognize that she is just as valuable as every other person and that her needs and feelings matter very much. Likewise she must come to see the wrongdoer as seriously confused about her status as a person." Holmgren (1993): p. 343.

[4] "[A] woman who wonders whether she might 'deserve' the beatings given her must first bring herself to protest them and challenge the idea that she should receive them before she is in a position to offer genuine forgiveness rather than mere condonation. But resentment is nonetheless an emotion which betrays weakness. Resenters mount a defense against a challenge to their value and rank to which they are in danger of succumbing. Hence their emotion needs to be 'overcome' in the sense of *transcended*: they must conquer the fear, inherent in the emotion, that the insulting message in the harmful action is correct." Hampton, J. (1988b), The Retributive Idea. In J. G. Murphy and J. Hampton, *Forgiveness and Mercy*. New York, NY: Cambridge University Press: p. 148.

[5] Cf. "We are, at least in part, social and socialized products—creatures whose sense of self is so much a part of our social setting that the idea of self-respect or self-esteem cannot be totally detached from a concern with how others (some others) regard and treat us . . . To think otherwise is to fall victim to the liberal myth of atomic individualism in its crudest form. A truly strong person will have the resources to fight off attacks on his self-esteem when they are unjustified, but no person is so 'strong' (so asocial) as to be totally indifferent to all such attacks—so indifferent that he does not even resent them." Murphy, J. G. (1988b). Hatred: a qualified defense. In J. G. Murphy and J. Hampton, *Forgiveness and Mercy*. New York, NY: Cambridge University Press: pp. 93-94.

[6] There is an alternative 'solution' to this 'catch-22' problem, which is, unfortunately, often recommended (if only implicitly) in a restorative justice setting. This approach involves the person harmed offering 'forgiveness' prior to hearing any apology; or, in the context of restorative justice, it involves a person harmed agreeing to take part in a restorative justice meeting even when there is no indication whatsoever that the person responsible has admitted fault or feels the slightest remorse. It is not impossible that this kind of 'blind trust' should inspire an otherwise unremorseful offender to see the error of his ways. But this is clearly a high-risk approach, requiring an enormous degree of self-confidence and vulnerability on the part of the person harmed. But given the very real possibility that the person responsible will remain unmoved, this cannot be recommended as best practice. Braithwaite offers what appears to be an example of this kind of pre-emptive move, although—given the definition of forgiveness given here—I would question whether the victim was actually offering 'forgiveness', as distinct from 'a willingness to forgive': "I have seen . . . victim forgiveness extended to a lost young person who is a remorseless offender, and then the forgiveness elicits remorse. . . . [W]hen we see

others express painful as opposed to aggressive emotions, we see them as human beings like ourselves. Empathy and compassion thus pave the path to healing." Braithwaite, J. (2006). Doing Justice Intelligently in Civil Society. *Journal of Social Issues*, 62, 2, 393-409: p. 404. Cf. "The assumption [that forgiveness can only follow a sincere apology eliminates a] seemingly plausible possibility: cases in which forgiveness *evokes*, rather than follows, repentance. . . . [However, it] might be that, if we spoke carefully, we would say that *mercy* may evoke repentance, but forgiveness always follows it." Hieronymi, P. (2001). Articulating an Uncompromising Forgiveness. *Philosophy and Phenomenological Research*, 62(3), 529-555: p. 540, n. 16.

[7] Cf. "An apology should be delivered in a humble manner. . . There are three aspects to the attitude of humility. First, I may metaphorically or literally bow my head as an expression of the shame of my having done wrong. Second, in bowing my head, I attribute special respect to you and I thereby try to make up for the deficit of respect with which I treated you through my wrongdoing. Third, in bowing my head, I relinquish power to you in that I let you be in charge of restoring my moral stature." Bovens, L. (2015). XII—Apologies. *Proceedings of the Aristotelian Society*, Vol. 108, Part 3, 219-239: pp. 230-31.

[8] To protect ourselves against manipulation, the extent to which we feel empathy for someone who has wronged us will usually be incremental, as the evidence for their sincerity builds and as we begin to gain trust. Cf. "The contagious quality of affect is so powerful that the normal adult has built a shield for protection from the affective experience of another person, a mechanism I call the *empathic wall*. It is a skill, a learned mechanism by which we can tune out the affect display of others. One way of building the empathic wall would be by refusing to mimic the facial or bodily display of affect we see in other people . . . . [Or] we might decide to shift our attention to something else . . . or we can limit [the effective resonance] over carefully graduated levels of connectedness. . . . If the empathic wall is too rigid, we will be immune to the feelings of others; if too flimsy, we will tend to be taken over by powerful feelings broadcast from outside ourselves." Nathanson (1992): pp. 111-12.

[9] Cf. "[R]emorse is a painful emotion, commanding sorrow for the situation, compassion for one's victim, and self-loathing." Pugh and Maslen (2017): p. 502

[10] Cf. "Even in those situations where my empathic thinking results in a relatively full understanding, and I do indeed come to see from your point of view and to share some of your feelings, . . . I may come, in the process, to understand just how selfish your behaviour was, how cruel, and the extent to which you delight in, and continue to gain from, your malevolence. And on grasping this, I am even more degraded by your past behaviour and your current lack of concern for what you have done to me. As a result, my feelings of resentment and anger may quite properly intensify." Novitz (1988): p. 311.

[11] Cf. "We can gain compassion and empathy for a wrongdoer when we come to admit to ourselves that we have all harmed other people, that we may be guilty of the same or similar acts as those that have been done to us." Engle (2001): p. 104. Forgiveness can be particularly difficult when we were at least partly responsible for what happened, and refuse to acknowledge that fact: "If we make the [wrongdoer] all bad, we don't have to face our part in the interaction or any of our own shortcomings

that might have contributed to the problem. Holding onto unforgiveness becomes a protective defense against self-examination." Engle (2001): p. 93.

[12] Cf. "Confronting the ones who hurt you enables you to take back your power, proving to yourself that you are no longer going to allow anyone to frighten, control, or mistreat you. It provides an opportunity to set the record straight, to communicate what you need from now on." Engle (2006): p. 111. Cf. Foster, C. A., and Rusbult, C. E. (1999). Injustice and power seeking. *Personality & Social Psychology Bulletin*, 25, 834–849.

[13] Cf. "In reaching a state of genuine forgiveness the victim extends an attitude of real goodwill towards the offender as a person. He does not extend an attitude of goodwill towards the type of action she performed. As Augustine puts it, he separates the 'sinner' from the 'sin'." Holmgren (1993): p. 347.

[14] As Dworkin puts it, the duty to treat people as equals is not the duty to treat them equally. I can respect someone as a person and acknowledge their dignity without needing to agree with their point of view or approve of their actions, or treat them as if they are more skilled or knowledgeable than they really are. See Dworkin, R. (1977). DeFunis v. Sweatt. In *Equality and Preferential Treatment*. ed. M. Cohen, et. al. Princeton, NJ: Princeton University Press: pp. 67-68.

[15] "Cf. "In a successful [apology], most victims will probably feel restored in dignity and in citizenship. The intruder on their dominion recognizes that his or her behaviour was wrong and is willing to put in an effort to repair what can be repaired. Emotions of revenge in the victim can fade. Whereas revenge emotions are a drive to respond to humiliation by a counter-humiliation, there is less reason for this any more: the offender has in fact diminished the victim's humiliation through his or her apology, which was a kind of self-humiliation." Harris Walgrave and Braithwaite (2004): p. 203; "If [the wrongdoer] come[s] to separate or divorce themselves from their own evil act? (True repentance is a clear way of doing this.) Then the insulting message is no longer present—no longer endorsed by the wrongdoer. We can then join the wrongdoer in condemning the very act from which he now stands emotionally separated. . . . [This separation would] represent grounds for forgiveness that are compatible with self-respect and respect for the rules of moral order." Murphy (1988a): p. 25.

[16] A study by Davis et.al. found that "when a romantic partner apologizes with remorse, perceptions that they are unlikely to repeat the behavior increase both empathy and forgiveness. Conversely, unconvincing remorse increases the perceived likelihood of a repeat offense and decreases empathy and forgiveness." Davis, J. R. and Gold, G. J. (2011). An examination of emotional empathy, attributions of stability, and the link between perceived remorse and forgiveness. *Personality and Individual Differences*, 50(3), 392-397: p. 395.

[17] "Instead of seeing him or her through the lens of anger and bitterness, the person's humility and apology cause us to see him or her as fallible and prone to [wrongful] acts, not as [an evil person]; we see him or her as in need of mercy, not revenge." McCullough, M., Sandage, S. and Worthington, E. (1997). *To Forgive is Human*. Downers Grover, Il.: Intervarsity Press: p. 133.

[18] "Victims who attended [a restorative justice conference] frequently commented on the relief they experienced at seeing who the offenders really were. One said 'You realise they aren't the monsters you'd made them out to be. . . . I don't have to feel conscious of people walking past and thinking, are they the ones? Are they the enemy?' Strang, H. and Sherman, L. (1997). The Victim's Perspective. *RISE Working Papers: Paper No. 2.* Australian National University, Canberra April.

[19] Cf. "No apology can undo a wrongful act. However, an apology can 'unstate' the implicit claim that the wronged person has no moral worth and merits no moral consideration. It is the cancellation of this profoundly insulting and potentially humiliating message that can inspire the ending of anger and resentment on the part of the victim. For one who has been humiliated or treated as worthless, such acknowledgment of dignity and human worth is profoundly significant." Govier, T. and Verwoerd, W. (2002a). The Promise and Pitfalls of Apology. *Journal of Social Philosophy*, 33(1), 67-82: p. 70.

[20] "There is often an instant rush of sympathetic and positive feelings toward the offender in response to what is commonly regarded as the gift of the apology." Lazare, A. (2004). *On Apology.* Oxford: Oxford University Press: p. 242.

[21] Cf. "Each of us, if honest, will admit two things about ourselves: (1) We will within the course of our lives wrong others—even others about whom we care deeply; and (2) because we care so deeply about these others and our relationships with them, we will want to be forgiven by them for our wrongdoings. In this sense we do all need and desire forgiveness and would not want to live in a world where the disposition to forgive was not present and regarded as a healing and restoring virtue." Murphy (1988a): p. 32.

[22] Cf. "When a wrongdoer confesses and apologises, . . . we see [them] as more like us, and this moves us. . . . [T]he more we are forgiven, the more likely we are to have compassion toward our wrongdoers and to forgive them." Engle (2001): p. 83-4; "Apologies motivate forgiveness through the feelings of empathy and compassion they evoke in a victim for the difficulty that an offender is thought to have at offering an apology . . . ." Cowden, R. G., Worthington, E. L., Joynt, S. and Jakins, C. (2018). Do congruent apologies facilitate forgiveness? *South African Journal of Psychology*, 1–14: p. 3.

[23] There may not be a significant time-gap between experiencing and offering forgiveness. Indeed, perhaps one reason why the two are often confused is that they can occur at roughly the same time.

[24] I take 'the acceptance of an apology' to be equivalent in meaning to 'an offer of forgiveness'. The latter can be, and often is communicated by means of the former. But it is important to note here that *accepting* an apology is not the same as *acknowledging* an apology, which is merely to register that it has been received but not necessarily accepted. In a similar way, if someone offers me a seat on the train, I can acknowledge the offer, without necessarily taking (or accepting) the seat. It may also be helpful to distinguish between 'accepting an apology' and 'being persuaded that an apology is genuine'. The latter, as we have seen, is an essential part of what it is to experience forgiveness. But it is possible to be persuaded of the sincerity of an apology

(experiencing forgiveness) without telling the apologiser (offering them forgiveness). That requires the further step of overtly 'accepting the apology'.

[25] "[T]he forgiver is able to respond to the wrongdoer as someone other than 'the one who hurt me,' and the wrongdoer himself is able, thanks to this new perspective, to regard himself as liberated from his burden of moral debt. Such liberation puts the two parties on an equal footing once more, and makes possible renewed relationships." Hampton (1988a): p. 49; "Forgiveness mitigates the moral inferiority engendered by the role of perpetrators . . . and is a reassurance that they belong to the moral community to which their membership was questioned." Shnabel, N. and Nadler, A. (2008). A needs-based model of reconciliation. *Journal of Personality and Social Psychology*, 94, 1, 116-32: p. 117.

11. Forgiveness

[1] Cf. "[E]ven if I could not, as I now am, do what the offender did, nonetheless had my early (and ongoing) circumstances been less favourable, I might have become the kind of person who could act in this way." Garrard, E. and McNaughton, D. (2003). In defense of unconditional forgiveness. *Proceedings of the Aristotelian Society*, 103(1), 39–60: p. 54. This claim does not require or entail the view that our actions are *determined* by our circumstances. If that were the case, then we would not be morally responsible for our actions, in which case there would nothing to forgive.

[2] Cf. "If I really had developed into a vastly different person (in morally relevant respects), in what sense would the resulting person still be 'me' as I stand here now, the victim of a wrong? The reference of the 'I' in the thought 'I could be similar to the wrongdoer' is altogether unclear . . . ." Blöser, C. (2019). Human Fallibility and the Need for Forgiveness. *Philosophia*, 47(1), 1-19: p. 4.

[3] Cf. "[The] human being has enough guilt of his own to be greatly in need of [forgiveness] . . . [i]t is therefore a duty of men to be forgiving." Kant, I. (1797/1996). *Metaphysics of Morals* (trans: M. Gregor). Cambridge: Cambridge University Press: 208; 6: pp. 460-61.

[4] Cf. "Awareness of moral fallibility and moral luck creates awareness of similarity with the wrongdoer: We all have a need for forgiveness. Insofar as we wish to be forgiven, we should in principle be forgiving toward others. This 'wide duty' leaves room for cases where we refrain from forgiving without being open to rational criticism." Blöser (2019): p. 18. Empirical studies tend to confirm that having a general willingness to forgive ('dispositional or trait forgiveness') does not mean that we do not need a good reason to forgive in any particular instance ('state forgiveness'). "A recent meta-analysis found a moderate association between dispositional forgiveness and state forgiveness (r = .30), suggesting a person's general tendency to forgive may not always correspond with forgiveness for a specific offence . . . . Specifically, outcomes of forgiveness are moderated by contextual factors (e.g., offence characteristics), including the provision or receipt of an apology . . . ." Cowden, Worthington, Joynt and Jakins (2018): p. 3.

[5] Cf. "We can forgive a person without his knowledge or in his absence, merely by altering our attitudes and behaviour towards him." Downie, R. S. (1965). Forgiveness. *The Philosophical Quarterly*, 15(59), 128-134: p. 131.

[6] Cf. "It is not satisfactory to say that the mere uttering of the words 'I forgive you' constitutes forgiveness. . . . Unless the words are accompanied by the appropriate behavior we shall say that A has not really forgiven B." Downie (1965): p. 131.

[7] There is, of course, a similar issue with declarations of apology. Cf. "[A]n insincere offer [of apology] is arguably not an offer at all." Helmreich (2015): p. 103.

[8] Some words can, under the right circumstances, 'bring about what they say', including vows, pardons and promises. For instance, by saying 'I promise to do X', I will, in most cases, have *thereby* promised to do X. I may fail to live up to my promise, but I have nevertheless made the promise. But if I say 'I forgive you' even though my emotions and behavior demonstrate that I still hold your wrongdoing against you, then we would say that I had not forgiven you in the first place. Cf. "It is true that forgiving is like promising in that to say, 'I forgive you' is to raise certain expectations which may or may not be fulfilled. But if the expectations are not fulfilled in the case of promising it is still true that a promise has been given, although a false one, whereas if they are not fulfilled in the case of forgiving we do not allow that there has been forgiveness at all." Downie (1965): p. 131.

[9] Cf. "If a woman says 'I forgive you' to her husband, who has confessed an affair, but then continues to remind him of it, appeal to his unfaithfulness to score points in their domestic battles, and nag him about his comings and goings, all this goes to show that regardless of what she said, she has not forgiven him." Govier, T. and Verwoerd, W. (2002b). Forgiveness: The Victim's Prerogative. *South African Journal of Philosophy*, 21(2), 97-111: pp. 98-99.

[10] For this reason, I disagree with the following, insofar as it suggests that *faux* declarations of forgiveness can still be 'real cases of forgiving': "In a range of circumstances, forgiving apart from an attitudinal shift serves important purposes. Sometimes, the speech act will precede changing our attitudes and serve as a first step along the way. We may want our child to say 'I forgive you,' then later remind him that he forgave the person that he is now treating resentfully. On other occasions, the speech act may have important effects in terms of welcoming a person back into a group or community. For example, it may be important to declare that one forgives one's coworker so that others in the office can move on, even if one has not gotten over it oneself. It seems unnatural to claim that instances like these are not real cases of forgiving, or are somehow infelicitous forgiving." Cornell, N. (2017). The Possibility of Preemptive Forgiving. *The Philosophical Review*, 126(2), 241-272: p. 250.

[11] Roche gives a nice example of this: "The case concerned a car theft by a young offender. The offender spoke about his actions, the victims described the impact of the theft of their only car, and all participants expressed their disappointment at the offender's action but also their faith in him for the future. The offender showed remorse, and then in crescendo, the victim expressed his forgiveness. By way of conclusion the victim asked the offender. 'So do you think you'll ever steal a car again?

'Well', he said, 'I'm definitely not going to steal your car again'." Roche, D. (2003). *Accountability in Restorative Justice*. Oxford: Oxford University Press: p. 12, n. 14.

[12] Cf. "Let us suppose, then, that because of your penitence, I do not just accept your apology but find . . . that my earlier desire to see you suffer—my desire for revenge—has at last been satisfied, and that I feel relief and release as a result. . . . I have let your conscience exact the revenge that I had earlier desired. Since . . . forgiveness is never conditional on the satisfaction of one's demand for revenge, this cannot be a case of forgiveness." Novitz, D. (1988). Forgiveness and Self-Respect. *Philosophy and Phenomenological Research*, 58.2, 209-315: p. 307

[13] In the course of their argument for unconditional forgiveness, Garrard and Naughton suggest that any insistence on an apology as a pre-requisite for forgiveness is equivalent to wanting the wrongdoer to be 'lowered' relative to the forgiver. "To insist on an apology is to insist that the wrongdoer humble himself before one, and this implies that there is still some residual resentment. Any relishing of the wrongdoer's lowered standing in relation to the forgiver impugns the genuineness of the forgiveness." Garrard, E. and McNaughton, D. (2003). III—In Defence of Unconditional Forgiveness. *Proceedings of the Aristotelian Society*, 103(1), 39-60: p. 47. It is hard not to see this objection to conditional forgiveness as trading on a mis-reading of the term 'resentment'. The objection takes it to mean *offensive* anger (i.e. vengefulness), when any advocate of conditional forgiveness would always take it to mean *defensive* anger—which, by definition, *affirms* the equal 'standing' of the wrongdoer. Without this mis-reading, the claim that conditional forgiveness is effectively little more than 'satisfied vengeance' does not follow.

[14] A good example of this view can be found in the following: "Success in the task of forgiveness, we can now see, is only as durable as one's self-image. A different sense of self at some time in the future, that results either in higher or in lower self-esteem, may rekindle the feelings of anger and resentment that were previously believed to have been banished. One obvious consequence of this is that it is difficult to know that one has finally forgiven someone for their wrongs against you. But this should come as no surprise; time alone can tell whether the feelings which we have struggled to control are finally conquered, or whether what is vanquished today will return by the backdoor tomorrow. Whether or not such feelings do return, I have suggested, has much to do with our personal histories, and, as a result, with factors that fall beyond our rational control." Novitz (1988): p. 313.

[15] People who commit domestic violence routinely use apologies as a recurring tool of abuse (often called the 'apology cycle'). This strategy 'works' by exploiting the partner's fervent hope that the abuse will stop and their desire to stay in the relationship. Over time, the effectiveness of this strategy will diminish, as the partner loses hope and no longer trusts the *faux* remorse. Cf. "Domestic violence offenders often apologize for their violence afterward and ask for forgiveness from and reconciliation with their partner. Frequently, truly caring for and wishing to continue in their relationship with the offender, survivors are often persuaded by these apologies that he is truly remorseful and dedicated to change. Although these offenders may often feel transitory remorse for their actions and think that they will not engage in future battering, when these apologies are echoed following second, third, or fourth incidents of violence, their function in manipulating the survivor to

return to the relationship becomes patent." Koss, M. P. (2014). The RESTORE program of restorative justice for sex crimes: Vision, process, and outcomes. *Journal of Interpersonal Violence*, 29(9), 1629–1660: p. 714; "[T]he skill of contrite apology is routinely practiced by abusers in violent intimate relationships" Acorn, A. (2004). *Compulsory Compassion: A Critique of Restorative Justice*. Vancouver: UBC Press: p. 73.

[16] See e.g.: Derrida, J. (2001). *On Cosmopolitanism and Forgiveness*. New York: Routledge; Garrard and McNaughton (2002); Govier, T. and Hirano, C. (2009). A conception of invitational forgiveness. *Journal of Social Philosophy*, 39, 3: 429–44; and Pettigrove, G. (2004). Unapologetic forgiveness. *American Philosophical Quarterly*, 41, 3: 187–96.

[17] Cf. "Some wrongs and some perpetrators of those wrongs may be unforgiveable, some resentments justified and healthy, and some ruptured relationships may be utterly unworthy of restoration—a point that may be missed when the often uncritical boosters of universal forgiveness (a group that sometimes includes the famous and influential South African Bishop Desmond Tutu) heap praise on what they take to be the moral, spiritual and mental health exhibited by those who forgive, and thereby tacitly condemn even those who will not forgive grave wrongs by unrepentant perpetrators as exhibiting serious moral, spiritual or even psychological problems." Murphy, J. G. (2008). Foreword. In T. Brudholm, *Resentment's Virtue: Jean Amery and the Refusal to Forgive*. Philadelphia: Temple University Press: p. ix.

[18] Exline and colleagues found that the offender's response was the single largest predictor of forgiveness, and their apology was correlated with high forgiveness. See Exline, J. J., Yali, A. and Lobel, M. (1997). *Correlates of Forgiveness*. Unpublished Data. Stony Brook: State University of New York. Cf. "Real resistance to forgiveness does not spring up solely because it is emotionally difficult to overcome anger and vindictiveness. It could, for example, be grounded in completely sensible complaints about the lack of signs of remorse in the wrongdoer. . . ." Brudholm (2008): p. 33.

[19] Interestingly, the idea that forgiveness is a 'never-ending journey' fits extremely well with the notion of 'unconditional forgiveness'. If we try to forgive someone in the absence of any evidence of their remorse, then there will, in effect, be nothing to which we can anchor our forgiveness. We will never know whether our feelings are tracking reality, since there will be no reality for our forgiveness to track. The only thing keeping our anger in check will be our own will-power—along with, perhaps, a hefty dose of social pressure. This will invariably place 'forgiveness' on an ever-receding horizon. Thus, if those around you are suggesting that forgiveness is something that you should do 'for you', and that 'you don't need to wait for an apology', then you can also predict that, at some point, they will offer you the 'helpful' advice that your journey toward forgiveness will be 'a never-ending struggle', and that you just need to 'try harder'. As we will see, however, if you have not received a sincere apology, this doesn't mean you need to remain 'stuck' in your anger. There *are* ways of 'moving on'. But there is no need to muddy the waters by calling these strategies 'forgiveness'. This will only cause anguish, confusion and heartache to people who, very sensibly, find they cannot forgive without having a good reason for doing so.

[20] This view, or something very like it, is advocated in the following: "[A]ccording to philosophical orthodoxy, forgiveness must involve a causal process leading from the recognition of a suitable reason (e.g. a sincere apology) to the forswearing of

resentment (or some other suitable attitude). . . . Forgiving does not require (but is, of course, compatible with) such a causal history. Rather, we should think of forgiveness as the endorsement of one's lack of resentment in light of the recognition that the offender has undergone a change of heart. Hence, since such endorsement can be easy, forgiving can be easy too." Schönherr, J. (2018). When Forgiveness Comes Easy. *The Journal of Value Inquiry*, 1-16: p. 1, 16.

[21] Cf. "[A] too ready tendency to forgive may properly be regarded as a vice because it may be a sign that one lacks respect for oneself. Not to have . . . the 'reactive attitude' of resentment when our rights are violated is to convey—emotionally—either that we do not think we have rights or that we do not take our rights very seriously. . . . . If I count morally as much as anyone else (as surely I do), a failure to resent moral injuries done to me is a failure to care about the moral value incarnate in my own person (that I am, in Kantian language, an end in myself) and thus a failure to care about the very rules of morality." Murphy (1988a): pp. 17–18.

[22] On this definition of 'collective acts' see Clark, H. H. (1992). *Arenas of Language Use.* Chicago: University of Chicago Press: p. 149.

[23] Cf. "[W]ronging someone and continuing to relate to her exactly as before the offense—doing nothing to her in response to having wronged her (whatever that could be)—constitutes acting toward the victim as though it is acceptable to have wronged her." Helmreich (2015): p. 89; "If a society pays no heed to brutalities and offenses suffered by many of its citizens, it further damages these vulnerable people because moral contempt can be as devastating as the original wrong itself. In literature on the treatment of trauma, this lack of acknowledgment has been termed a second injury to victims, and its effects are referred to as the second wound of silence." Govier and Verwoerd (2002a): p. 71.

[24] Cf. "[I]n some circumstances, the preservation of outrage or resentment and the refusal to forgive and reconcile can be the reflex expression of a moral protest and ambition that might be as permissible and admirable as the posture of forgiveness." Brudholm (2008): p. 4

[25] Cf. "[W]e should respect, not chastise the person who preserves resentment when moral repair fails to be achieved and when the voicing of resistance invites demonizing and pathologizing responses. This kind of resentment should not be considered a moral taint on the person nor should it be reduced to an illness to be treated. Resentment can also be the reflex expression of an honorable emotional response to inexpiable evil or wrongs and legitimate moral expectations that have not been properly dealt with." Brudholm (2008): pp. 16-17.

[26] Nor should we judge those who prioritise justice over well-being. Cf. "Victims and survivors are concerned about more than the goals and values privileged in the therapeutic perspective. Some survivors might be fully aware that their preservation and expression of resentment are bad for their health, functioning, and ability to engage with other things than the atrocity of the past. Yet, they choose to hold on to their resentment because of a sense of moral duty to those who were murdered or as a protest in circumstances where the atrocity is followed by cheap reconciliation or the absence of punishment. When the therapeutic concern with victims' ability to get

on with their lives becomes blind or deaf to such aspects and reasons for continued resentment, it can add insult to injury." Brudholm (2008): p. 39.

[27] Cf. "[Where a sincere apology is not forthcoming, it] might be the task of the victim to remain angry, without letting that anger embitter or disfigure her, and then to so enlarge her life that her anger does not consume it." Hieronymi (2001): p. 540, n. 16. It should be noted that, whilst Hieronymi offers this option, she is not convinced that forgiveness *requires* a sincere apology.

[28] "If the victim truly respects himself and has worked through the process of responding to the wrongdoing . . . he will simply recognize that [the wrongdoer's] implicit claim [that he lacks worth] is mistaken. He can hope that she will overcome her confusion, [he can] regard her with compassion, and extend towards her an attitude of real goodwill, all without acquiescing in the judgment that he lacks worth." Holmgren (1993): p. 346, 347.

[29] Cf. "[P]eople can protect their self-integrity from threats by reflecting on other important values and sources of self-worth. Reflecting on core values allows people to adopt a more expansive view of the self, weakening the implications of a threat for their self-integrity. With their self-integrity intact, they can bypass defensive behaviors aimed at protecting the self from the threat." Schumann, K. (2014). An affirmed self and a better apology: The effect of self-affirmation on transgressors' responses to victims. *Journal of Experimental Social Psychology*, 54, 89-96: p. 91.

[30] Cf. "[P]eople who have been badly hurt, who have been scorched by the actions of others, may not be willing or able to think empathically and feel compassion. Their view of others may be permanently skewed, and . . . they will remain embittered . . . sometimes through no fault of their own." Novitz (1988): p. 314.

12. Moral Repair for Persons Responsible

[1] Cf. "If the apology or the showing of remorse is successful, then it may be inferred that the self that condemned the act is more real than the self that committed the act. Contrariwise, for those who are viewed as unapologetic or unremorseful, the act becomes their essence. If they do not separate themselves from the act or if their apology or show of remorse is not believed, then the transgression comes to define who they are—the self that committed the offending act is the true self." Weisman (2014): p. 9.

[2] "Shame acknowledgment is an admission that what has happened is wrong and shameful, and involves expressing remorse, while shame displacement takes the form of blaming others for the wrong and expressing anger toward them." Ahmed, E. and Braithwaite, V., (2006). Forgiveness, Reconciliation, and Shame: Three Key Variables in Reducing School Bullying. *Journal of Social Issues*, 62, 2, 347-70: p. 353. Cf. "Apology elements require transgressors to admit fault, recognize the harmful nature of their actions, promise change, convey emotions like shame or regret, and even offer a plea for forgiveness—all expressions that might diminish transgressors' sense of power and further threaten their self-integrity . . . . Transgressors may

therefore choose to avoid using these potentially threatening elements, and instead offer more perfunctory apologies or even refuse to apologize altogether. . . . [or] by responding with defensive strategies. These strategies include justifications (attempts to defend one's behavior), victim blaming (attempts to place some or all of the responsibility for the offense on the victim), excuses (attempts to mitigate responsibility for the offense), minimizations (attempts to downplay the consequences of one's actions), and denials (attempts to deny one's involvement in or the presence of an offense . . .)." Schumann (2014): p. 90.

[3] "[Repentance] is surely the clearest way in which a wrongdoer can sever himself from his past wrong. In having a sincere change of heart, he is withdrawing his endorsement from his own immoral past behavior; he is saying, 'I no longer stand behind the wrongdoing, and I want to be separated from it. I stand with you in condemning it.' Of such a person it cannot be said that he is *now* conveying the message that he holds me in contempt." Murphy (1988a): p. 26. Cf. "[A]pologies represent a splitting of the self into a blameworthy part and a part that stands back and sympathizes with the blame giving, and, by implication, is worthy of being brought back into the fold." Goffman, E. (1971). Remedial Interchanges. In *Relations in Public: Microstudies of the Public Order.* New York, NY: Basic Books, 95-187: p. 113.

[4] Cf. "[T]he outward displays of the different self-conscious emotions serve different appeasement functions. These displays serve as vital social signals that remediate social interactions that have gone awry. They provide information to observers that the individual is committed to social norms and morals and feels some remorse for the preceding transgression." Beer and Keltner (2004): p. 127.

[5] Cf. "All dimensions of the apology require strength of character, including the conviction that, while we expose vulnerable parts of ourselves, we are still good people." Lazare, A. (1995). Go ahead say you're sorry. *Psychology Today*, Jan, v28n1, 40-43: p. 43; "While [facing the person they violated] is often an uncomfortable position for offenders, they are given the equally unusual opportunity to display a more human dimension to their character." Umbreit, M. (1994). *Victim Meets Offender: The Impact of Restorative Justice and Mediation.* Monsey, NY: Willow Tree Press, Inc.: p. 9. See also: Lindsay-Hartz, J. (1984). Contrasting experiences of shame and guilt. *American Behavioral Scientist*, 27, 689–704: p. 700.

[6] Cf. "If an offender appears to provide a paint-by-numbers apology, we might question her intentions and the depth of her understanding of the gesture she enacts." Smith, N. (2008). *I Was Wrong: the Meaning of Apologies.* Cambridge University Press: p. 145. Although it is perhaps worth noting that if the person harmed tells the person responsible that they 'accept' an apology that has been 'merely recited', this *can* have the unanticipated effect of evoking remorse: "When we respond to a postured apology with acceptance, a curious development sometimes occurs. Offenders frequently dive into apology thinking they can control the process, but the apology process often takes over and controls them. The insincere apologizer is overtaken by the process itself and converted on the way there. The very act of apologizing, sincerely or not, is transformational." Kador, J. (2009). *Effective Apology.* San Francisco, CA: Berrett-Koehler Publishers: p. 21. Even so, to 'accept' an apology that one believes to be insincere will be itself insincere. We cannot *genuinely* accept an apology unless we are

first persuaded of its sincerity. Aside from this, 'accepting' an insincere apology in the hope of evoking genuine remorse is a high-risk strategy. It is far more likely to 'block' or make no difference to the level of remorse in the person responsible: most will just feel as if they have 'gotten away with it'. And *this* outcome will make the person harmed feel as if they have betrayed themselves. An insincere apology should be challenged, not simply 'accepted'.

[7] Cf. "Explaining that 'I was wrong' may identify my offense, affirm the breached underlying value, and accept blame for the harm. To the victim all of this may seem abstract, distant or cold. Empathy snaps into focus the suffering of a particular person by bringing us to understand 'how she feels.' Rather than simply sharing rules, we share feelings. We connect emotionally as well as intellectually." Smith (2008): p. 100; "[Jenny] realized . . . that [her father] would never really apologise because he was incapable of having any empathy for her and her pain. It was all about him. It was all about trying to appease her so that she'd continue to see him. It was all about trying to appear to be the good father who would do anything for his daughter, while all along he was just thinking about himself." Engle (2001): pp. 58-59.

[8] Cf. "Wholehearted apology emphasizes compassion for the victim rather than redemption. That means you are grounded in the experience of the other person. . . . Your authentically remorseful statements are free of self-loathing and a self-centered preoccupation with guilt. Your focus is not on a mission of personal redemption (although that might come) nor of moral or opportunistic advantage." Kador (2009): p. 17; "Without empathy, the apology . . . may appear to be *about* and *for* the offender and the value at issue rather than taking its orientation from the victim and her lived experiences." Smith (2008): pp. 100-101; "Having empathy for the person you hurt or angered is the most important part of your apology. When you truly have empathy, the other person will feel it. Your apology will wash over him or her like a healing balm. If you don't have empathy, your apology will sound and feel empty." Engle (2001): p. 66.

[9] Cf. "When I empathize with the offended, I better appreciate the consequences of my acts because I am attuned to what it feels like to suffer such harm. . . . I may be more likely to appreciate why my actions were unjustifiable [and this may trigger] a sympathetic desire to ameliorate such suffering [by] undertak[ing] remedial actions." Smith (2008): p. 101.

[10] Cf. "Because there is little to go on, except their experience in a previous conference, many young people and their parents do not know what is expected of them. The potential for restorativeness is greater when participants, and especially offenders, have taken time in advance to think about what they want to say. Yet, as we learned from the interviews [in the SAJJ evaluation], over half the YPs hadn't at all thought about what they'd say to the victim. . . . Most did not think in terms of what they might offer victims, but rather what they would be made to do by others." Daly, K. (2003). Mind the gap: restorative justice theory in theory and practice. In *Restorative Justice and Criminal Justice: Competing or Reconcilable Paradigms*. ed. A. von Hirsch, J. Roberts, A. Bottoms, K. Roach and M. Schiff. Oxford: Oxford University Press: pp. 232-33.

[11] "Compassion is the response that assists the worst of us to put our best self forward. It helps us to build out from whatever ethical strengths continue to be

defined as part of our self." Harris, Walgrave and Braithwaite (2004): p. 204; "Apology has the power to bring down the wall of even the most arrogant, defensive person. When we apologize, we humble ourselves before the person we have harmed, and this helps us to regain our dignity and our humanity." Engle (2001): p. 137.

¹² This is consistent with empirical studies: e.g. "[A]pologies perceived by victims as lacking sufficient empathy may appear dishonest or insincere, thereby maintaining and aggravating victims' emotional rancour . . . . Accordingly, the likelihood of an apology being accepted is heightened when it reflects a level of empathic understanding of the victim's feelings and suffering that is consistent with the victim's needs. . . . perpetrators' apologies appear to be most impactful when they are expressed with concern for victims and openly admit to the distress their actions have caused." Cowden, Worthington, Joynt, and Jakins (2018): pp. 10-11.

¹³ Cf. "In compassion, I feel sadness and distress at the other person's suffering and desire it to be overcome. In cases of remorse, at the same time as I feel the compassion (or possibly not until some time later, depending on the way in which the matter is disclosed to me), I realize or acknowledge that I am responsible for the suffering, that my own actions caused that suffering. . . . [So if] a person claimed to be remorseful but, upon being questioned, said they felt no compassion or sympathy for their victim, we would reject their claim of remorse as either insincere or deluded. Thus, compassion can be said to be part of remorse." Proeve and Tudor (2010): pp. 36-37.

¹⁴ Cf. "If the offended fails to accept the apology, the offender might be able to turn to the surrounding community for a recognition of his change of heart." Hieronymi, P. (2001): p. 550, n.38; "[T]he hope is that the offender will feel that all the vindication born of compassion from loved ones must mean that 'I am basically a good person'. That is, while defects in the self, in the ethical identity of the person, are revealed by the offence and its condemnation, these defects in a mostly good self can be repaired. Through their compassion supporters are saying 'you are not irredeemably bad and that is why we are standing beside you'." Harris, Walgrave and Braithwaite (2004): p. 203.

¹⁵ Cf. "[I]f we understand one's identity as at least partially constituted by how one is perceived by others, then we can both start to make sense of remorse and start to see why one's repentance and change in heart requires ratification by others. If the one offended trusts the sincerity of the offender's apology, she might now see it within her power to change the significance of the past event by joining forces with the offender. In accepting the apology, the offended in some way ratifies, or makes real, the offender's change in heart. . . . [which] will leave the original meaning of the event in the past." Hieronymi, P. (2001): p. 550; "[F]orgiveness can [liberate] the wrongdoer from the effects of the victim's moral hatred. If the wrongdoer fears that the victim is right to see them as cloaked in evil, or as infected with moral rot, these fears can engender moral hatred of themselves." Hampton (1998a): p. 86.

¹⁶ Cf. "Taking responsibility for our actions instills pride and self-respect. We feel better about ourselves when we do the right thing. Even though we may feel more shame at the moment, when we admit we were wrong and apologize for our behaviour that feeling of shame will be replaced before long with a feeling of self-respect and genuine pride (as opposed to false pride)". Engle (2001): p. 133. See also: "In a reintegration ceremony, disapproval of a bad act is communicated while sustaining

the identity of the actor as good." Braithwaite, J. and Mugford, S. (1994). Conditions of successful reintegration ceremonies. *British Journal Of Criminology*, 34, 2, 139-171: p. 142.

[17] Cf. "[Our research] indicates that a victimizing episode makes victims feel less powerful and perpetrators feel more morally inadequate. Thus, the main psychological resource that is damaged for victims is their sense of power, whereas the main psychological resource that is damaged for perpetrators is their sense of belongingness and social acceptance. Consequently, a social exchange interaction that restores the respective psychological resources of the adversaries facilitates their willingness to reconcile." Shnabel and Nadler (2008): pp. 129-30.

[18] Cf. "In restorative justice processes, victim vindication is the path to discharging victim shame . . . and, when it elicits remorse and apology from offenders, this also helps offenders to discharge their shame." Harris, Walgrave and Braithwaite (2004): p 198; "The [victim] may feel helpless, rejected, powerless, or inadequate because of the treatment received; the [offender] may feel unworthy because he or she has injured the other. All these terms have been rated as encoded references to shame. . . . The function of apology under these conditions is to allow both parties to acknowledge and discharge, rather than deny, the burden of shame they are carrying with respect to the injurious act." Retzinger, S. and Scheff, T. (1996). Strategy for community conferences: Emotions and social bonds. In *Restorative Justice: International Perspectives*. ed. B. Galaway and J. Hudson. Monesy, NY: Criminal Justice Press: p. 35.

[19] Cf. "The apology 'makes things right' between the parties both emotionally and cognitively; it repairs the breach in the [social] bond. The success of the action of repair is felt and signaled by both parties; they both feel and display the emotion of pride." Scheff (1994): pp. 135-37.

PART 2. Restorative Justice

1. Designing Restorative Justice Processes

[1] Cf. "[T]here is every reason to believe that we can construct social institutions that will encourage forgiveness rather than revenge" McCullough (2008): p. 19.

[2] Scheff (1994): pp. 135-36.

[3] After having written this section on the analogy between restorative justice and jazz, I came across a similar comparison made by Braithwaite: "It is this localism that makes the restorative movement to justice as jazz is to music". Braithwaite, J. (2002). *Restorative Justice and Responsive Regulation*. Oxford: Oxford University Press: p. 10.

[4] As McCullough puts it: "To forgive a stranger or a sworn enemy, we have to activate the same mental mechanisms that natural selection developed within the

human mind to help us forgive our loved ones, friends and close associates. To encourage more forgiveness in our communities, and on the world stage, we must create the social conditions that will activate those mechanisms." McCullough (2008): p. 16

[5] Cf. "It seems possible that differences in the order of who speaks in a conference, for example, will affect the order in which the emotional sequences described will occur." Harris, Walgrave and Braithwaite (2004): p. 206, n.4.

[6] This phenomenon is well illustrated by the number of videos that have been produced showing, in my view, poorly structured meetings or conferences, that are nevertheless promoted as good (even 'ideal') examples of restorative justice.

2. Mechanisms for Releasing Shame

[1] Cf. "It is commonly agreed that shame must be acknowledged and owned if it is to be healed. Without insight and knowledge into the nature of shame a person will be unable to get rid of, or dissipate it." Pattison, S. (2000). *Shame: Theory, Therapy, Theology.* Cambridge: Cambridge University Press: p. 166. See also Lewis, M. (1992). *Shame: The Exposed Self.* New York, NY: The Free Press: p. 127ff.

[2] Cf. "Children who were emotionally abused or deprived almost always internalize the negative parental messages they received. In order to eliminate these negative internal messages we need to identify their presence." Engel (2006): p. 96.

[3] Cf. "Negative beliefs and negative thought patterns can continue to affect your identity and self-concept unless you consciously work on changing them." Engel (2006): p. 99, 102.

[4] Cf. "[Emotions] can and usually do begin without our awareness of the processes involved . . . If the process were slower, we might be aware of what was happening inside our brain . . . But we wouldn't survive near-miss car accidents; we wouldn't be able to act quickly enough. In that first instant, the decision or evaluation that brings forth the emotion is extraordinarily fast and outside of awareness." Ekman (2003): pp. 20-21.

[5] Cf. "[S]elf-conscious emotions . . . are evoked by . . . self-evaluation [based upon how others see us]. This self-evaluation may be implicit or explicit, consciously experienced or transpiring beneath the radar of our awareness." Tangney, J. P., Stuewig, J. and Mashek, D. J. (2007a). Moral Emotions and Moral Behavior. *Annual Review of Psychology*, 58, 345–72: p. 347.

[6] See Engle's similar approach to healing the self from shame memories: First, she asks the client to make a list of all the ways in which they were abused or neglected as a child. Then she suggests the following exercise: "Return to your list and for each item write about the following: How you felt at the time. The effect the neglect or abuse had on you at the time. How you feel now as you remember the experience. What effect you believe the experience has had on you long term. As you write about each incident of neglect or abuse, allow yourself to feel whatever emotions come up

for you. It is appropriate for you to feel angry, enraged, afraid, terrified, sad, grief-stricken, guilty, ashamed, or any other emotions you may feel." Engle (2006): p. 90.

[7] Cf. "Sometimes the simple act of talking about an emotional episode will cause us to re-experience the emotion all over again." Ekman (2003): p. 34.

[8] "[D]o not become alarmed if you do not feel anything. Survivors of childhood abuse and neglect often numb themselves to their feelings as a self-protective mechanism." Engle (2006): p. 1.

[9] Cf. "Allowing yourself to feel and express your hidden emotions from the past will help heal your wounds from the past." Engle (2006): p. 89.

[10] Cf. "Most victims [do] not have what is called a compassionate witness to their pain and anguish. Telling a loved one about what happened to you and receiving your loved one's support and kindness can be a major step in the healing process." Engle (2006): p. 90; "The skillful therapist must recognize the inevitability of this discomfort [of shame arising from disclosure] and provide for the patient the type of relational safety that fosters both the emergence of whatever must be disclosed and the healing balm of love that soothes the inevitable pain associated with disclosure. It is fascinating to note that most of the great teachers of therapy have stressed this point without even mentioning shame. When Carl Rogers taught us to treat the patient within an atmosphere of 'unconditional positive regard,' he was creating a counter-shaming attitude. All of the great psychoanalytic masters stressed the need to treat patients with infinite respect. All of the regulations about the nature of 'privileged communication' are veiled references to the importance of shame within the therapeutic encounter." Nathanson (1992): p. 319.

[11] Cf. "[T]here is a tendency for the observer of another's shame to turn away from it." Lewis, H. B. (1971). *Shame and Guilt in Neurosis*. New York, NY: International Universities Press: p. 16.

[12] In any restorative justice process, this 'positioning' can be difficult to avoid entirely, simply by virtue of the asymmetrical relationship between the 'facilitator' (as helper) and the 'participant' (as a person seeking help): "The contrast between the imperturbable, benign listener who has adopted an almost saintly acceptance of the patient, and the patient himself, with all his guilty, 'irrational' thoughts and feelings, particularly evokes shame on the part of the patient." Lewis (1971): p. 15.

[13] There is empirical evidence that "shame displacement (or avoidance) escalates when social disapproval is not expressed in a respectful manner." Shin, H. (2003). *Workplace practice and shame management*. Paper presented at the 11th European Congress on Work and Organizational Psychology. Lisboa, Portugal, May. Quoted in Ahmed and Braithwaite, V. (2006): p. 353.

[14] "Therapeutic passivity—the decision to remain silent in the face of a humiliated, withdrawn patient—will always magnify shame because it confirms the patent's affect-driven belief that isolation is justified." Nathanson (1992): p. 325.

[15] "It actually seems more likely that wrongdoers will repent in an atmosphere of acceptance and compassion than in an atmosphere of rejection and resentment." Holmgren (1993): p. 348.

[16] A study by Schumann found that: "[r]elative to control participants, those who had previously been affirmed offered responses that included more apology elements and fewer defensive strategies. Observers also rated these responses as being more sincerely remorseful, suggesting that self-affirmation can promote transgressor responses that might be judged as more sincere (and thus more deserving of forgiveness) by victims." Schumann (2014): p. 92.

[17] According to Carl Rogers, originator of the 'Person-Centered' approach to counselling and psychotherapy, the three 'Core Conditions' below are qualities of a counsellor that are considered vital for therapeutic change in a client. *Genuineness*: Being oneself (open, transparent, authentic); not hiding behind a mask of professionalism; being sincere, warm and non-defensive. *Unconditional Positive Regard*: Acceptance of the client without being judgmental, stereotyping, labelling, making assumptions, or jumping to conclusions. It involves caring for, valuing and respecting the client as a unique human being with intrinsic dignity and worth, irrespective of how offensive or uncomfortable their words or behaviour are. *Empathetic understanding*: This is the ability to step into the client's world or frame of reference—as if you are in their shoes—without becoming enmeshed in their world or so involved as to lose your objectivity. Adapted from Sutton, J. and Stewart, W. (2002). *Learning to Counsel*. Oxford: How to Books: Ch. 2; and Palmer, S. ed. (2001). *Introduction to Counselling and Psychotherapy*. Great Britain: Sage Publications: pp. 178-79.

[18] Cf. "When someone says: 'I have a wound', it implies a distance between my whole being and the wound, a distance that lets me react and heal myself. On the other hand, when I state: 'I am wounded,' I identify my whole being with the wound and thus make myself unable to react." Monbourquett (2000): p. 102; "No one is all good or all bad. We all have good and bad qualities; we all share the capacity to do both good and evil. . . . We need to accept our humanity and that of others with all its imperfections." Engle (2001): pp. 94-95.

[19] Cf. "Although no one can bestow self-esteem on you, the validation of friends and lovers can help you feel better about yourself so that you can bestow esteem on yourself. In other words, using external validation can become a tool for helping you raise your self-esteem. . . . [My patient] Lorraine had used my voice as her nurturing voice until she could develop her own." Engle (2006): p. 202, 160; "[One] advantage to conversation with an empathetic person [is that] their unconditional acceptance will better dispose you to accept yourself compassionately." Monbourquette (2000): p. 94; "Whenever possible, I try to catalogue (and get the patient to agree to the existence of) the good features of the self that remain. This helps reduce the dominance of the bad self that was depicted during the cognitive phase of shame." Nathanson (1992): p. 325.

3. Commitment

[1] E.g. "The experience of being caught for an offense and being charged will be sufficient to incite a degree of regret in most offenders (if only out of self-pity). The task of the [restorative justice] scheme is then to build on this spark of remorse to encourage even more insightful realization of the harm caused and thereby to make that remorse deeper, more genuine, and less self-centered." Marshall, T. and Merry, S. (1990). *Crime and Accountability—Victim/Offender Mediation in Practice.* Home Office, HMSO, London: p. 97.

[2] Cf. "[T]elling someone about [what happened] lets you relive the painful event more calmly. This will help you become aware of the emotions that are just below the surface of your being. The past comes alive and is made present. You relive the present experience, but this time in a safe context. Thanks to the trust you place in your confidant, you will become more confident. Your perception of the offence changes: you will find it seems less threatening and more bearable." Monbourquette (2000): p. 93.

4. Preparation

[1] Cf. "The whole point of asking for an apology [or agreeing to take part in a restorative justice process] is for you to find out whether the person who wronged you is truly remorseful so that you can open your heart and move toward forgiveness. It is not to force another person to humble herself before you so that you can feel you have power over her. . . . While it is true that hearing the apology will make you better able to forgive, you need to do your part be being willing to forgive. Otherwise, no matter how sincerely the offending party apologizes, you may not be able to forgive. Your pride, your anger, and your need for revenge will get in the way and you will sabotage your opportunity for healing." Engle (2001): p. 124.

[2] Cf. "It is important to prepare yourself for any result when you apologize. . . . The person you have wronged may tell you that she is unable to forgive you, or that even though she accepts your apology, it is going to take a great deal of time before she can once again trust you, or that although she accepts your apology she no longer wishes to have any kind of relationship with you. By being prepared for any outcome you won't be as devastated if you receive one of these latter responses. . . . . [T]he fact that you were able to admit your wrong to the person harmed . . . in itself will be healing to you, no matter what the outcome. You will be freed from the guilt and shame you've been carrying around, and you will gain self-respect because you were willing and able to take responsibility for your actions." Engle (2001): p. 76. See also p. 155.

[3] Cf. "Apologizing to the person you hurt or harmed will no doubt help you to forgive yourself, especially if he or she is able to forgive you. But, paradoxically, you will need to begin the process of forgiving yourself if your apology is to be effective. If you approach the person you wronged feeling overwhelmed with guilt, you will be

distracted from where your focus needs to be—on the person you wronged and his or her feelings." Engle (2001): p. 70.

[4] Cf. "[A] weeping offender can leave the victim so uncomfortable that she offers exculpation simply to bring the spectacle to an end." Smith (2008): p, 105; "The self-blamer cleverly manages to make the offended party feel sorry for him for being so hard on himself. Not only do most people temporarily forget about the offense, but they end up taking care of the person who is apologizing. This nullifies the apology entirely." Engle (2001): p. 61; "If someone does refuse to accept your apology, work on releasing this person and releasing any negative feelings you have toward him or her." Engle (2001): p. 155.

[5] Cf. "If in your heart you feel that what you did was justified, or as a result of what the other person did, then you should not apologise." Engle (2001): p. 65.

[6] Cf. "A common obstacle that many people encounter when they attempt to make amends to someone in their past is that their own resentment toward the other person for his or her part in the disagreement or conflict gets in the way. Then they're likely to bring up the other person's mistakes and end up insulting him or her. Thus, it is vitally important that you make sure you have forgiven the other person before attempting to make your amends." Engle (2001): p. 153.

[7] Sadly, this kind of situation is not uncommon in some restorative justice services. If it were otherwise, Victim Support UK, for example, would not have felt the need to issue the following statement: Cf. "Victim Support believes that it is essential that victims' interests, wishes and preferences be given primary consideration in all restorative justice initiatives. It is essential that the use of restorative justice to reduce re-offending or to rehabilitate the offender should be secondary considerations after this. If in fact the objective is merely to confront the offender with the consequences of his/her behaviour with a view to preventing further offending, this should be clearly stated at the outset, so that the victim can make a choice." Victim Support (2003). *Victim Support UK Policy on Restorative Justice In Criminal Justice*: p. 1.

[8] Cori, J. L. (2008). *Healing from Trauma*. New York, NY: Marlowe & Company: pp. 121-22.

[9] Cf. "Although your confrontation [with the person responsible for harming you] may include expressing your anger along with your other feelings, it is generally important that you have released a great deal of your anger in constructive ways before you confront, because you will be better able to communicate your feelings in a strong, clear, self-assured manner. You will also be less likely to explode or lose control." Engle (2006): p. 111.

[10] "On the one hand, [research has found that] excessive displays of anger, be they physical or verbal, often produce the following illnesses: heart attacks, degenerative arthritis and peptic ulcers. On the other hand, people who repress their fear and their anger are subject to skin diseases, rheumatoid arthritis and ulcerative colitis. . . . asthma, diabetes, high blood pressure and migranes." Monbourquette (2000): p. 112.

[11] Cf. "After committing an offense, transgressors' need to protect their self-integrity might prevent them from offering an appropriate response, thus further threatening the well-being of the relationships they care about. But with their self-integrity protected by self-affirmation, transgressors appear to be less likely to defend their

negative behavior and more likely to apologize in a comprehensive manner that will likely encourage forgiveness." Schumann (2014): p. 95.

5. Communication

[1] E.g. "[The victim's] expression of painful feelings can have a profound effect on the offender, since they reveal the inner person of the victims: wounded, suffering beings like the offender." Retzinger and Scheff (1996): p. 329.

[2] Cf. "The therapeutic 'graduate' may be able to function and over time may feel his wound less acutely. Deep inside, however, the residual effects of the injury may continue to poison him in the form of mistrust of others or misplaced anger. (Some people fly into fits of rage years after they have been injured at the simple mention of their offender's name.) Wrongs righted in the self do not right wrongs between people who harm each other; they remain in silent places, waiting for the transaction of forgiveness [and apology] and the relief it bears." Flanigan (1992): p. 10.

[3] Cf. "When an enemy apologizes, this person is admitting he was wrong, and this takes away his power and the threat that he will continue to be our enemy." Engle (2001): p. 31.

[4] Cf. "Apology may start as a feeling, a desire to make matters right, but apology requires a commitment to move that desire into practice, to actually take on the great courageous task of showing compassion to others. . . . If the experience is internal or through a intermediary, what you have is confession. Confession is good, but it's not apology." Kador (2009): pp. 15-16.

6. Action

[1] In the RISE project, of those victims who did receive an apology, whether in a conference or not, 23% felt the apology was insincere. Sherman, L. and Strang, H. (2007). *Restorative Justice: The Evidence*. The Smith Institute: p. 63. In a South Australian restorative justice pilot, Kathleen Daly reported that only 27% of victims felt that apologies from offenders were sincere. Daly (2003): p. 224.

[2] Obviously there will be the cases in which an apology cannot (or need not be) understood as a promise about future actions, such as 'death-bed apologies' or when we apologise to strangers we are unlikely to ever meet again. As Helmreich puts it: "Such apologies say nothing about the offender's future behavior, nor does it seem to matter if they do. Their future relationship is beside the point: [they are] apologizing for the past, so as to make things right for now. . . . yet [this can still be a] sincere and meaningful apology that justifies forgiveness and reconciliation." Helmreich, J. S. (2015). The Apologetic Stance. *Philosophy & Public Affairs*, 43(2), 75-108: p. 85. One way of absorbing such cases into our account would be to use a counter-factual formulation: e.g. 'To apologise to someone entails promising not to repeat one's offending behavior against them, *should the opportunity arise*'. This is a solution that

Helmreich also seems to countenance: e.g. "The son apologizing to his dying father . . . can still be a sincere . . . as long as he is genuinely disposed to act that way should his father miraculously recover, or should their final moments together be extended, or should he find a way to treat his father that way after he dies (as when he writes the eulogy or records a family history)." Helmreich (2015): p. 102. Cf. "A simple test for determining whether 'I apologize' is an apology in the formal sense of the word is to ask whether the person making the statement would repeat the behavior if a similar situation arose." Lazare (2004): p. 26.

[3] Cf. "[Y]ou need to complete your amends for your wrongful actions of the past by changing your actions in the future. . . . To apologize for our actions and then to go right back to hurting those we are close to would make our words empty indeed." Engle (2001): p. 157.

[4] Cf. "Accepting an apology is in essence a vote of confidence on your part, since you are saying that you believe in the basic goodness of the other person and in his or her ability to change." Engle (2001): p. 35.

[5] "If the offender breaks her promise to reform and provide redress over her lifetime, her gesture would not rise to the level of a categorical apology. . . . We should meet urges to prematurely judge apologies with suspicion and scrutinize the motivations behind such haste. We should be especially wary of offenders who attempt to simplify the exchange so that they can 'put it behind them'." Smith (2008): p. 145.

[6] "Sometimes, offenders have been adjudicated (whether by a trial or plea-bargaining) as being guilty, but the judge offers the offender the option of entering a VOM [i.e. Victim Offender Mediation] program instead of facing 'traditional' sentencing. Given the unknown 'traditional' sentence, and given that usually judges seem to drastically reduce sentences when using VOM programs, it seems that the 'choice' offered the offender is particularly coercive. If this is true, then the offender (striving to successfully complete the VOM program) seems particularly likely to feign repentance and fake his or her way through the mediation program." Andersen, J. D. (2003). *Victim Offender Settlements, General Deterrence, and Social Welfare.* The Harvard John M. Olin Discussion Paper Series: No. 402 01: p. 17.

[7] A study by Jehle et. al. found that "actual victims adjust their perceptions of the offender based on the apology's level of voluntariness . . . [V]ictims will likely appreciate an apology if the apology can appear to be motivated by the offender's desire to demonstrate true regret for his actions rather than merely to reduce his sentence." Jehle, A., Miller, M. K., Kemmelmeier, M. and Maskaly, J. (2012). How voluntariness of apologies affects actual and hypothetical victims' perceptions of the offender. *The Journal of Social Psychology*, 152(6), 727-745: p. 747, 742.

[8] Cf. "[S]ome trends on [restorative justice] processes existing in international research emphasize that mere material compensation has an important function in inducing the victim to enter the [restorative justice] process, but it can become much less important, even incidental, during the interaction, where the victim can develop new aims, such as the expression of one's own emotions, the possible experience of forgiveness, and the potentialities of reinforcing one's own self, and so forth." Centomani, P. and Dighera, B. (1992). The new juvenile penal procedure code and the reparation-reconciliation process in Italy: A chance for a possible change. In H.

Messmer and H. U. Otto eds. *Restorative Justice on Trial: Pitfalls and Potentials of Victim-Offender Mediation* International Research Perspectives. Netherlands: Kluwer Academic Publishers: p. 363.

[9] Cf. "The final task for the victim of wrongdoing is to determine whether she wants to seek restitution from the offender. In order to respect herself the victim must recognize that she has been wrongfully harmed and deserves to have any loss she has suffered made good. Respect for her own integrity also requires that she look objectively (and with some compassion) at the wrongdoer's situation. She must then make a reasoned judgment about how she wants to proceed. If the victim bypasses this task in an attempt to forgive her offender, she exhibits a lack of self respect. A state of genuine forgiveness is also forestalled in this case, as the victim has not achieved a full internal resolution of the issue. The incident will not be over for her until she determines her own course of action with respect to seeking restitution." Holmgren (1993): p. 344.

7. Designing Speaking Turns

[1] Adapted from Bowen, H., Boyack, J. and Hooper, S. (2000). *New Zealand Restorative Justice Practice Manual*. Auckland, New Zealand: Restorative Justice Trust: p. 92; and O'Connell, T., Wachtel, B. and Wachtel, T. (1999). *Conferencing Handbook: The New REALJUSTICE Training Manual*. Pipersville, PA: The Piper's Press: p. 58.

[2] Bird, S. (1999). *Conference Convenor Training Package*. Sydney, NSW: Dept. of Juvenile Justice: p. 13.

[3] "[I]t is necessary to talk through consequences [suffered by people as a result of the crime]. Unless we do this, we will not know who and what has to be restored." Harris, Walgrave and Braithwaite (2004): p 198.

[4] "The major parties attend the conference in the roles of victim or offender. The labels of 'victim' and 'offender' may gradually be removed, and the conference process may begin that longer process of restoring the moral equality between them." Moore, D. B. (1996). Transforming Juvenile Justice Transforming Policing: The Introduction of Family Conferencing in Australia. In *Comparative Criminal Justice: Traditional and Nontraditional Systems of Law and Control*. ed. C. B. Fields and R. H. Moore. Prospect Heights, IL: Waveland: p. 595.

[5] "Confronting the shamefulness of these hurts is necessary to vindicate victims. Any failure to do so that is motivated by a desire to coddle the fragile sensibilities of offenders may be seen as a denial of victim vindication that amounts to a form of stigmatizing shaming for the offender who cannot face the music." Harris, Walgrave and Braithwaite (2004): p 198.

[6] "An apology is premature if sufficient time has not been taken to consider fully the consequences of the wrongdoing." Engle (2001): p. 60.

[7] "[T]he wrongdoer is ultimately responsible for her own moral development. Although we may force her to refrain from certain types of behaviors, it is up to her to assess her own past actions and to revise her own attitudes. No one can perform this task for her, and even if someone could, it would be a gross violation of her autonomy to do so. It is of fundamental importance for all of us as autonomous moral agents to perform this task for ourselves." Holmgren (1993): p. 348.

[8] "[T]he parents in a Canberra shoplifting case also expressed incredulity that their son could be a thief, but indirectly. Most of their comments seemed geared to distance them from the offender, their son, because they saw themselves as hardly the kind of people to be spending time in a police station." Retzinger and Scheff (1996): pp. 324-25.

[9] "Most English-speaking people find it normal to cancel grudges at the moment of a physical act of compensating wrongdoing by uttering the word 'sorry'. Faced with such an utterance, only unusual victims resist the imperative to return a word of forgiveness, to 'let bygones by bygones', or at least to show acceptance, thanks, or understanding." Braithwaite and Mugford (1994): p. 154.

[10] Cf. "While we may intuitively know that we should accept an apology as the gift that it is . . . it will likely take more work and more time before we can truly forgive. We may need time to assimilate the apology, to examine our emotions, and to discover whether we feel the person's words seemed sincere." Engle (2001): p. 82. I take Engle to be referring here to the *acknowledgement* of an apology as a 'gift', rather than its *acceptance* (which requires being persuaded that it is genuine).

[11] "In [one] case, the facilitator . . . reported that [during refreshments] the victim had patted one of the offenders on the shoulder after he had made a tearful apology to her." Retzinger and Scheff (1996): p. 317.

[12] "Forgiveness must always be freely chosen and should never be understood as obligatory." Govier, T. (2002). *Forgiveness and Revenge*. London: Routledge): p. 77; "[If] victims of bullying and other wrongs [have] the feeling that they are expected to forgive . . . [this] undermines the power of forgiveness because it strips it of the generosity and compassionate spontaneity that gives forgiveness its special meaning as a gift from the wronged to the wrongdoer." Braithwaite (2006): p. 404.

[13] In the following quote, I take Engle to be referring to the *acknowledgement* of an apology, rather than its *acceptance*. "When we *accept* an apology, it usually follows that we are willing to forgive the person for the wrongdoing, even if we can't forgive him or her at the moment. In fact, for most people, accepting an apology opens the door to forgiveness. . . . It may take some time, but at least there is a willingness on [our] part." Engle (2001): p. 81. In other words, in acknowledging an apology I am only registering to the person responsible that their apology has been received and that I will consider it (somewhat like acknowledging the offer of a seat on the train). This does not—and should not be taken to—imply that I have *as yet* accepted that apology (I may choose not to take the seat). This additional step requires that I am persuaded that their apology is genuine and thus have experienced forgiveness (which may 'take some time'). The acceptance of apology, in this sense, is effectively the same as an offer of forgiveness. So what Engle means, as I understand it, is that by acknowledging

your apology (rather than ignoring it or immediately rejecting it), I am saying that I am at least *willing* to forgive you.

[14] If the person harmed does accept the apology or offer forgiveness, then this completes what has been called the 'core sequence' of a restorative justice process: that is, (a) the person responsible expressing remorse and apologising for their actions; followed by (b) the person harmed being persuaded that the apology is sincere and accepting the apology or offering forgiveness. "Even though the emotional exchange that constitutes the core sequence may be brief -- even a few seconds -- it is the key to reconciliation, victim satisfaction, and decreasing recidivism. . . . It is the vital element that differentiates conferences from all other forms of crime control. . . . Without the core sequence, . . . whatever settlement is reached . . . leaves the participants with a feeling of arbitrariness and dissatisfaction." Retzinger and Scheff (1996): pp. 316-17.

Appendices

1. Shame vs. Guilt

[1] Tangney, Stuewig and Mashek (2007b): p. 26. Cf. "What arouses guilt in an agent is an act or omission of a sort that typically elicits from other people anger, resentment, or indignation. . . . What arouses shame, on the other hand, is something that typically elicits from others contempt or derision or avoidance." Williams, B. (1993). *Shame and Necessity*. Los Angeles, CA: University of California Press: pp. 89–90; "[Shame] pertains to the whole self, rather than to a specific act of the self [but guilt] takes an act, rather than the whole person, as its primary object." Nussbaum (2004): p. 184.

[2] Cf. "People are highly motivated to maintain their sense of self-worth and integrity . . . , but the act of harming another person can threaten one's identity as a good and appropriate person . . . . Because of this threat, transgressors are likely motivated to avoid associating themselves with wrongful actions." Schumann (2014): p. 90.

[3] Cf. "[A] person can genuinely accept responsibility only if they also accept that their behavior has implication for who they are . . ." Harris, Walgrave, and Braithwaite (2004): p. 196. See also: "If someone feels guilt about having hurt another person it would seem odd if they did not also feel some shame because their actions had threatened their perception of the kind of person they are and their perception of how others judge them." Harris, N. (2001). Shaming and shame: regulating drink driving. In E. Ahmed, N. Harris, J. Braithwaite, and V. Braithwaite, *Shame Management through Reintegration*. Cambridge: Cambridge University Press: p. 124; "[I]n our typical experiences of guilt and shame the two are so intimately intertwined that they cannot be distinguished from one another. We routinely experience our transgressive

acts as wrongdoing and, simultaneously, as failures of character. We see not only our acts but also ourselves as open to blame." Pettigrove, G. and Collins, J. (2011). *Apologizing for Who I Am. Journal of Applied Philosophy*, 28(2), 137-150: p. 143; "[T]he experience of pure guilt *as Tangney defines it* [i.e. without shame] is at most a fairly mild emotion; intense guilt, Rodion Romanavitch Raskolnokov guilt, *that* guilt, we suggest, has as its bite shame. Tangney's analysis too thoroughly dissociates shame from guilt, character from action. Acts for which we are guilty (and don't just in some weak sense feel guilty), do involve the self. And because they involve the self they involve shame." Sabini, J. and Silver, M. (1997). In Defense of Shame: Shame in the Context of Guilt and Embarrassment. *Journal for the Theory of Social Behavior*, 27, 1, 1–15: p. 8. I would agree with Sabini and Silver here, except to say that, if guilt is a kind of shame, then there is no such thing as 'pure guilt'. If there are occasions when guilt is a 'fairly mild emotion', then that is not due to the fact that shame is absent. Rather, it is because the kind of shame we call 'guilt' is sometimes experienced as 'fairly mild'. Shame is not always of the 'biting' intensity experienced by Rodion Romanavitch Raskolnokov.

⁴ Cf. "[T]hese results suggest that in the context of criminal offending the distinction between guilt and shame may not be as important as has been suggested." Harris (2001): p. 124.

⁵ Some argue that there is a difference between shame and embarrassment: e.g. "Shame involves evaluation of a 'core' self whereas embarrassment involves evaluation of more transient, less central aspects . . . shame involves a serious moral transgression whereas embarrassment is a matter of a breach of convention. . . . Shame involves a serious character flaw whereas embarrassment involves a less serious flaw, something that can be 'put right'. . . . The emphasis here is on the individual's perception of the public implications for the self of his or her action. If core attributes of the self are involved, then shame will be experienced, if peripheral or transient aspects are involved, embarrassment." Crozier (1998): pp. 278-79. See also Miller, C. (2011). Guilt, Embarrassment, and the Existence of Character Traits. In *New Waves in Ethics*. ed. T. Brooks. Palgrave Macmillan UK: p. 155f. But this analysis assumes that shame comes in only one 'flavour' or level of intensity. What is common to both shame and embarrassment, on Croziers description, is that the self believes that it is flawed or has a defect. On the analysis preferred here, that is precisely what is common to all types of shame. Crozier is therefore simply describing two types of shame: one is guilt ('moral transgression') the other is embarrassment ('breach of convention').

⁶ Tangney, Stuewig and Mashek (2007a): p. 353. Cf. "If feelings of guilt concentrate on the deed or the omission then the thought that some repayment is due is in place here as it is not in the case of shame. If I have done wrong then there is some way in which I can 'make up' for it, if only by suffering punishment. . . . [But] how can I possibly make up for what I now see I am? There are no steps that suggest themselves here. Therefore is nothing to be done, and it is best to withdraw and not to be seen. This is the typical reaction when feeling shame. Neither punishment nor forgiveness can here perform a function." Taylor (1985): p. 90.

⁷ Rawls, J. (1999). *A Theory of Justice*. Rev. edition. Cambridge, MA: Harvard University Press: p. 424.

[8] Tangney, Stuewig and Mashek (2007a): p. 352-53.

[9] Tangney, Stuewig and Mashek (2007a): p. 353.

[10] Tangney, Stuewig and Mashek (2007b): p. 26.

[11] Tangney, Stuewig and Mashek (2007b): p. 26.

[12] Tangney, Stuewig and Mashek (2007b): p. 27.

[13] Tangney, Stuewig and Mashek (2007b): p. 26.

2. Terminology

[1] "Notwithstanding the humane ideals of restorative justice, the unpalatable but inescapable fact is that restorative justice programmes are embedded in a contemporary cultural and political context where punitive and exclusionary punishment is dominant . . . . One pertinent manifestation of this dominance is the widespread resurgence of shaming penalties . . . . The precise form of these penalties varies—from punishing people who urinate in public by requiring them to scrub a street with a toothbrush . . . to newspapers 'naming and shaming' convicted paedophiles—but the basic goal is the same: to subject an offender to extreme shame and humiliation. Though such penalties are grossly offensive to the overwhelming majority of restorative justice practitioners, to many citizens they are not." Roche (2003): p. 18.

[2] There is evidence that this has already been happening. See, e.g., Young, R. (2001). Just Cops Doing 'Shameful' Business? In *Restorative Justice for Juveniles: Conferencing, Mediation and Circles*. ed. A. Morris and G. Maxwell. Oxford: Hart Publishing.

[3] Neiderbach, S. (1986). *Invisible Wounds: Crime Victims Speak*. New York, NY: Harrington Park Press: p. 3.

[4] "Psychopaths are without conscience and incapable of empathy, guilt, or loyalty to anyone but themselves." Babiak and Hare (2006): p. 19.

[5] Cf. "I am convinced that shame plays a major role in much offending as well as in how those who offend experience justice. I'm also convinced that it often plays a significant role in victims' trauma and the negative ways they often experience justice." Zehr, H. (2009). Shame and restorative processes. Restorative Justice Blog, July 26th: <http://emu.edu/blog/restorative-justice/2009/07/26/shame-and-restorative -processes> accessed June 30, 2010.

[6] Ahmed, Harris, Braithwaite, J., and Braithwaite, V. (2001): p. 5

[7] Quoted in Neiderbach (1986): p. viii. Cf. "Alice Miller notes that when children are asked to forgive abusive parents without first experiencing their emotions and their personal pain, the forgiveness process becomes another weapon on silencing. The same is true of adults who rush to forgiveness. Many people have been brainwashed

into submission by those who insist that they are 'less than' if they don't forgive." Engle (2006): p. 113-14.

[8] Cf. "Although we must accept the wrongdoer *as a person* in order to forgive, we need not accept him into a more intimate relationship with us. For example, a woman may forgive her husband for repeated acts of violence against her and still decide to divorce him. She may understand why he engages in this pattern of abuse, overcome any negative feelings towards him, and continue to love him, but at the same time decide she can no longer live in this manner. Likewise the owner of a business may forgive an employee for embezzlement but decide she can no longer risk retaining the employee. To forgive a wrongdoer is to reach an acceptance of that person as a person, not as a husband, an employee, etc." Holmgren (1993): p. 342.

[9] "[W]hile justice concerns itself with re-establishing the rights of an injured party on an objective basis, forgiveness depends primarily upon freely expressed good will. . . . Forgiveness that does not fight injustice, far from being a sign of strength and courage, shows weakness and false tolerance. It encourages the offender to repeat the crime." Monbourquette (2000): p. 38.

[10] Moore, K. D. (1989). A Retributivist Theory of Pardon. In *Pardons: Justice, Mercy, and the Public Interest.* New York: Oxford University Press, 89-196: p. 185.

[11] "Either forgiveness is free or it does not exist. But there is a strong temptation, especially among some preachers, to force people to forgive freely. One day I was listening to a bishop who was giving the homily in a televised Sunday Mass . . . Interspersed throughout his homily were such expressions as 'we *must* forgive', 'we *must* forgive others', 'the *commandment* about loving your neighbour,' and 'the Christian *precept.*' The cameras sweeping over the audience caught people fidgeting rather uncomfortably. One could only guess at their inner turmoil as the desire to forgive collided with the hesitation brought on by their feelings and emotions that were also clamouring to be heard." Monbourquette (2000): p. 34.

[12] Braithwaite claims that: "restorative justice programs that do not set out with the direct objective of eliciting forgiveness and apology roughly double the prospects of both and also quadruple prospects that apologies which are given will be perceived as sincere by victims." Braithwaite (2006): p. 407. But there is a radical difference between 'eliciting' in the sense of *compelling, pressuring* or *requiring* participants to 'forgive' or 'apologise', as compared to *offering a process that is designed to enable them to do so safely and effectively, if they so choose.* It seems clear that the evidence that Braithwaite cites refers to the former type of 'elicitation', rather than the latter.

[13] "Forgiveness must always be freely chosen and should never be understood as obligatory." Govier (2002): p. 77.

[14] Minow, M. (1998). *Between Vengeance and Forgiveness: Facing History after Genocide and Mass Violence.* Boston: Beacon Press: p. 17. Quoted in Roche (2003): p. 36.

[15] Cf. "[A] person's attempt at forgiveness might end up, for reasons outside her control, appearing to the wrongdoer as acquiescence to the disrespectful treatment or as signaling that the wrong was not very serious." Lueck, B. (2019). Forgiveness as institution: a Merleau-Pontian account. *Continental Philosophy Review.* doi.org/10.1007/s11007-019-09464-x.

[16] Cf. "To be too eager to forgive . . . may not be rationally warranted, [and] may very well signal a willingness to condone what is immoral, and may not only underestimate one's own worth but, in the process, may perpetuate and aggravate the harm and the wrong that one has suffered, and may do so in ways that preclude eventual forgiveness." Novitz (1988): p. 314.

[17] See, e.g.: "[I]n forgiveness the offended, relative to the offender, *recognizes* that the equality of their commonly shared humanity existed before, during, and after the hurtful event." Enright, R. D., Gassin, E. A. and Wu, C. (1992). Forgiveness: A Developmental View. *Journal of Moral Education* 21, 99-114: p. 112; "[I]t is the act of forgiving . . . that allows the victim to put a closure on the unfortunate experience, to draw a line under the balance-sheet, and to start to lead a normal life again." Marshall and Merry (1990): p. 3.

[18] Cf. "[P]roponents of the value of forgiveness in restorative justice in general, of in the [Truth and Reconciliation Commission] in particular, often stress that forgiveness can and should never be demanded or imposed. This is however— unwittingly or not—a kind of smoke screen, because the real issue, in terms of victims' complaints about the proceedings, is precisely the use of subtle and covert pressures— what is not demanded directly but is clearly expected—and ways of speaking and examples [e.g. about continued resentment or unforgiveness] that are provided or ignored or forgotten." Brudholm (2008): p. 41.

3. The Ethics of Shame

[1] Crozier (1998): p. 276.

[2] "[W]e may become extremely embarrassed when other people perceive us in an undesired fashion even when we know that the other people's perceptions of us are inaccurate. . . . Similarly, others can make us feel guilty or ashamed even though we know that we did absolutely nothing wrong. . . . Positive self-conscious emotions, such as pride, may also arise from approbations that, deep down, we know are not fully deserved. People experience self-conscious emotions not because of how they evaluate themselves but rather because of how they think they are being evaluated or might be evaluated by others." Leary, M. R. (2004). Digging Deeper: The Fundamental Nature of 'Self-Conscious' Emotions. *Psychological Inquiry*, 15, 2, 129-131: p. 130.

[3] "What is crucial is the actor's attribution to the audience, the recognition and endorsement of the fact that his or her behaviour is being, or can be, judged in a manner that reflects badly upon him or herself. It is not necessary that an observer is actually present . . . or that an observer actually takes an adverse view of the actor's behaviour . . . ." Crozier (1998): p. 276.

[4] "The real presence of an evaluating other may be necessary for the initial early development of self-representations, however when these representations are fully

internalized they can be activated when individuals are alone." Tracy, J. L. and Robins, R. W. (2004). Keeping the Self in Self-Conscious Emotions: Further Arguments for a Theoretical Model. *Psychological Inquiry*, 15, 2, 171–177: p. 173. Cf. "The social roots of self-conscious emotions may become obscured as the developing child learns to apply abstract standards and internalized norms in their conscious self-evaluation. . . . [For example] a child worried about pleasing parents and others might, indeed, a year later engage in self-cognition ('I feel stupid') with no explicit social referent. Still the ultimate source of the emotion is the anticipation (conscious or implicit) of positive or negative social outcomes. This social outcome expectation may not be experienced consciously, as it may function entirely implicitly via overlearned procedural knowledge . . . however it is the root cause of the affective response." Baldwin and Baccus (2004): p. 140.

[5] For this view, see O'Hear, A. (1976–1977). Guilt and Shame as Moral Concepts. *Proceedings of the Aristotelian Society*, 77 73–86; Kekes, J. (1988). Shame and Moral Progress. In *Ethical Theory: Character & Virtue*, ed. P. A. French, T. E. Uehling Jr., H. K. Wettstein. Midwestern Studies in Philosophy, vol. 13. Notre Dame, IN: University of Notre Dame Press; Aldrich, V. C. (1939). An Ethics of Shame. *Ethics*, 50, 57–77.

[6] "Moral shortcomings must first be exposed to public view before they can be the source of shame; or at the very least, the contempt that others would show us were our shortcoming exposed must be clearly imaginable. The primary fears attached to shame are fears of being ridiculed, made the subject of gossip, subjected to demeaning treatment, and of being ostracized or abandoned. Thus, shame is strongly connected with the desire to conceal failings from others' view, with fear of exposure, and with anxiety about 'how it will be for one's life with others' if one acts shamefully. . . . [Hence the] real objects of shame . . . are failures to meet moral standards that are also held by other people. Shaming moral failures are paradigmatically ones that might, if exposed, reduce one's social standing in some actual group and might degrade the quality of one's social interactions." Calhoun, C. (2004). An Apology for Moral Shame. *The Journal of Political Philosophy*, 12, 2, 127–146: p. 131.

[7] For this view, see Williams (1993).

[8] It is possible, on this view, for a mature moral agent to feel shame even though they disagree with the specific criticism of others. In such cases, the agent must at least have come to respect, independently, the others' general capacity to evaluate well, their moral reasoning skills and perceptiveness in order to feel 'mature shame'. This preserves their ethical autonomy.

[9] "Morality is also fundamentally a social enterprise. While hypothetical moral worlds of ideally rational agents are heuristically useful in evaluating the justifiability of moral principles and norms, morality is only practiced in real social worlds. Morality regulates interactions between real social actors. Even if particular social practices of morality seem flawed from the individual's critical, normative perspective, the social practice of morality is the only moral game in town. It is only in real social worlds that I have a moral identity." Calhoun, C. (2004): p. 144–5. See also Calhoun, C. (2000). The Virtue of Civility. *Philosophy and Public Affairs*, 29, 251–75; Calhoun, C. (1999). Moral Failure. In *On Feminist Ethics and Politics*, ed. C. Card. Lawrence:

University of Kansas Press); and Calhoun, C. (1995). Standing for Something. *Journal of Philosophy*, 92, 235–60.

[10] Even people with whom we disagree violently have the power to shame us, so long as our identities are somehow linked to how they see us. Hitler chose to commit suicide rather than be captured and paraded as a 'loser' by his enemies. This was surely because Hitler invested so much of his identity into his role and how the world–including his enemies–saw him. To be seen as an evil man and an incompetent leader was too shameful for him to handle.

[11] "People typically believe they are entitled to more respect from in-group members than from out-group members . . . . Furthermore, the indignation produced by disrespectful acts by out-group members tends to be different than that aroused by disrespectful acts by in-group members . . . . An insult from an out-group member is more likely to be perceived as insolent and to provoke a 'How dare they?' response, whereas an insult from an in-group member is more likely to seem like a betrayal and to provoke a 'How could they?' response. . . . The nature of the audience who witnesses an insult also affects the intensity of the victim's feelings of injustice. For example, a worker criticized in front of coworkers will experience stronger feelings of injustice than when the worker is criticized either in private or in front of others whose good opinion the worker cares less about." Miller, D. T. (2001): p. 540.

[12] "The power to shame is a function of our sharing a moral practice with the shamer and recognizing that the shamer's opinion expresses a *representative viewpoint* within that practice. The shamer's opinion tells us who we are for any number of co-participants within a social practice of morality that we take ourselves to be a part of. Shaming criticisms have, in this sense, practical weight. . . . [V]ulnerability to shame has more to do with our sharing a moral practice with others than it does with accepting another's criticism . . . As a result, even if in one's own view one has nothing to be ashamed *of*, one may nevertheless have *reason* to feel ashamed." Calhoun, C. (2004): p. 141, 143.

[13] Calhoun claims that there is reason to be pessimistic about whether a 'lone moral voice' can be heard, given that they will have little or no power to shame. "[T]he power to shame is likely to be concentrated in the hands of those whose interpretations are socially authoritative. . . . In other cases, interpretations are socially authoritative because of their sheer conventionality; they express what generally 'goes without saying' . . . . By contrast, those who lack social status or who voice controversial or idiosyncratic moral criticisms often lack the power to shame." And yet, Calhoun also suggests that it is possible to stand up against social conventions or authoritative viewpoints that shame people unjustly. That must be not because we can *resist* these feelings of shame, but rather because we can *respond* to those feelings by engaging in moral challenge, protest and reform. "Because shaming criticisms that articulate representative viewpoints are not something that people can just steel themselves against, we need to take very seriously the sexism, heterosexism, racism, and the like that are embedded in ongoing moral and political practices. We need to take seriously the deformed identities that the subordinate inhabit and the practical importance of contesting defective moral understandings and struggling to achieve their reform." Calhoun, C. (2004): p.146.

4. Preparing for an Apology

[1] Bowen, Boyack and Hooper (2000): p. 93.

[2] Cf. "Most people would rather receive a genuine heartfelt apology that took many hours, months, or even years than one that came within seconds of an offense and was given with no thought or feeling." Engle (2001): p. 60.

[3] Cf. "[I]t is very important that you plan and prepare for your apology in order to maximize the possibility of it being a positive experience for both you and the person you wronged. . . . There will, of course, be occasions when a spontaneous 'I'm sorry' is very appropriate. But for those bigger mistakes and transgressions, impulsiveness and spontaneity may convey disrespect and may cause you to botch your efforts at apology." Engle (2001): p. 72. Cf. "The apology carries no weight if the context for its delivery has not provided for a meeting of the minds on its composition, its purpose, and its method of delivery. Teaching the offender specific skills to deliver an effective apology, for example, and helping victims understand the anxieties experienced by the offender in framing, composing and delivering the apology is likely to end in a meaningful experience for both: Offenders can express and accept their responsibility and victims can believe in a process that has adhered to the fundamental principle of being victim-centered. In essence, taken as a whole, enhanced knowledge and skill on the part of the mediator is more likely to result in a more 'victim-centered' approach to the delivery of apologies by offenders. This may lessen the anxiety of the juvenile and his or her parents, and has the potential of leaving the victims feeling more satisfied that the process was indeed both respectful of the loss experienced and supportive of the victim's right to reparations. Thus, it is critical that offenders be educated about how to effectively compose and deliver an apology to the victims who will judge their sincerity." Choi, J. J. and Severson, M. (2009). 'What! What kind of apology is this?': The nature of apology in victim-offender mediation. *Children and Youth Services Review* 31, 813–820: p. 819.

[4] E.g. "An unremorseful or defiant offender can immediately cause greater anger in the victim and others, which will sometimes lead to more moralizing or stigmatization being directed towards the offender." Harris, Walgrave and Braithwaite (2004): p. 200; Umbreit's study found that some victims did not find the restorative justice process "helpful", due to the "the negative, non-repentant attitude of their specific offender. 'I felt he wasn't owning up to it.' 'He just slouched all the way down and just sat and half-heartedly gave answers'." Umbreit (1990): p. 56; "[W]hen the harm-doer apologised for her wrongdoing, in contrast to when she did not, the subjects generally had more favorable impressions of her, felt more pleasant and refrained from severe aggression toward her." Ohbuchi, K., Kameda, M. and Agarie, N. (1989). Apology as aggression control: Its role in mediating appraisal of and response to harm. *Journal of Personality and Social Psychology*, 56, 2, 219-227: p. 222.

[5] "[T]hose offenders who failed to apologise to victims were more likely to be reconvicted than those who had apologised." Morris, A. and Maxwell, G. (1998). Restorative Justice in New Zealand: Family Group Conferences as a Case Study. In *Western Criminology Review*, 1, 1.

⁶ Cf. "[O]nce a societal convention meets the moral demand for some kind of apology-like act—some way of respecting a victim's right not to have been wronged and treated as though it is acceptable to do so—it becomes established practice. As a result, it becomes an expected behavior of repentant wrongdoers. That, however, adds to the moral reasons to apologize, and to do it in the specific way established. After all, if that's what people tend to do when they recognize their wrongful behavior, then failure to do so is to single out a particular victim as not entitled to the same respect. It is to act toward her as an exception to the established convention for redressing wrongs done to victims. And that makes it additionally wrong not to apologize to her, or, put differently, that fact puts in place a new duty to apologize and to do so in whatever way is conventional." Helmreich (2015): p. 107.

⁷ Coercion would be humiliating, and so the predictable outcome would be an insincere apology that functions more as a self-protecting shame-reaction, rather than a shame-releasing gesture. Cf. "Mandating apology denudes its power as a gift from the person who places themselves as wrongdoer by apologizing to the wronged. If we apologize because we are required to, the apology ceases to be a manifestation of a vulnerable emotion. We distrust a coerced apology as insincere, as papering over a deeper truth of aggressive emotion." Braithwaite (2006): p. 407; "Their apology fulfilled [the young offenders'] expectations; they were punished by an authority figure; they were powerless to prevent the process; they acquiesced; they then, in order to retain peer-group status and keep their egos intact, retrospectively recreated the encounter as one in which sullen obeisance was transformed into heroic resistance." Blagg, H. (1985). Reparation and Justice for juveniles. *British Journal of Criminology*, 25, 267-279, quoted in Davis, G., Messmer, H. and Umbreit, M. (1992). *Making Amends: Mediation and Reparation in Criminal Justice*. London and New York: Routledge: p. 143. Cf. O'Connell, Wachtel, B. and Wachtel, T. (1999): p. 66.

⁸ "[D]o we hesitate to repent of our crimes precisely because we fear it will be interpreted by our victims as a kind of victory over us which lowers us, or which is, in an of itself, an admission of our inferiority?" Hampton (1998a): p. 69.

5. Facilitator Scripts

¹ Cf. "A major debate among restorative justice administrators is whether facilitators should be trained to follow a script to ensure that these are the kinds of questions that are always asked, as opposed to questions that might be more likely to elicit aggressive emotions. Another reason some defend script-based training is to prevent facilitators descending into lecturing of wrongdoers, especially if they are police or youth justice officials who must unlearn lifetime habits of telling young offenders what to do. Of course the argument against scripting is that it inhibits flexibility, responsiveness to cultural difference, and the greater authenticity of more spontaneous forms of communication such as humor, which can be such an asset in tense encounters for those who have the gift to use it without offense." Braithwaite (2006): p. 404-5.

Bibliography

Acorn, A. (2004). *Compulsory Compassion: A Critique of Restorative Justice*. Vancouver: UBC Press.

Ahmed, E. and Braithwaite, V. (2004). 'What, Me Ashamed?' Shame Management and School Bullying. *Journal of Research in Crime and Delinquency*, 41, 269-94.

Ahmed, E. and Braithwaite, V. (2006). Forgiveness, Reconciliation, and Shame: Three Key Variables in Reducing School Bullying. *Journal of Social Issues*, 62, 2, 347-70.

Ahmed, E., Harris, N., Braithwaite, J. and Braithwaite, V. (2001) *Shame Management through Reintegration*. Cambridge: Cambridge University Press.

Alder, J. (1992). *The Urgings of Conscience*. Philadelphia: Temple University Press.

Aldrich, V. C. (1939). An Ethics of Shame. *Ethics*, 50, 57–77.

Alston, W. (1989). *Epistemic Justification*. Ithaca and London: Cornell University Press.

Andersen, J. D. (2003). *Victim Offender Settlements, General Deterrence, and Social Welfare*. The Harvard John M. Olin Discussion Paper Series, 402, 01.

Babiak, P. and Hare, R. D. (2006). *Snakes in Suits: When Psychopaths Go to Work*. New York, NY: HarperCollins.

Baldwin, M. W. and Baccus, J. R. (2004). Maintaining a Focus on the Social Goals Underlying Self-Conscious Emotions. *Psychological Inquiry*, 15, 2, 139-144.

Baskin-Sommers, A., Stuppy-Sullivan, A. M. and Buckholtz, J. W. (2016). Psychopathic individuals exhibit but do not avoid regret during counterfactual decision making. *Proceedings of the National Academy of Sciences*, 113(50), 14438-43.

Batson, C. D. (2009). These Things Called Empathy. In *The Social Neuroscience of Empathy*. ed. J. Decety and W. Ickes. Cambridge, Massachusetts: MIT.

Beck, E., Britto, S. and Andrews, A. (2007). *In the Shadow of Death: Restorative Justice and Death Row Families*. Oxford: Oxford University Press.

Beer, J. S. and Keltner, D. (2004). What Is Unique about Self-Conscious Emotions? *Psychological Inquiry*, 15, 2, 126-129.

Best Practice Standards for Restorative Justice Facilitators. (2009). Victorian Association for Restorative Justice.

Best Practice Guidance for Restorative Practitioners and their Case Supervisors and Line Managers. (2004). UK Home Office.

Bird, S. (1999). *Conference Convenor Training Package*. Sydney, NSW: Dept. of Juvenile Justice.

Blagg, H. (1985). Reparation and Justice for juveniles. *British Journal of Criminology*, 25, 267-279.

Blöser, C. (2019). Human Fallibility and the Need for Forgiveness. *Philosophia*, 47(1), 1-19.

Bovens, L. (2015). XII—Apologies. *Proceedings of the Aristotelian Society*, Vol. 108, Part 3, 219-239.

Bowen, H., Boyack, J. and Hooper, S. (2000). *New Zealand Restorative Justice Practice Manual*. Auckland, New Zealand: Restorative Justice Trust.

Braithwaite, J. (1989). *Crime, Shame and Reintegration*. New York: Cambridge University Press.

Braithwaite, J. (2002). *Restorative Justice and Responsive Regulation*. Oxford: Oxford University Press.

Braithwaite, J. (2006). Doing Justice Intelligently in Civil Society. *Journal of Social Issues*, 62, 2, 393-409.

Braithwaite, J. and Mugford, S. (1994). Conditions of successful reintegration ceremonies. *British Journal Of Criminology* 34, 2 139-171.

Brookes, D. (2009). *Restorative Justice and Work-Related Death: A Literature Review*. Melbourne, Victoria: Creative Ministries Network.

Brudholm, T. (2008). *Resentment's Virtue: Jean Amery and the Refusal to Forgive*. Philadelphia: Temple University Press.

Buck, R. and Miller, M. (2015). Beyond Facial Expression: Spatial Distance as a Factor in the Communication of Discrete Emotions. In *The Social Psychology of Nonverbal Communication*. ed. A. Kostic and D. Chadee. Palgrave Macmillan.

Burns, D. D. (1999). *The Feeling Good Handbook*. New York, NY: Penguin Books.

Bushman, B. J., and Baumeister, R. F. (1998). Threatened egotism, narcissism, self-esteem, and direct and displaced aggression: Does self-love or self-hate lead to violence? *Journal of Personality and Social Psychology*, 75, 219-229.

Buss, S. (1999). Appearing Respectful: The Moral Significance of Manners. *Ethics*, 109, 4, 795-826.

Calhoun, C. (1995). Standing for Something. *Journal of Philosophy*, 92, 235–60.

Calhoun, C. (1999). Moral Failure. In *On Feminist Ethics and Politics*. ed. C. Card. Lawrence: University of Kansas Press.

Calhoun, C. (2000). The Virtue of Civility. *Philosophy and Public Affairs*, 29, 251–75.

Calhoun, C. (2004). An Apology for Moral Shame. *The Journal of Political Philosophy*, 12, 2, 127–146.

Centomani, P. and Dighera, B. (1992). The new juvenile penal procedure code and the reparation-reconciliation process in Italy: A chance for a possible change. In *Restorative Justice on Trial: Pitfalls and Potentials of Victim-Offender Mediation*. ed. H. Messmer and H. U. Otto. International Research Perspectives. Netherlands: Kluwer Academic Publishers, pp. 355-366.

Choi, J. J. and Severson, M. (2009). 'What! What kind of apology is this?': The nature of apology in victim-offender mediation. *Children and Youth Services Review*, 31, 813–820.

Clark, H. H. (1992) *Arenas of Language Use*. Chicago: University of Chicago Press

Cori, J. L. (2008). *Healing from Trauma*. New York, NY: Marlowe & Company.

Cowden, R. G., Worthington, E. L., Joynt, S. and Jakins, C. (2018). Do congruent apologies facilitate forgiveness? *South African Journal of Psychology*, 1–14.

Crozier, R. W. (1998). Self-Consciousness in Shame: The Role of the 'Other'. *Journal for the Theory of Social Behaviour*, 28, 3, 273-286.

Daly, K. (2003). Mind the gap: restorative justice theory in theory and practice. In *Restorative Justice and Criminal Justice: Competing or Reconcilable Paradigms*. ed. A. von Hirsch, J. Roberts, A. Bottoms, K. Roach and M. Schiff. Oxford: Oxford University Press.

Davis, G., Messmer, H. and Umbreit, M. (1992) *Making Amends: Mediation and Reparation in Criminal Justice*. London and New York: Routledge.

Davis, J. R. and Gold, G. J. (2011). An examination of emotional empathy, attributions of stability, and the link between perceived remorse and forgiveness. *Personality and Individual Differences*, 50(3), 392-397.

Decety, J. and Ickes, W. ed. (2009). *The Social Neuroscience of Empathy*. Cambridge, Massachusetts: MIT.

Derrida, J. (2001). *On Cosmopolitanism and Forgiveness*. New York: Routledge.

Downie, R. S. (1965). Forgiveness. *The Philosophical Quarterly*, 15(59), 128-134.

Dworkin, R. (1977). DeFunis v. Sweatt. In *Equality and Preferential Treatment*. ed. M. Cohen, et. al. Princeton, NJ: Princeton University Press.

Einhorn, S. (2006). *The Art of Being Kind*. Great Britain: Sphere.

Eisenberg, N. and Eggum, N. D. (2009). Empathetic Responding: Sympathy and Personal Distress. In *The Social Neuroscience of Empathy*. ed. J. Decety and W. Ickes. Cambridge, Massachusetts: MIT.

Ekman, P. (2003). *Emotions Revealed: Understanding Faces and Feelings*. Great Britain: Weidenfeld & Nicolson.

Elison, J., Lennon, R. and Pulos, S. (2006). Investigating the Compass of Shame: The development of the Compass of Shame Scale. *Social Behavior and Personality*, 34, 3, 221-238.

Engle, B. (1989). *The Right to Innocence: Healing the Trauma of Childhood Sexual Abuse*. New York, NY: Random Publishing House.

Engle, B. (2001). *The Power of Apology*. New York, NY: John Wiley & Sons.

Engle, B. (2006). *Healing your Emotional Self*. New York, NY: John Wiley & Sons.

Enright, R. D., Gassin, E. A. and Wu, C. (1992). Forgiveness: A Developmental View. *Journal of Moral Education*, 21, 99-114.

Exline, J. J., Yali, A. and Lobel, M. (1997). *Correlates of Forgiveness*. Unpublished Data. Stony Brook: State University of New York.

Feinberg, J. (1973). *Social Philosophy*. Englewood Cliffs, New Jersey: Prentice-Hall.

Feinberg, J. (1987). *The Moral Limits of the Criminal Law, Volume I: Harm to Others*. Oxford: Oxford University Press.

Feinberg, J. (1988). *The Moral Limits of the Criminal Law, Volume IV: Harmless Wrongdoing*. Oxford: Oxford University Press.

Flanigan, B. (1992). *Forgiving the Unforgivable*. New York, NY: MacMillan.

Foster, C. A., and Rusbult, C. E. (1999). Injustice and power seeking. *Personality & Social Psychology Bulletin*, 25, 834–849.

Frieze, I. H., Hymer, S. and Greenberg, M. S. (1987). Describing the Crime Victim: Psychological Reactions to Victimization. *Professional Psychology: Research and Practice*, 18, 4, 299-315.

Garrard, E. and McNaughton, D. (2003). In defense of unconditional forgiveness. *Proceedings of the Aristotelian Society*, 103(1), 39–60.

Goffman, E. (1971). Remedial Interchanges. In *Relations in Public: Microstudies of the Public Order*. New York, NY: Basic Books.

Govier, T. (2002). *Forgiveness and Revenge*. London: Routledge.

Govier, T. and Hirano, C. (2009). A conception of invitational forgiveness. *Journal of Social Philosophy* 39,3: 429–44.

Govier, T. and Verwoerd, W. (2002a). The Promise and Pitfalls of Apology. *Journal of Social Philosophy*, 33(1), 67-82.

Govier, T. and Verwoerd, W. (2002b). Forgiveness: The Victim's Prerogative. *South African Journal of Philosophy*, 21(2), 97-111.

Grayling, A. C. (2007). *Towards the Light: The Story of the Struggles for Liberty and Rights That Made the Modern West*. Great Britain: Bloomsbury Publishing.

Grice, P. (1975). Logic and conversation. In *Syntax and Semantics Volume 3, Speech Acts*. ed. P. Cole and J. Morgan. New York, NY: Academic Press: pp. 41–58.

Gruenewald, T. L., Kemeny, M. E., Aziz, N. and Fahey, J. L. (2004). Acute Threat to the Social Self: Shame, Social Self-esteem, and Cortisol Activity. *Psychosomatic Medicine*, 66, 915-924.

Hampton, J. (1988a). Forgiveness, Resentment and Hatred. In J. G. Murphy and J. Hampton, *Forgiveness and Mercy*. New York, NY: Cambridge University Press.

Hampton, J. (1988b). The Retributive Idea. In J. G. Murphy and J. Hampton, *Forgiveness and Mercy*. New York, NY: Cambridge University Press.

Hampton, J. (1997). The Wisdom of the Egoist: The Moral and Political Implications of Valuing the Self. *Social Philosophy and Policy*, 14, 21-51: p. 28.

Harris, S. (2010). *The Moral Landscape*. Great Britain: Simon & Schuster.

Harris, N. (2001). Shaming and shame: regulating drink driving. In E. Ahmed, N. Harris, J. Braithwaite, and V. Braithwaite, *Shame Management through Reintegration.* Cambridge: Cambridge University Press

Harris, N., Walgrave, L. and Braithwaite, J. (2004). Emotional Dynamics in Restorative Conferences. *Theoretical Criminology,* 8, 191-210.

Helmreich, J. S. (2015). The Apologetic Stance. *Philosophy & Public Affairs,* 43(2), 75-108.

Hieronymi, P. (2001). Articulating an Uncompromising Forgiveness. *Philosophy and Phenomenological Research,* 62(3), 529-555.

Holmgren, M. R. (1993). Forgiveness and the Intrinsic Value of Persons. *American Philosophical Quarterly,* 30, 4, 341-352.

Jehle, A., Miller, M. K., Kemmelmeier, M. and Maskaly, J. (2012). How voluntariness of apologies affects actual and hypothetical victims' perceptions of the offender. *The Journal of Social Psychology,* 152(6), 727-745.

Kador, J. (2009). *Effective Apology.* San Francisco, CA: Berrett-Koehler Publishers.

Kekes, J. (1988). Shame and Moral Progress. In *Ethical Theory: Character & Virtue.* ed. P. A. French, T. E. Uehling Jr., H. K. Wettstein. Midwestern Studies in Philosophy, vol. 13. Notre Dame, IN: University of Notre Dame Press.

Koss, M. P. (2014). The RESTORE program of restorative justice for sex crimes: Vision, process, and outcomes. *Journal of Interpersonal Violence,* 29(9), 1629-1660.

Kostic, A. and Chadee, D. (2015). *The Social Psychology of Nonverbal Communication.* Palgrave Macmillan.

Lamb, S. and Murphy, J. G. eds. (2002). *Before Forgiving.* New York: Oxford University Press.

Lazare, A. (1995). Go ahead say you're sorry. *Psychology Today,* 28, 1, 40-43.

Lazare, A. (2004). *On Apology.* Oxford: Oxford University Press.

Leary, M. R. (2004). Digging Deeper: The Fundamental Nature of 'Self-Conscious' Emotions. *Psychological Inquiry,* 15, 2, 129-131.

Lerner, H. (2005). *The Dance of Anger.* New York, NY: Perennial Currents.

Lewis, H. B. (1971). *Shame and Guilt in Neurosis.* New York, NY: International Universities Press.

Lewis, M. (1992). *Shame: The Exposed Self.* New York, NY: The Free Press.

Lindsay-Hartz, J. (1984). Contrasting experiences of shame and guilt. *American Behavioral Scientist,* 27, 689-704.

Lueck, B. (2019). Forgiveness as institution: a Merleau-Pontian account. *Continental Philosophy Review.* doi.org/10.1007/s11007-019-09464-x.

Lyons, W. (1980). *Emotions.* Cambridge: Cambridge University Press.

Manusov, V., Docan-Morgan, T. and Harvey, J. (2015). Nonverbal Firsts: When Nonverbal Cues Are the Impetus of Relational and Personal Change in Romantic Relationships. In *The Social Psychology of Nonverbal Communication*. ed. A. Kostic and D. Chadee. Palgrave Macmillan

Marshall, T. and Merry, S. (1990). *Crime and Accountability—Victim/Offender Mediation in Practice*. London: Home Office, HMSO.

Martens, W. (2005). A Multicomponential Model of Shame. *Journal for the Theory of Social Behaviour*, 35, 4, 399-411.

McEwan, I. (2001). *The Guardian*, September 13th.

McCullough, M., Sandage, S. and Worthington, E. (1997) *To Forgive is Human*. Downers Grover, Il.: Intervarsity Press.

McCullough, M. (2008). *Beyond Revenge: The Evolution of the Forgiveness Instinct*. San Francisco, CA: Jossey-Bass.

Melville, H. (1851/2003). *Moby Dick*. London, England: Penguin Books.

Messmer, H. and Otto, H. U. ed. (1992). *Restorative Justice on Trial: Pitfalls and Potentials of Victim-Offender Mediation*. International Research Perspectives. Netherlands: Kluwer Academic Publishers

Miller, A. (1987). *For your Own Good: The Roots of Violence in Child-Rearing*. Great Britain: Virago.

Miller, D. T. (2001). Disrespect and the experience of injustice. *Annual Review of Psychology*, 52, 527-53.

Millon, T., Simonsen, E., Birket-Smith, M. and Davis, R. D. (1998). *Psychopathy: Antisocial, Criminal, and Violent Behaviour*. New York, NY: Guildord Press.

Minow, M. (1998). *Between Vengeance and Forgiveness: Facing History after Genocide and Mass Violence*. Boston: Beacon Press.

Monbourquette, J. (2000). *How to Forgive*. Canada: Novalis.

Moore, D. B. (1996). Transforming Juvenile Justice, Transforming Policing: The Introduction of Family Conferencing in Australia. In *Comparative Criminal Justice: Traditional and Nontraditional Systems of Law and Control*. ed. C. B. Fields and R. H. Moore. Prospect Heights, IL: Waveland.

Moore, K. D., (1989). A Retributivist Theory of Pardon. In *Pardons: Justice, Mercy, and the Public Interest*. New York, NY: Oxford University Press.

Murphy, J. G. (1988a). Forgiveness and Resentment. In J. G. Murphy and J. Hampton, *Forgiveness and Mercy*. New York, NY: Cambridge University Press.

Murphy, J. G. (1988b). Hatred: a qualified defense. In J. G. Murphy and J. Hampton, *Forgiveness and Mercy*. New York, NY: Cambridge University Press.

Murphy, J. G. and Hampton, J. (1988). *Forgiveness and Mercy*. New York, NY: Cambridge University Press.

Murphy, J. G. (2008). Foreword. In T. Brudholm, *Resentment's Virtue: Jean Amery and the Refusal to Forgive*. Philadelphia: Temple University Press.

Nakashima, R. and Lettini, G. (2012). *Soul Repair: Recovering from Moral Injury After War*. Boston: Beacon Press.

Nathanson, D. L. (1992). *Shame and Pride*. NY and London: W.W. Norton & Co..

Neiderbach, S. (1986). *Invisible Wounds: Crime Victims Speak*. New York, NY: Harrington Park Press.

Novitz, D. (1988). Forgiveness and Self-Respect. *Philosophy and Phenomenological Research*, 58.2, 209-315.

Nussbaum, M. C. (2004). *Hiding from Humanity: Shame, Disgust and the Law*. Princeton, NJ: Princeton University Press.

O'Connell, T., Wachtel, B. and Wachtel, T. (1999). *Conferencing Handbook: The New REALJUSTICE Training Manual*. Pipersville, PA: The Piper's Press.

Ohbuchi, K., Kameda, M., Agarie, N. (1989). Apology as aggression control: Its role in mediating appraisal of and response to harm. *Journal of Personality and Social Psychology*, 56, 2, 219-227.

O'Hear, A. (1976–1977). Guilt and Shame as Moral Concepts. *Proceedings of the Aristotelian Society*, 77, 73–86.

Palmer, S. ed. (2001). *Introduction to Counselling and Psychotherapy*. Great Britain: Sage Publications.

Parrott, W. G., (2004). Appraisal, Emotion Words, and the Social Nature of Self-Conscious Emotions. *Psychological Inquiry* 15, 136–138.

Pattison, S. (2000). *Shame: Theory, Therapy, Theology*. Cambridge: Cambridge University Press.

Pettigrove, G. (2004). Unapologetic forgiveness. *American Philosophical Quarterly* 41,3: 187–96.

Pettigrove, G. and Collins, J. (2011). Apologizing for Who I Am. *Journal of Applied Philosophy*, 28(2), 137-150.

Piers, G. (1953). Shame and Guilt: Part I. In *Shame and Guilt: A Psychoanalytic Study*. ed. G. Piers and M. B. Singer. Springfield, Il.: Charles C. Thomas.

Preckel, K., Kanske, P. and Singer, T. (2018). On the interaction of social affect and cognition: empathy, compassion and theory of mind. *Current Opinion in Behavioral Sciences*, 19, 1-6.

Proeve, M. and Tudor, S. (2010). *Remorse*. London: Routledge.

Pugh, J. and Maslen, H. (2017). 'Drugs That Make You Feel Bad'? Remorse-Based Mitigation and Neurointerventions. *Criminal Law and Philosophy*, 11(3), 499-522.

Radzik, L. (2009). *Making Amends: Atonement in Morality, Law, and Politics*. Oxford: Oxford University Press.

Rawls, J. (1999). *A Theory of Justice*. Rev. edition. Cambridge, MA: Harvard University Press.

Retzinger, S and Scheff, T. (1991). *Emotions and Violence: Shame and Rage in Destructive Conflicts.* Mass: Lexington Books.

Retzinger, S. and Scheff, T. (1996). Strategy for community conferences: Emotions and social bonds. In *Restorative Justice: International Perspectives.* ed. B. Galaway and J. Hudson. Monesy, NY: Criminal Justice Press.

Roche, D. (2003). *Accountability in Restorative Justice.* Oxford: Oxford University Press.

Sabini, J. and Silver, M. (1997). In Defense of Shame: Shame in the Context of Guilt and Embarrassment. *Journal for the Theory of Social Behavior,* 27, 1, 1–15.

Scheff, T. (1994). *Bloody Revenge: Emotions, Nationalism, and War.* Oxford: Westview Press.

Schönherr, J. (2018). When Forgiveness Comes Easy. *The Journal of Value Inquiry,* 1-16.

Schumann, K. (2014). An affirmed self and a better apology: The effect of self-affirmation on transgressors' responses to victims. *Journal of Experimental Social Psychology,* 54, 89-96.

Seligman, M. E. (2002). *Authentic Happiness: Using the New Positive Psychology to Realize Your Potential for Lasting Fulfillment.* Australia: Random House.

Shakur, S. (1993). *Monster: The Autobiography of an L.A. Gang Member.* New York, NY: Penguin.

Sherman, L. and Strang, H. (2007). *Restorative Justice: The Evidence.* The Smith Institute.

Shin, H. (2003). *Workplace practice and shame management.* Paper presented at the 11th European Congress on Work and Organizational Psychology. Lisboa, Portugal, May.

Shnabel, N. and Nadler, A. (2008). A needs-based model of reconciliation. *Journal of Personality and Social Psychology,* 94, 1, 116-32.

Silver, M. (2007). Coping with guilt and shame: a narrative approach. *Journal of Moral Education,* 36, 2, 169–183.

Smith, N. (2008). *I was Wrong: The Meaning of Apologies.* Cambridge: Cambridge University Press.

Strang, H. and Sherman, L. W. (1997) The Victim's Perspective. RISE Working Papers: Paper No. 2. Australian National University, Canberra.

Sutton, J. and Stewart, W. (2002). *Learning to Counsel.* Oxford: How to Books.

Tangney, J. P., Stuewig, J. and Mashek, D. J. (2007a). Moral Emotions and Moral Behavior. *Annual Review of Psychology,* 58, 345–72.

Tangney, J. P., Stuewig, J. and Mashek, D. J. (2007b). What's Moral about the Self-Conscious Emotions? In *The Self-Conscious Emotions: Theory and Research.* ed. J. L. Tracy, R. W. Robins and J. P. Tangney. NY and London: The Guilford Press.

Taylor, G. (1985). *Pride, Shame, and Guilt.* Oxford: Clarendon Press.

The Universal Declaration of Human Rights. (1948).

Thwaites, T., Davis L. and Mules, W. (1994). *Tools For Cultural Studies: An Introduction.* Melbourne: Palgrave Macmillan.

Tracy, J. L. and Robins, R. W. (2004). Keeping the Self in Self-Conscious Emotions: Further Arguments for a Theoretical Model. *Psychological Inquiry,* 15, 2, 171-177.

Tracy, J. L., and Robins, R. W. (2008). The nonverbal expression of pride: Evidence for cross-cultural recognition. *Journal of Personality and Social Psychology,* 94, 3, 516–530.

Tracy, J. L. and Robins, R. W. (2007). The Self in Self-Conscious Emotions: A Cognitive Appraisal Approach. In *The Self-Conscious Emotions: Theory and Research.* ed. J. L. Tracy, R. W. Robins and J. P. Tangney. NY and London: The Guilford Press.

Tracy, J. L., Robins, R. W. and Tangney, J. P. ed. (2007). *The Self-Conscious Emotions: Theory and Research.* NY and London: The Guilford Press.

Tyler, S. (1978). *Said and the Unsaid: Mind, Meaning and Culture.* New York: Academic Press.

Umbreit, M. (1994). *Victim Meets Offender: The Impact of Restorative Justice and Mediation.* Monsey, NY: Willow Tree Press, Inc..

Vecina, M. L. and Marzana, D. (2016). Always looking for a moral identity- The moral licensing effect in men convicted of domestic violence. *New Ideas in Psychology,* 41, 33-38.

Victim Support (2003). *Victim Support UK Policy on Restorative Justice In Criminal Justice.*

Vlastos, G. (1969). Human Worth, Merit, and Equality. In *Moral Concepts,* ed. J. Feinberg. Oxford: Oxford University Press.

Walker, M. U. (2006a). The Cycle of Violence. *Human Rights and Negative Emotions: Special Issue of Journal of Human Rights,* 5, 1, 81-105.

Walker, M. U. (2006b). *Moral Repair.* Cambridge: Cambridge University Press.

Weisman, R. (2014). *Showing Remorse.* London: Routledge.

Williams, B. (1993). *Shame and Necessity.* Berkeley and Los Angeles, CA: University of California Press.

Wink, W. (1992). *Engaging the Powers: Discernment and Resistance in a World of Domination.* Minneapolis MN: Augsburg Fortress.

Young, R. (2001). Just Cops Doing 'Shameful' Business? In *Restorative Justice for Juveniles: Conferencing, Mediation and Circles.* ed. A. Morris and G. Maxwell. Oxford: Hart Publishing.

Zehr, H. (2009). Shame and restorative processes. Restorative Justice Blog, July 26th: <http://emu.edu/blog/restorative-justice/2009/07/26/shame-and-restorative-processes> accessed June 30, 2010.

Index of Authors

Subject Index